making

DOCUMENTARY
FILMS *and*
REALITY VIDEOS

Also by Barry Hampe
Video Scriptwriting

BARRY HAMPE

making

DOCUMENTARY

FILMS *and*

REALITY VIDEOS

: A PRACTICAL

: GUIDE TO

: PLANNING,

: FILMING,

: AND EDITING

: DOCUMENTARIES

: OF REAL EVENTS

AN OWL BOOK

Henry Holt and Company

New York

Henry Holt and Company, Inc.
Publishers since 1866
115 West 18th Street
New York, New York 10011

Henry Holt® is a registered
trademark of Henry Holt and Company, Inc.

Library of Congress Cataloging-in-Publication Data
Hampe, Barry.
    Making documentary films and reality videos: a practical
guide to planning, filming, and editing documentaries
of real events / Barry Hampe.
        p.   cm.
    Includes bibliographical references and index.
    1. Documentary films—Production and direction.
2. Video recordings—Production and direction.   I. Title.
PN1995.9.D6H26   1997   96-17746
070.1'8—dc20   CIP

ISBN 0-8050-4451-5

Henry Holt books are available for special promotions and
premiums. For details contact: Director, Special Markets.

First Edition—1997

Designed by Victoria Hartman

Printed in the United States of America
All first editions are printed on acid-free paper. ∞

10 9 8 7 6 5 4 3

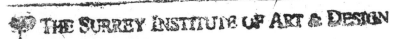

On the principle that the important people in one's life never receive enough recognition, I gratefully dedicate this book with love to three of them.

To my sister Barbara Hempleman, who helped me to love reading and then writing . . .

And to my brother Warren Hampe, who not only helped me to see behavior as it is, but has always been a wonderfully challenging guy to talk with . . .

And to the memory of my teacher, colleague, and friend Sol Worth, who taught me that a craftsman values the work. I owe so much to you, and I miss you.

CONTENTS

PREFACE

I got into documentary by accident because I was looking for a better job. I was working as a promotion copywriter at the *Philadelphia Bulletin* and doing lunchtime job interviews with ad agencies around town, all of which seemed to end with the statement, "You're a good writer, but you don't know anything about film, so we can't use you. If you get some film experience, give us a call."

Through a lot of financial juggling and a certain amount of sacrifice by my wife, my sons, and my father, that fall I entered the master's program at The Annenberg School of Communications at the University of Pennsylvania. Annenberg is not now and never has been a film school. But it did offer a documentary film laboratory in which I enrolled. It was taught by Sol Worth, a photographer, filmmaker, and painter, nursing a secret desire to be a scholar. That year we both achieved our goals. Sol wrote the proposal for the study with anthropologist John Adair that would result in their book, *Through Navajo Eyes*. And I got a better job.

Unfortunately, it was not one that paid better; it was a labor of love. I became Sol's assistant in the documentary film lab on a graduate fellow's pittance. This led to my first documentary *The Trouble with Adults Is* . . . and eventually to a series of other behavioral documentaries.

It was a good time. From Sol I learned a way to think about film and filmmaking. I learned how to see what was really there in the footage. And I learned some important things about doing creative work—that you had to combine the playfulness and desire to experiment of a young child with an absolutely adult willingness to persist at the task until you had it right. It was no accident that Sol had the highest percentage of dropouts in the graduate school because many students got so excited about making films after taking his course that they left without completing a degree. But he also had the highest percentage of students who went on to a doctorate, because after you had spent a year making a documentary for Sol, writing a dissertation was a piece of cake.

This book is a way of giving back some of what I have learned.

A NOTE ON USAGE

Throughout this book I have made distinctions wherever necessary between the process of producing a documentary on film and the quite different process of doing it on video. But the distinction between the two media becomes less clear every day. Today, most programs, even if originally recorded on motion picture film, are shown on a video screen. And our language has extended the verb *to film* to refer to the process of recording any sort of sound-image material. People talk of *filming* a video, and I have used the term this way.

I have also tried to keep my manuscript as gender-free as I could without getting into the syntactic distortions that have become the style of memos written by faculty committees on diversity. It may be worth noting that when I began working in documentary, the only camera operators and sound recordists I knew were men, so it was very natural to think of them as cameramen and soundmen. Indeed, the only documentarians I knew were men. So it was also natural to think of a documentarian as a *he*. Today all that is changed. Women are making just as many great documentaries— and just as many bad ones—as men.

So I have tried to refer to people in the book as *he or she* or *him or her.* If I haven't done it everywhere, it is because I think of myself as a writer first, and I sometimes just can't face stuffing in a *himself or herself* to demolish the rhythm of an otherwise well-crafted sentence or piling up multiple uses of *he or she* without end, like a legal brief. Therefore, if you find a *he* without an *or she* or a *him* without an *or her,* please accept that this is grammatical gender only and still the convention in English, but can be read, if you so desire, as *she or he* and *her or him.*

Feedback

On-line, you can reach Barry Hampe by E-mail at **WriteHampe@aol.com.**

If you are not on-line, you can write to:

Barry Hampe
Making Documentary Films & Reality Videos
Henry Holt and Company
115 W. 18th Street
New York, NY 10011

ACKNOWLEDGMENTS

Everything I know about documentary begins with my great teacher and good friend Sol Worth, who taught me his love of film, and who paid me the supreme compliment when he went on sabbatical of asking me to teach the class in documentary film that he had created. As a teacher, I have had the opportunity to learn from the work and questions of many very bright and truly creative students. As a documentarian, I have been privileged to work with some fine film- and videomakers over the course of my career, and I must acknowledge the contribution that Jack Behr, Andy Dintenfass, and Tim Bradley have made to my understanding of making documentaries. I am also indebted to Calvin Pryluck for forcing me to think about documentary ethics when I would much rather just get a signed release and move on. And I am grateful to Betsy McLane and the staff of the International Documentary Association for being there whenever I had a question and for creating and sponsoring such valuable events as the International Documentary Congress. I must thank my agents, Michael Larsen and Elizabeth Pomada, for their belief in my work and their effort on my behalf, and for bringing my book proposal to Cynthia Vartan at Henry Holt and Company, who has been a patient and truly encouraging editor. Finally, everything I write has to pass beneath the critical eye and flashing red pen of my long-time partner in life and work, Sylvie Hampe. Whenever she announces, "This doesn't make sense," I've learned not to argue, but to rewrite. Over the years she and I have learned how to give and receive criticism and still remain best friends. Thanks, love.

PART I

MAKING ANALOGS
OF REALITY

I used to think that the documentary films
I was making were real. But as I looked
at what I was doing, I saw I was
making analogs—I was making models
of the situation I was filming.

· · · · · · · · · ·

—*Bob Young, documentary filmmaker,*
118th SMPTE Technical Conference

1

IT LOOKS SO EASY

From the outside, making a documentary seems like the easiest thing in the world. You just go where something interesting is happening, turn on the camera, and record it.

Looked at that way, the most successful American documentarian would be Abraham Zapruder, the Dallas garment manufacturer whose home-movie camera was pointed at President John Kennedy as he was being shot. His three-hundred-plus frames of Super-8 film have probably been the most talked about and widely shown bit of footage in the history of nonfiction film.

Certainly, if you can get camcorder shots of a tornado flattening a town or a brushfire wiping out million-dollar homes, you can be on TV.

And yes, if you can put together a series of interviews with the right kinds of people sounding concerned about the right kinds of social problems—from AIDS to zoolatry—you can become the darling of the special interest video festivals.

But, unfortunately, reality footage of a tornado really isn't a documentary. It's a news clip.

And long interviews with earnest proponents of any sort of social change usually don't make a documentary either. What they make is a dull video sermon, acceptable only to those who already side with the speakers. That's called preaching to the choir.

IT TAKES MORE

Making a successful documentary film or video requires much more.

It starts with the camera. You have to have good footage—visual evidence that sets forth the statement of the documentary in visual terms. Tornado footage is good, but it is not sufficient. In their *VolcanoScapes* documentaries about the destruction of the lovely Hawaii coastal town of Kalapana by Kilauea Volcano, Artemis and Mick Kalber had incredible footage of homes destroyed by a slow-moving river of lava. But they focused their story on the people who had chosen to live and build their homes downhill from an active volcano.

And you have to have an idea, a concept that expresses the point of view of the documentary. Interviews may help define the point of view, but they are usually a terribly cumbersome way to get the documentary idea across. In spite of what you see nightly on PBS, interviews do not a documentary make, because they don't *show* the topic; they show people *talking about* the topic.

It takes pictures. For instance, immediately after the opening title, Ken Burns's *The Civil War* shows a series of dramatic photographs of war after a battle. The camera moves slowly across each photo, letting you know that in this documentary much of what you will see will come from still pictures, and you will be given time to see what is there. On the sound track we hear a violin—no speech—as the documentarian shows us that the pictures can speak for themselves.

Then you have to have a structure—an ordered progression of images and sounds that will capture the audience's interest and present the point of view of the documentary as a visual argument. For instance, *The War Room*, a film by Chris Hegedus and D. A. Pennebaker, about the 1992 Clinton campaign, opens with a series of scenes in New Hampshire showing the problems facing candidate Clinton. No interviews; just interactions that show what is happening in the campaign at that time. As the film develops, we see the campaign overcoming obstacles on the way to a Clinton victory.

THE CAMERA WON'T DO IT FOR YOU

I once worked as house audiovisual guy for a teacher training project. When the project put on a conference, I'd take Polaroid snapshots of each day's activities and display them on the bulletin board the next morning. The teachers told me how much they liked the pictures. And, invariably, the next thing they'd say was, "What kind of camera did you use?"

As if that mattered.

It was the simplest, thirty-dollar, wide-angle-lens, no-frills camera that Polaroid made. But it wasn't the camera that made the pictures interesting. It was what the people were doing.

A persistent problem for the modern documentary has been the almost mystical belief of many would-be documentarians that the *camera* somehow does it all. I vividly recall one academic authority on documentary who questioned whether I was "in sympathy with the cinema verité filmmaker's desire to shoot a wealth of footage as a passive observer, in order to report as self-effacingly as possible as a journalist."

Well, no. Because that formulation reduces the documentarian to something of a media janitor in charge of an image vacuum machine. Just turn on the machine and it will suck the essence of the event through the lens and store it on videotape or film. Then all you have to do is reverse the flow and blow your documentary back in the audience's faces.

If it were only that easy!

Yes, I'm in favor of shooting a lot of footage, but always as an active, decision-making participant in a process of communication that begins with an idea and ends with an audience. Inexpensive video equipment has placed the possibility of making a documentary within the reach of anyone. But the equipment won't make your footage interesting. And digital effects and nonlinear editing systems can't turn random shots or hours of talking heads into a dramatic documentary statement.

GOOD IMAGES DON'T JUST HAPPEN

I began planning this book while working on the script for *Defenders of Midway*, a documentary focused on a group of veterans of the famous World War II naval battle. At the start of that project, UPS delivered to my apartment two boxes of VHS windowprint dubs covering 120 half-hour field tapes shot at Midway Atoll. The problems I found with this footage are typical of the problems to be avoided in making a documentary: lack of planning, inadequate visual evidence, poor interview technique, and obtrusive crew interference with the people in the video.

Much of the footage was shot by an award-winning commercial director who wouldn't dream of shooting a thirty-second spot without extensive preproduction planning. But who, at least from the evidence in his footage, went off to shoot an hour documentary with little or no preparation.

It is precisely when you don't *know* what is going to happen that preproduction planning is most important.

A group of veterans had returned to Midway fifty years after the historic battle. They had been young marines, sailors, and airmen in 1942. Now they were men in their late sixties and seventies who had come to dedicate a memorial and to reminisce with one another. I'm sure the producers believed that if the video crew just followed these veterans around and recorded whatever they did and said, they'd have a great documentary. And the notes I received from one of the producers suggest that he believed they had accomplished exactly that. Unfortunately, his optimism wasn't borne out in the footage.

Lack of preproduction planning left the project without a unifying concept. And without that, there was no apparent strategy for gathering visual evidence related to the theme.

The Interview Problem

Half of the tapes were interviews with veterans. Now, a major problem with interviews is that they're about people talking when your goal should be to *show* things happening. Still, this was a historical documentary, and each of these men had a story to tell. Unfortunately they were asked to tell their stories in a static interview conducted by a historian who specialized in oral histories.

Two problems there: First, a static interview is visually boring. Nothing happens. It's a talking head. Second, an oral history gathers the facts of a story to be listened to on tape or to be published. That makes it the exact opposite of a documentary interview. In an oral history, the interviewer usually has a checklist of items to cover and often will use leading questions, since a yes or no answer still provides the facts. But showing someone listening to an interviewer read a question and then answering yes or no—or possibly just shaking their head—does not make dramatic documentary footage.

The way you get good stuff in a documentary interview is by encouraging people to tell you stories, not by interrogating them. You avoid leading questions because you want the person being interviewed to tell the story in his or her own words. And while you always have a checklist of questions to refer to, the most important thing is to follow up on *whatever* the person is most interested in talking about.

The *Midway* interviewer, unfortunately, asked many leading questions, which elicited information in a form that was useless for the documentary. Even worse, when any of the veterans got excited and started to tell a story about something not on the checklist, the interviewer would often say, "We'll come back to that, but first I want to ask you about . . ." And he'd go on with his prepared list of questions, often forgetting to follow up on the topic which had excited the veteran.

He didn't understand that the reason you can go with whatever the subject is excited about is precisely because you have your checklist questions written down. You can *always* get back to them.

Many of the interviews seemed so dull—and these were guys talking about their experiences in combat at the start of World War II!—that the camera operator got bored and began being *cre-*

ative. For instance, he'd take the camera off the subject to point at the wall, and then slowly pan back to the subject's face. Murphy's Law suggests that the camera would be pointing at a blank wall just when the subject said something we'd like to use, and, of course, that's what happened.

Shooting static interviews can be the toughest job in the world for a camera operator. The camera must remain steady and must show the person being interviewed. You change composition only during questions—never during answers—so that you will have an image of the speaker available whenever you find something you want to use.

In other footage, the veterans went on a boat trip to visit Eastern Island, where several of them had been stationed. And the camera crew went along—with the camera operator asking questions, giving directions, and generally talking all over the sound track. This would have been an excellent opportunity to do some good on-site interviews as the veterans reminisced about their service on the island, but that opportunity was lost.

In spite of the problems in the footage, *Defenders of Midway* ended up a good documentary, and I'm proud of my part in making it. But if the producers and the crew that shot the footage had known more at the beginning about making a documentary, it could have been far better.

And that's how this book got started.

A NEW INTEREST IN DOCUMENTARIES

Today, people who don't know anything about video or film technology, and whose only knowledge of how to create a finished program has come from watching television, have begun making documentary films and reality videos. And, frankly, they need help.

You may be one of them.

Last year I wrote an hour documentary for a twenty-five-year-old producer who had absolutely no production experience. He had taken his savings and hired a crew to shoot ten hours of videotape about infantry recruit basic training. Only after the tape was shot and his funds were running out did he realize he didn't know how to turn what he had into a finished program.

Three trends have come together to create this new interest in nonfiction video and film production.

The first is the growing belief that, today, many people can't— or won't or don't have time to—read. The popular wisdom is that they *can* be reached by video.

The second is the growth of reality programming on television. This started with silly home videos, expanded to include videos made by eyewitnesses to disasters and unique events, and now has grown to include tabloid news programs.

The third is the accessibility and apparent ease of use of video technology. Writers and editors accustomed to working in print are being asked to create videos instead of brochures. Corporate communicators are being asked by their managements to document their institutions' activities on video. Artists, writers, and other creative people are finding new outlets for their creativity in the current video explosion.

But even those who have knowledge and experience with video and film technology—for example from producing sales or training videos or TV commercials—can find themselves lost when they turn to documentary. Unfortunately, many people think that because they are making a film about actual events, the *truth* will jump inside their cameras and will automatically reveal itself on the screen to their audience.

This never happens.

DOCUMENTARY GENRES

Documentaries can range from those shot in a hot situation, happening *right now* with the outcome in doubt, to fully scripted reenactments or re-creations shot with the same preparation and attention to detail as a feature film or television program. And these two different approaches to the nonfiction film have existed from the earliest days of documentary.

History and Biography

Documentaries have always looked at historical events and the biographies of important or interesting people. Today, television and the education market make these prime areas for documentarians. History and biography are after-the-fact reports on past events. The problem for the documentarian always is to find a way to make such documentaries visually interesting. For people and events of the twentieth century, there may be stock footage or photographs. Before that, there may be a few paintings or drawings, but hardly the wealth of visual material needed to fill a half-hour or hour documentary.

The documentarian often fills in by interviewing experts, by going to the site of the event or the home or working place of the biographical character. Today we also find documentarians borrowing footage from feature films to illustrate the period, person, or event.

Another approach is reenactment, re-creating the historical time or the people and events of the biography. Reenactment in documentary should follow the same rules as re-creation in a historical or biographical text. What is shown should be accurate and the truth as the documentarian understands it.

What about Docudrama?

There is nothing new about basing a dramatic presentation on a historical person or event. But films such as *Cromwell, The Longest Day, JFK,* and others are not documentaries. They may be related to actual events, but these films are not bound by the historical truth of those events. They are works of fiction derived from the lives of real people and the history of real events. Docudrama is no more documentary than a can of "real draft" beer is a draft beer. These are terms dreamed up by a marketing person to make you believe something is what it isn't.

Documentaries of Behavior

The ability to go anywhere with lightweight recording equipment made it possible to follow people around and observe on film or videotape whatever they do. In the early days of direct cinema, there were a lot of films made about ordinary people living out their ordinary lives. Films such as the Maysles' *Salesman*, Alan King's *A Married Couple*, and the PBS series *An American Family*. This became a kind of anthropology of ourselves.

One of my first films, and the one I remain the proudest of, *A Young Child Is . . .* , made in 1972, set out to observe how very young children grow and learn. Until then, those who wanted to look at the behavior of children were stuck with works such as the McGraw Hill *Ages and Stages* series, which took prevailing child development theory and *illustrated* it by having children act out whatever the experts said children did at that age. One unforgivable offshoot of this series was hanging the name "the terrible twos" on two-year-olds, when they are actually terrific, not terrible. Anyone observing without preconceived expert theory would recognize that this is the age when babies become people in their own right. And people don't always do what someone else wants them to.

The behavioral documentary is very much with us today. And much of this book will deal with recording human behavior.

Documentaries of Emotion

As the behavioral documentary pushed us in new directions, some documentarians began to explore another kind of behavior, which might be called the documentary of emotion. For example, Allie Light, in her brilliant film *Dialogues with Madwomen*, explores the emotional dimension of mental illness.

Reality Videos—
A *New Role for Direct Cinema*

With competition squeezing their production budgets, network and syndicated broadcast television producers have discovered reality videos. What started with several comedy shows based on silly home videos has resulted in a new interest in the actuality documentary. Programs such as "Cops," "LAPD," and "Real Stories of the Highway Patrol" are bringing direct cinema to the home screen nightly.

And this has reopened questions of truth versus reality, which burned so brightly in the early cinema verité era and remain a primary concern today.

ABOUT THIS BOOK

This book is written for the person who wants to make a documentary, for whatever reason, and especially for those interested in recording behavior out there in the real world, either for production of a documentary or for research of some sort.

It brings into focus what I have learned from making and watching documentaries and from trying to help others organize the documentaries they've shot. It's based on a lifetime of love for the nonfiction film in all its permutations.

My teacher and colleague at The Annenberg School of Communications, the late Sol Worth, once said he'd never seen a film he didn't like. Because Sol was a scholar first and a filmmaker second, I think he meant that he'd never seen a film he couldn't learn something from. And I'd go along with that. Some of my best documentary ideas have been sparked by films I absolutely hated.

But I have loved *making* documentaries from the first time I sat down at an editing table and spliced selected pieces of film into a visual statement. I have shot, directed, edited, and written scores of documentary films and videos. And in the quiet hours of the night while I cut film or edited video, I've thought a lot about what goes into a successful documentary. And by "successful" I mean a documentary that communicates to an audience exactly what you intended.

That means I'm a theory maker. I don't think of making a documentary as a technical—by which I mean equipment—problem. It is always, from initial concept to final print, a communication problem.

Generally we learn how to operate our technology long before we really have any clear idea of *what we want to do with it*. Put another way, you can get so caught up in the problems of shooting that you forget about showing. And it is the documentary the audience sees, not the one the documentarian shoots (or wishes he or she had shot), that counts.

Doing a documentary requires:

- planning the visual evidence that needs to be recorded,
- recognizing it when it occurs, and
- selecting and organizing what has been recorded to present a visual argument to your audience.

So a substantial portion of this book is devoted to (1) planning what you're going to do before shooting, and (2) after shooting, selecting and organizing what has been shot into the visual evidence of your documentary.

It should go without saying that the introduction of lights, microphones, a camera, and three or four technical people into any situation can have a profound effect on that situation. So a part of the book is devoted to problems and techniques involved in filming people who are not actors in actual situations on their home grounds.

Much of what I have learned about documentary filmmaking has been learned under pressure—on location with a small budget and a tight schedule, where every mistake cut deeply. So for every chapter in the book, somewhere, I've got a scar.

Shooting a documentary is a lot of fun. I'm always up when I set off for a new location to start a documentary. There's a kind of automatic status that goes along with being a documentarian.

When you walk in with the lights, the sound equipment, and the camera, people assume you know what you're doing. Even if it's your first documentary, you are automatically accorded the status of professional. That's pretty heady stuff.

But a documentarian must never forget that the end of this exciting process is a program that an audience is going to look at— without any explanation from you. The audience will never know how much fun—or how much trouble—you had in getting the pictures. Nor should they.

The audience can be concerned only with the documentary you show them.

2

HOW THINGS GOT THIS WAY

These days, when a high-8 camera fits in the palm of the hand and can render crisp pictures of a ghost in a cave, it is hard to imagine the problems of early filmmakers, and especially documentarians, who wanted to record real people and real events in the real world. Many of the problems of making documentaries are related to the evolution of film, sound, and video technology, and the ways in which the available technology caused documentarians to think about what they were doing.

Great visual films were made in the silent era because all the filmmaker had to work with was the image. Almost all of the techniques for telling a story visually had been worked out in the first decade of the motion picture medium's existence. By the 1920s, film was a sophisticated art form and communication medium. Robert Flaherty's *Nanook of the North* remains a classic. Joris Ivens's *The Bridge* is a clinic on observing actuality with a movie camera. And Walter Ruttman's *Berlin, Symphony of a Great City* became the model for all subsequent city films.

In some ways, making a documentary in the silent era was similar to making one today. Filmmakers went out with their hand-cranked cameras and recorded whatever interested them. But then things changed.

THE HOLLYWOOD MODEL

Starting with the sound era in the 1930s, the model for all film-making became the way films were made in the big movie factories in Hollywood. They were—and still are—technological marvels. Battalions of expert technicians could create a frontier town or burn Rome overnight. If the light outdoors wasn't exactly right, they moved the production onto a huge sound stage, where it could be high noon, twenty-four hours a day.

Slow film, bulky cameras, and masses of sound equipment kept the scene being shot pinned down to a tightly defined location. Actors had to "hit the mark" where the light was right and a microphone was positioned to record what they said. Film was shot in short takes, starting with the master scene. Then the set was relit and everything was moved around for the next take, and so on.

In documentary, it was a lot easier to shoot silent footage with a lightweight camera, get some wild sound with a nonsynchronous recorder for use in the background, and limit sound-on-film shooting—if used at all—to a few carefully staged, convenient sequences that would give an air of naturalism to the film.

There were good technical reasons for this. Equipment to synchronize camera and sound was heavy and unwieldy. It was also expensive. Shooting sound on film raised the cost of a film by an order of magnitude. It meant that a lot more film had to be shot, because people speaking the lines of a script would make mistakes. Or, if there was no script, the crew had to keep shooting until the person being interviewed said something worthwhile. The problems of editing sound on film also raised the editing time by several-fold.

As a result, narration and music dominated the sound tracks of nonfiction films from the '30s well into the '60s. There were many good films made this way. These included classics such as John Grierson's *Night Mail*, Pare Lorentz's *The Plow That Broke the Plains* and *The River*, and Willard Van Dyke's *The City* in the '30s; the many great war documentaries of the '40s; and the early television documentaries of the '50s, such as the award-winning Fred Friendly–Edward R. Murrow program *See It Now*.

But there were a lot more bad ones. The pictures were technically perfect. The sound was crisp and clear. The narrator was lucid and informative. But all too often the film itself was a dull, illustrated lecture.

According to the Hollywood model, a picture had to be perfect, or it couldn't be shot. Everything was scripted. Suppose the documentary was about a world-famous author, a Nobel Prize winner who would never let anyone else write, or change, a line in his books. Nevertheless, a scriptwriter would write the words for the famous person to say, and the world-famous author would memorize them—and say them.

Believe it or not, actors were often used instead of the actual personalities, because the actors were considered "more believable on film."

Hollywood Rules

Filmmaking—and later television—was boxed in by *rules* that everyone knew and everyone followed. A stray sunbeam in the lens, a long pause while someone thought of the answer to a question, the wrong kind of light, ambient noise on the sound track—anything that would take away from the high gloss of the finished product— was justification for a retake, or to stop filming.

The statement of the film often had to be subservient to the technology with which it was being made.

I first became involved with filmmaking as this era was coming to a close. Through great good luck, I found myself in the documentary film laboratory at The Annenberg School of Communications, studying under Sol Worth. Sol was a commercial photographer and innovative documentarian who knew all the rules by heart and firmly believed they had *nothing* to do with making a documentary.

Filming by the Rules

Here's a story Sol used to tell from the rules period.

He swore that it's true.

Once upon a time there was a film company in New York that had a contract with a major airline to produce travel films. It had an immense library of stock footage from all over the world. It had thousands of feet of color film of the airline's planes taking off, landing, and flying over scenic countryside. And each year it would send a film crew to several foreign cities to update the stock footage.

One year it scheduled a film crew to shoot in Rome and Tokyo. Almost a year before the trip to Rome, the company had sought, and been granted, permission to place a camera in the best possible position for filming the Vatican. This was a balcony that commanded a view of everything.

Just before the crew arrived in Rome, the pope died. And the day the perfect balcony was reserved was the day of the election of a new pope. Suddenly the location from which they planned to shoot some scenes for a travelogue had become the premium piece of real estate in Rome for news coverage of the election.

"Great!" said the director. "We'll shoot all the film we've got, and sell it to the news media. It's a once-in-a-lifetime chance."

He had a Mitchell 35mm camera, a first-class union cameraman, and a lot of very slow color stock. In these days of fine-grain, high-speed color film, it's hard to imagine there was once a time when color stock had an exposure index of ten, but there was. Getting a decent picture took bright daylight or massive studio lighting. This story takes place back then.

"Hold on," said the cameraman. "I'm a first-class union cameraman. I have to guarantee the footage that I shoot. If there's enough light, I shoot. If not, I won't."

"I'll take the responsibility," said the director. (He had already tried to buy some high-speed black-and-white film, but there was none available. It was sold out to the newspeople.) "Look, if there isn't enough light, we'll shoot at sixteen frames per second, or eight frames per second. Just so we get pictures of the smoke coming up, signifying the election of a new pope."

"Hold on," replied the cameraman. "If you think I'm going to change the speed of this camera when I've got to take it all over the world, you're crazy. This isn't a toy. Once the speed is changed, we might never get it right again. I'll shoot at twenty-four frames per second if there is enough light to expose the film properly. Otherwise, I don't shoot."

The day the new pope was elected was dark, dull, and overcast. The director stood on the perfect balcony, next to his adamant cameraman, watching a once-in-a-lifetime opportunity and praying the sun would come out. He pleaded, begged, commanded, and tried to bribe the cameraman to shoot. But the sun never came, and the cameraman stood there all day long and never exposed a frame of film.

Technology had triumphed over common sense, and the opportunity was lost forever.

That story seemed ridiculous when I first heard it, and I'm sure it seems downright impossible to believe today. But it is part of our filmmaking heritage and illumines the mind-set that led up to the direct cinema revolution.

The epilogue to the Rome story occurred a month later in Tokyo. The director and cameraman had filmed everything in the script except for a shot of the Imperial Palace with Mount Fuji in the background. It was their last day in Japan—a perfect day, clear sky, a light haze in the valley, a few white clouds over the mountain—a day like a Japanese silk print.

The director thought the shot of the palace would be more interesting if the clouds over Fuji seemed to be moving. But their movement was so slow that they appeared stationary in any take of a reasonable length.

If we shoot at a slower speed, he reasoned, the clouds will seem to be moving.

Once again he asked the cameraman to change the speed of the camera. "I'll take the responsibility," he said. "It's the last shot before we go home. If the camera jams, we haven't lost anything. We already have the scene at normal speed. Slow the camera down to eight frames per second, and we'll have an even better shot."

"Hold on," said the cameraman. "I'm supposed to shoot at twenty-four frames per second, and I won't take a chance on jamming the camera. Besides, if I slow the camera speed now, and nothing goes wrong, you'll say I should have done it in Rome."

And that was that.

The spark of life was missing from films made this way, crushed out under the pressure of technology. I don't think we realized this, completely, back then. Perhaps we sensed that something was missing. But the audience—no less than the filmmakers—knew that this was how nonfiction films had to be.

The Traditional Documentary

Whether filmed in process or re-created, the documentary film until the 1960s was a show-and-tell affair. It was Grierson who in the 1930s first used the term *documentary*, derived from the French word *documentaire*, which means travelogue. Even the highly acclaimed CBS *See It Now* documentaries of Edward R. Murrow and Fred Friendly were closer in structure to the dull travelogues shown in junior high social studies classes than to modern documentary videos and films.

These films did let you see things you might otherwise never know about, but always as an after-the-fact report. The nonfiction film was like the nonfiction magazine article or book, a report from those who knew what had happened to those who didn't.

BREAKING THE RULES

But at the same time that technical domination of filmmaking was reaching a peak, there were filmmakers already breaking the "rules."

Army Signal Corps cameramen went into battle armed with spring-wound, one-hundred-foot capacity, 16mm Bell and Howell or 35mm Eyemo cameras. They shot what was happening and brought it back. They risked their lives to get the picture as it happened. And not all of them returned.

Anthropologists were experimenting with film. Even silent footage, they believed, was a better document of behavior than their laborious note-taking systems.

The Influence of Television

One could argue that it was television that made possible the development of the documentary of human behavior. The nature of television—live television—is the instantaneous transmission of whatever happens in front of the camera. Some selection is possible, of course, but no editing, no polishing and refining, and no delay in presentation to the audience.

We watched the Gulf War on CNN, even though there was little to see, and we watched O. J. Simpson cruising the freeways of Los Angeles in the white Bronco while very little happened on screen, simply because *we didn't know what might happen next.*

It was television, and specifically the "Tonight Show," that showed us that people talking about things they cared about could be intensely interesting. The entire program, which was broadcast live in its early years, was an exercise in spontaneity. (Now, of course, it is that wonderful TV oxymoron *live on tape.*) The various segments were planned as to who would appear, but no one knew who would say what to whom or when a topic would suddenly catch fire and stretch on long beyond the allotted time.

TV's Effect on the Classic Documentary

The environment of spontaneous presentation created by television changed forever the way we looked at the traditional documentary. The technical polish, the carefully worded script spoken by a mellifluous voice-of-god narrator, and the obvious pretense that the camera wasn't there, all contributed to a structural message which seemed to say, "We know something you don't know." When what was shown had some importance, this came across as arrogance. When it wasn't very important, it seemed almost silly that so much effort could be expended with so little result.

TV Sports

It is the sense of process, of watching while it happens with the outcome in doubt, that has raised television coverage of sporting events to an art form. Understand that these are instantaneous documentaries. A live broadcast on TV is not just the next best thing to being there in person. It's an entirely different experience. When it is well done, you can see, hear, and know far more about what is happening at the event than would ever be possible from a seat in the stands.

Keep the presentation of sports on TV in mind as a model for recording and structuring a documentary.

CINEMA VERITÉ CHANGED THE WORLD

New technology opened a new world for documentarians. They could go into the field with lightweight equipment and capture on film people as they were and events as they happened. The only limitations were the sensitivity of the film—you had to have *some* light—the cost of film stock and processing, and the cooperation of those involved. At *Life* magazine, Robert Drew put together the first direct cinema production company and with other pioneers such as Ricky Leacock and the Maysles brothers began to shoot a new kind of documentary that broke all the rules. I can still remember the physical shock of seeing the French cinema verité film *Chronicle of a Summer, 1960* as a student at The Annenberg School of Communications, the exultation I felt at viewing Wolf Koenig's *Lonely Boy*, my incredulousness at the intimacy of the Drew Associates' classic direct cinema documentary *Primary*, and the potential I saw in Arthur Barron's *The Berkeley Rebels*. These films might seem fairly tame today—after all, documentarians have been copying their techniques for more than thirty years— but they were earth-shaking at the time because they showed a completely new way of making a documentary. In essence, these documentarians put their research on film and showed the audience whatever they found.

And when video technology caught up with and surpassed film, it became possible to record with as little as a half foot-candle of light and shoot forever on inexpensive videotape without the crushing costs of film processing.

With these developments, filmmakers could—and did—record events as they happened. And because they filmed real people (not actors) doing real things in a real situation, it was almost inevitable that they began to think of nonfiction filmmaking as documenting reality. Because the footage was *real*, it seemed to be the best evidence of its own truth. *Cinéma* became *vérité*, the camera couldn't lie, and an entire generation of filmmakers went about trying to get reality to fit into a little box.

It seemed so easy.

It wasn't.

THE REALITY PROBLEM

The biggest problem in the development of direct cinema and the behavioral documentary came from the undeniable fact that it was shot in a real situation. That became the justification, if not the outright excuse, for any number of conceptual errors.

Confusing Actuality with Truth

One was the error of trying to stuff reality into a box, which came from confusing the *truth* of the documentary with the *actuality* of the situation in which it was shot. If it happened, it's real, the argument went. And if it's real, it's true.

Not really.

It may be worth noting that the French chose the term *vérité*, not *réalité*, to describe *cinéma* as found in the behavioral documentary. What is shot bears only an ideal relationship to what is shown. The documentary shown to an audience is a carefully constructed analog that has been abstracted from the footage that was shot. It has been tempered by the overall truth of the situation as the documentarian understands it and, indeed, by the *honesty* of the documentarian in constructing the program.

The distinction between truth and reality was an obvious and necessary one in the early days of documentary film. The technology simply didn't permit much direct filming of actual events. So a documentary was expected to be *true* in the sense that it was based on fact and its accuracy could be verified. But it wasn't expected to be *real*. Most documentaries were re-creations of events, using actors and written scripts, and were often shot in a studio just like fiction films.

The documentary film—from *Battleship Potemkin* to *The River* to *Harvest of Shame*—was clearly an analog to the event being shown. It was "documentary" because it was based on documented facts that were a matter of record and not just the product of a scriptwriter's imagination. In those days a documentary was expected to be true, but not necessarily to be real, because reality was usually too fleeting and elusive to be captured by slow film stocks, heavy cameras, and cumbersome, inadequate sound systems.

Cinema verité showed a new way to film behavior. A subtle shift developed, away from the technological stance in which the film that was to be made controlled the action in front of the cameras, toward a new notion of letting the action control the film. Naturally, what you might anticipate happening, did happen. Everyone wanted to try it, and as the '60s passed into the '70s, there was a rush to take cameras somewhere—anywhere!—turn them on, and let events record themselves.

In various communities, kids were given 8mm cameras and a few minutes of instruction and were told to go out and make a movie. Hospitals and mental health institutions bought videotape equipment and began to record hours and hours of human behavior. Public schools jumped into videotape and film with a vengeance.

The "subtle shift" had become a vicious backswing away from technological control and all that went with it. And that, unfortunately, included technical competence and planning. In a sense, filmmaking was trapped in a new kind of technological tyranny, which posed as complete freedom. These beginning filmmakers quite literally were saying, "We don't need all that. We'll just point the camera at something interesting, and it will make the film for us."

In a move that later became a habit, Public Broadcasting in the mid-sixties spent more than a million dollars and two years making a multipart documentary about the members of a single family. And when the furor over *An American Family* died down, the notions of cinematic truth and cinematic reality had taken some heavy blows to the body, and all that remained was the conviction that what was shown in the series had, in fact, happened—somewhere, sometime—while a camera was running.

But the belief in the "realness" of a documentary came—as it always has—from the way in which the director, camera operator, and film editor selected what was to be shot and shown, and organized it for presentation to an audience as an accurate analog of the situation that was filmed.

Glorifying Grab Footage

The new film technology provided the illusion of recording reality by letting filmmakers shoot candid, unstaged, undirected, sound footage of people, events, and places that previously had been impossible to get. And this led to the error of justifying poor footage on the basis that it was shot in a real situation—on the fly as it were.

I'm guilty along with the rest. I shot with high-speed film under fluorescent lights and got images that looked like fifty-year-old wallpaper. In fact, in a triumph of form over content, I stuck a swish pan and focusing zoom that went nowhere into the final version of my first behavioral documentary just because I thought it gave the feel of actuality filming to an otherwise fairly humdrum scene.

Winging It

There is the recurring error of believing that recording an event as it happens does away with any need to plan the shoot in advance. Quite the opposite is true.

Serendipity plays a part in documentary just because you are working with actuality. And every now and then, someone chances to turn on a camera just as something interesting happens in front of the lens. But the good stuff—including the "unplanned" good stuff—is most often the result of a shooting plan that puts camera and crew in situations where something interesting is likely to happen. Indeed, the less you know about what will happen, the more essential it is to plan for contingencies.

Talking Heads

The ability to shoot sound on film wherever you went opened a new concern with talk. When people talking were difficult and expensive to record, documentarians either ignored interviews or planned for them very carefully. But now some documentarians began to concentrate on what people *said* rather than on what they *did*, which brought the phrase *talking head* into the language. I'm referring to the interview as a set piece where the subjects are placed in front of the camera and asked questions, like the veterans at Midway. I'm not referring to people talking to each other—or even to themselves—as they go about their lives.

If it costs several hundred dollars to shoot a ten-minute interview sequence on film, few of us, except those darlings of the culture mafia who seem to have more grant money than anyone ought to be allowed, are going to shoot interviews promiscuously. But when videotape brings the cost of stock down to less than a dollar a minute, interviews tend to proliferate. I have seen too many documentaries where the documentarian has gone out with a camera and interviewed everyone he or she could think of. And then edited the interviews into a presentation.

When I hear a producer or director talking about shooting lots of interviews and then having them transcribed so he or she can work from the transcript in editing the documentary, I cringe. Because usually what will result is something that may be more than a Q & A magazine article, perhaps even more than the sort of thing you might hear on talk radio, but it will definitely be something less than a film.

Talk is cheap. Show us what the people did.

TWO MAJOR APPROACHES TO DOCUMENTARY

Throughout its history, the documentary has followed two different approaches. One is anthropological—showing people, institutions, and cultures as they are, or at least as they seem, when a camera is pointed at them. The other is historical—trying to bring to life on film or video significant people and events from the past.

Nanook, San Pietro, and *Hoop Dreams* are anthropological. *Potemkin, The Sorrow and the Pity,* and *Baseball* are historical.

Robert Flaherty took his camera into the frozen Arctic in the early '20s to observe behavior for *Nanook of the North.* At about the same time, in the Soviet Union, Sergei Eisenstein was "documenting" the Bolshevik revolution with reenactment films such as *Battleship Potemkin* and *October: Ten Days that Shook the World.*

John Huston's combat cameramen shot *The Battle of San Pietro* as it happened in World War II Italy. Marcel Ophuls went back to re-create the sense of that tragic time in occupied France in *The Sorrow and the Pity* through interviews conducted two decades after the war.

Hoop Dreams follows the lives and athletic careers of two young basketball players as they unfold before the camera over a period of several years. *Baseball: A Film by Ken Burns* uses interviews with players, fans, and friends of the filmmaker, along with photographs and stock footage, to portray the director's lengthy view of the history of the sport.

History and Biography

Historical documentaries and biographies usually require some kind of re-creation. There may be stock footage available to cover some parts of the story. There may be still pictures, drawings, or graphics. But mostly what will exist are precisely what you'll find in books of history and biography—words. And words by themselves, no matter how well written, no matter how eloquently spoken, do not make a film. On very rare occasions what someone has to say about a person or an event will be the best possible way to present the person or event. *Very rare occasions.*

The documentarian always has the responsibility to find a way to portray this person or event in a manner that is visually interesting. And this always means more than finding some *visuals* to illustrate the words. In the PBS series *FDR*, for example, the second hour deals with the period in Franklin Delano Roosevelt's life when he contracts polio and learns to live with it. In my opinion there is less than a minute of interesting footage in this hour. Interesting footage should be revealing; it should show us something we otherwise wouldn't know. It must always go beyond illustrating the text.

History and biography need to be tightly organized and require a carefully crafted structure. I have no problem with Ken Burns's *The Civil War* covering nine volumes for a total of eleven and a third hours. It's a big topic. But then his *Baseball: A Film by Ken Burns* uses the same nine-volume structure and runs several hours longer. It includes interviews with people who have very little to do with the sport and actually repeats the same stories and the same scenes in more than one volume.

From the standpoint of being visually interesting, *FDR* and *Baseball* are not the models to use for biography or history.

Filming Behavior

From the early Edison short *Mother Washing a Baby* to Flaherty's *Nanook* to *In the Street* by Levitt, Loeb, and Agee to Rouch and

Morin's *Chronicle of a Summer, 1960* to Galan's *The Blue Minority* to Warhol's *Sleep* to the body of work by Frederick Wiseman and others to contemporary documentaries such as *The War Room* and *Hoop Dreams*, the goal of many documentarians has been, and is, to show people as they are. To record and reveal human behavior.

A tremendous body of work was created by film and video documentarians as they tested, revised, and refined the behavioral documentary through practical experience in the field. And while it was possible to see the results of the work of these early practitioners, it was not at all easy to determine how the results were achieved. In the beginning it seemed like magic, and we often asked, "Did the people know the camera was there?" We had never seen everyday people bare their souls so completely on film.

Three decades later, the shock value of personal revelation has been blunted by tabloid TV and talk shows whose hosts and guests hold *nothing* sacred. But the desire—and the need—to document behavior as it happens, remain.

There is a way to film people so that their speech and behavior are consistent with their personality and beliefs, even when they know that a camera and recorder are running. It's not such a difficult task that it requires spy technology and hidden cameras. Nor is it so easy that anyone can do it just by turning on a video camera and letting it run. Recording human behavior takes work, intelligence, an understanding of human nature, a cooperative crew—and practice.

And there are dozens—maybe hundreds—of ways to do it wrong.

. . . .

3

REALITY IS NOT ENOUGH

If you're serious about doing documentary, you're going to have to come to grips with the reality problem. You can start by getting rid of a couple of notions that have had great influence on making documentaries but simply don't hold up on close examination.

The Camera Doesn't Lie

The first of these is that the camera doesn't lie. Which is nonsense. Cameras don't tell the truth, either. They simply record a very coarse analog of the light patterns in front of the lens.

What is a picture? On film it's the result of the clustering of silver halide or dye molecules into black dots or points of color. Look closely enough, and the image disappears. On videotape it is a magnetized signal that will cause a video tube to create a pattern of light, dark, and color on a television screen. In digital video it is a stored pattern of ones and zeroes yielding the same effect: a display of light and color on the screen.

It is only the mind of the viewer, making inferences from these shadows and color patterns, that gives them meaning.

Actuality Equals Truth

The second notion, in all its eloquent and complex permutations, has accounted for thousands of silly, unintelligible, and stupid films and videos. It is this: *What was filmed really happened; therefore it is true, and will be accepted by an audience as true.*
Which is simply not true.

Even if we define reality as whatever happens when the camera is on that is spontaneous, unplanned, unrehearsed, and undirected—which neatly sidesteps several thousand years of philosophical speculation about the nature of reality—there is no reason to assume that what was captured by the camera is *true.*

At the most obvious level, if we film someone telling a lie, then what is the truth of the scene? We've documented that the person said whatever he or she said. But we may have no way of knowing whether what they've said is true. Even if we know the person is lying, we may not know why. Perhaps it's just a joke. Perhaps they are psychotic and don't know they are lying. Or perhaps they are simply repeating what they have been told and believe to be true. While we have recorded a piece of what happened, its mere existence tells us little or nothing about its truth value.

How about this: In a dusty village, a person with his hands bound behind his back kneels in a dirt road. A man in uniform takes a pistol from his holster and shoots the kneeling man through the head. Cold-blooded murder? Perhaps. Or maybe a legal execution according to the laws of that country or the mores of that culture. Again, we have recorded a piece of what happened, but may need a great deal more information to communicate meaning and to define the truth of what we've filmed.

Even if what we've recorded *is* documentably true, it is dangerous to assume that an audience will judge the truth of a sequence in a documentary on the basis of its objective *realness*. The person telling the truth may behave on film like a liar. The scene of an execution in the middle of the street may look staged to an audience.

THE FORM OF REALITY

A nonfiction video or film, every bit as much as a Hollywood movie or a Broadway play, must work within the framework of audience beliefs, conventions, and expectations. The images on the screen may be both *real* and *true*, but if they lack the appearance of truth, you are setting up a credibility gap with your audience that you may never overcome.

For example, in the early days of the cinema verité movement, documentaries were shot on film. The only way to record any kind of image in the low light of most practical locations—even *with* some minimal production lighting—was to shoot what was then called high-speed black-and-white film. The resulting images were coarse grained, often very contrasty, and with little or no production value to the lighting. And for a time this became the *look* of the reality documentary: black and white, grainy—often scratchy—images with bad lighting. For reasons of his own, which I do not understand, Douglas Keeve adopted this convention for his 1994 documentary *Unzipped,* about fashion designer Isaac Mizrahi.

Today we have *shaky-cam,* which yields a jumpy image that never settles down to let the action unfold in front of it because it is too busy emulating a camcorder in the hands of a hyperactive child. Actuality, we are led to believe, comes handheld, badly lit, and with muffled sound, even though today's technology allows us to record rock-steady, well-lit scenes with decent sound—even in hot situations.

Does this mean you have to use the shaky-cam convention to make a believable documentary? No. But it does mean you have to be aware of such formal elements in shaping the documentary communication you will eventually show your audience. It means you may even have to be cognizant of conventions from fiction such as *verisimilitude*—the appearance of truth—in order to make a documentary statement that is not only true, but believable.

HIGH DEGREE OF ABSTRACTION OF FILM AND VIDEO

At the start of this chapter I suggest that a picture is a pattern of molecules, iron filings, or digital formulae, arranged to create light and shadow, which can be recognized as an analog to something the viewer might recognize.

"Yes," the viewer says, looking at a snapshot, "that's Aunt Mary."

Well, no, it isn't. It's a piece of paper with a dot pattern on it. It is a highly abstract analog of a small piece of something which may have existed in the real world. Indeed, this picture doesn't even show all of Aunt Mary. It only shows her head. And not all of her head —just one side of it.

The core of the matter is not the picture, but the human being who looks at this tiny bit of data and says, "Yes, that's Aunt Mary."

One final example. I'll make it simple. In your office is a blank, white wall. You want to show the reality of this wall to someone. You take a motion picture camera and carefully record your wall. Have you captured its reality on film?

Let's take a look at the film, before it is projected. Is there a white wall recorded there for all to see?

No, there isn't.

What *is* recorded on the film?

Nothing.

Nothing?

That's right. In order to represent the white wall you photographed, the motion picture film has nothing on it. The light of the projector shines through the empty plastic of the film to represent your white wall as simply light falling on a white screen.

There is no reality recorded on the film. There is only a high level of symbolic abstraction, which by implication may be made to represent an analog of something that was recorded in the real world.

I'm carrying this to an extreme because if you want to make good, believable, useful documentaries or reality videos, you have to get over the idea that you can suck reality into a camera and blow it back at your audience.

DIGITALLY ENHANCED IMAGES

Not long ago, the existence of an image was at least evidence that what was shown had happened. No longer. Digitized images and powerful computers can create scenes of things that never were, in such a way that no one may be able to judge whether what is shown is a record of something that exists or an artist's fantasy.

Novelist and filmmaker Michael Crichton explores this problem in his novel *Rising Sun*. Detective Peter James Smith, who tells the story, talks with Dr. Phillip Sanders at the University of Southern California:

> I said, "These copies are exact?"
> "Oh, yes."
> "So they're legal?"
> Sanders frowned. "Legal in what sense?"
> "Well, as evidence, in a court of law—"
> "Oh, no," Sanders said. "These tapes would never be admissible in a court of law."
> "But if they're exact copies?"
> "It's nothing to do with that. All forms of photographic evidence, including video, are no longer admissible in court."
> "I haven't heard that," I said.
> "It hasn't happened yet," Sanders said. "The case law isn't entirely clear. But it's coming. All photographs are suspect these days. Because now, with digital systems, they can be changed perfectly. *Perfectly.* And that's something new. . . .
> "Photographs always had integrity precisely because they were impossible to change. So we considered photographs to represent reality. But for several years now, computers have allowed us to make seamless alterations of photographic images. A few years back the *National Geographic* moved the Great Pyramid of Egypt on a cover photo. The editors didn't like where the pyramid

was, and they thought it would compose better if it was moved. So they just altered the photograph and moved it. Nobody could tell. But if you go back to Egypt with a camera and try to duplicate that picture, you'll find you can't. Because there is no place in the real world where the pyramids line up that way. The photograph no longer represents reality. But you can't tell. Minor example."

"And someone could do the same thing to this tape?"

"In theory, any video can be changed."

EVERY FRAME REQUIRES A DECISION

For the present, at least, reality is out of the box, and documentarians can return to their proper job of recording good images and organizing them in a forceful way to make a statement to an audience. Reality is not enough. We are obliged to document as well as to record.

So let's agree that whatever the terms mean, *reality* in the external world and *truth* in video and film are not the same thing.

The verifiable truth of a video or film depends on the honesty of the documentarian in presenting an accurate analog of the situation as he or she understands it. But that is still no guarantee that the audience will accept the documentary as *true*. It takes a lot of hard, professional work to turn your record of what happened when the camera was on into a documentary that will be believed by an audience.

4

. . . .

RECORDING HUMAN BEHAVIOR

When my oldest son, Jeffrey, was about six years old, I took him to the TV studio at The Annenberg School of Communications, where graduate students were prepping a project in which several artists would demonstrate their work.

We arrived before taping began. In the center of the studio a sculptor had set up an armature loaded with wet clay which he was smoothing with a curved tool. Jeff was enthusiastic about anything to do with art, and he was fascinated by the sculptor. He stopped to watch, while I wandered off to talk with some friends.

The next time I noticed my son, he was standing on an apple box with a wire tool in his hand, reaching up over his head to smooth the clay just as the sculptor had been doing. He appeared to be totally absorbed in the work and made such an interesting picture that the students moved in video cameras to photograph him.

I went to master control to watch on the monitors there. You could see his intense concentration as he carefully worked the clay, and the students working as control room crew were ecstatic. "Look how natural he is!" they said. "How unselfconscious! He's not even paying any attention to the cameras."

In a little while I went back down to the studio. Jeff had been working with the clay for at least fifteen minutes.

"How's it going?" I asked him.

"My arms are killing me," he said without looking up, barely moving his lips.

"Then quit," I said, "and we'll go up to my office and get a Coke."

"I can't," he said.

"Why not?"

"The cameras are still on."

It makes you wonder what the truth is about recording behavior. Does it require a hidden camera to get real behavior? Or can we go into a situation with camera running and expect to record behavior that not only looks genuine but has the ring of truth to it?

Good documentary images don't just happen. You have to plan for them. You have to hunt them out. You have to be disciplined when you are shooting. And you have to come to grips with the tremendous power you exercise just because you and your crew have come onto the scene.

WHAT IT TAKES

Recording human behavior requires sufficient mastery of the recording technology—whether video or motion picture—to allow you to concentrate on the people being filmed.

It requires a contract—not only unwritten, but perhaps never spoken—with these people that you will be a professional and will not abuse their amateur standing. You will let them do whatever they are doing without bothering them with your production problems.

It requires a separate contract with the audience that you will show them the truth as you know it to be, and will not knowingly fool them.

It requires the ability to plan for the unexpected and the ability to discard preconceptions when they don't fit what people are doing in front of the camera.

It requires a high tolerance for uncertainty—a willingness to turn the camera on and let videotape or film run through it with the clock running and production costs mounting in the optimistic belief that something interesting will happen.

It requires an understanding of what is happening in the filming situation, and how that relates to the edited film that will be shown to an audience.

HOW NOT TO RECORD BEHAVIOR

I was shooting a simple interview with a police captain in Wilkes-Barre, Pennsylvania. I had hired a highly professional film crew that had shot many industrial films. But we had never worked together. The camera operator turned out to be the best I've ever worked with at getting clean, well-exposed, nicely composed footage. The camera assistant was an obsessive about keeping the slates and camera log in order, and a tyrant about cleanliness. The sound recordist could get a useable sound bite inside a cement mixer.

The film was focused on community reaction to a plan to provide care and treatment for mental patients in their home communities rather than in large, state-operated institutions. We had picked Wilkes-Barre because this subject had already evoked strong feelings there. I was after community reaction, and I wanted people to be as spontaneous as possible on camera. In briefing the crew, I had told them I wanted an invisible wall between us and anyone we were filming, so that the subjects would not try to be actors.

On that first day, we went to the center square of Wilkes-Barre to interview the police captain. He was a man in his late forties, responsible for police-community relations and also a member of the board of directors of the local mental health organization. I was after his comments on reports that former mental patients had been gathering in the square and annoying other residents.

A Crack in the Invisible Wall

Because I hoped to use his answers to my questions as a kind of running narrative, I was not in the picture. The captain wore a wireless microphone, but I didn't. As we got ready to shoot, the sound recordist said, "Captain, would you repeat the question before you start to answer, so I'll get it on tape?"

That's not my style, because it's a crack in the invisible wall, but it didn't seem too much to ask, so I let it pass. I certainly wasn't going to *prompt* him to repeat the questions, but if he could remember to do it, editing the film might be a little easier.

We slated the first take and began walking and talking. After I had gotten his name and occupation, I asked, "Captain, what about the reports of former mental patients hanging out in the square? Has this been much of a problem?"

"Well, it really hasn't been a problem," he started.

"Repeat the question!" yelled the sound recordist.

"Oh, right," said the captain. "Well, let's see. Has there been much of a problem . . ."

"Could you walk a little faster?" asked the camera operator.

At that point, with the invisible wall crumbling, I yelled, "Cut!"

"It looks terrible," the camera operator said. "You're hardly walking."

"And try to remember to repeat the question," the sound recordist added.

We started again, got through the next couple of questions, and were in the middle of the third when the camera operator took the camera down from his shoulder.

"The film ran out," he said.

Although the film camera was an Eclair NPR, which boasted a five-second magazine change, we stood around for about two minutes while the camera assistant pulled the lens, checked the gate for cleanliness, changed magazines, and set a new slate.

"The walking just doesn't look good," the camera operator told me.

"Okay," I said, "let's pick a spot and stand there and talk."

Death of an Interview

We found a good spot in front of some old people sunning themselves on a bench and started again.

"What was I saying?" the captain asked.

"You were answering the question about police training," the sound recordist told him.

"Better start again," the camera operator said. "It's a new location."

CAPTAIN: Well, the officers . . .

SOUND: Repeat the question!

CAMERA: Could you cheat this way a little more?

CAPTAIN: How's this?

CAMERA: That's good.

SOUND: Remember to repeat the question.

CAPTAIN: What was I saying?

SOUND: Police training.

CAPTAIN: The Wilkes-Barre Police Department has implemented a comprehensive, communitywide, innovative program of . . .

We got through it with several more interruptions. The tape ran out and we had to wait while the sound recordist put in a new reel. A noisy truck went by and we had to repeat a question and answer. But by then it didn't matter. I was no longer interviewing a police captain who knew a great deal about the problem we had come to film. I was playing a bad scene with an amateur actor who was trying to please my crew. In the rushes, the picture was sharp and well composed and the sound was clear. But the captain had been reduced to a boring bureaucrat, spouting officialese and qualifying every statement. His film debut had to be postponed indefinitely.

A SET OF IDEAS ABOUT DOCUMENTING BEHAVIOR

In directing and editing my own documentaries, in viewing hundreds of videos and films made by others, and in teaching documentary production in both video and film, I've come up with a set of ideas about documenting behavior. Let's look at these one at a time.

When We Photograph People, It Is Behavior That We Record on Videotape or Film, and Nothing Else

We don't record personality, or the way people are, or what they believe, or what they think. Those things must be *inferred* from the behavior we observe. We *see* physical behavior, including the way in which a person dresses and grooms himself. We *hear* verbal behavior; not just the words themselves, but the way in which the words are spoken. And that is all. In documentary, as in life, this is the evidence from which we infer the essence of a person's character.

People Behave Differently in Different Situations

How people act, their body posture, facial expression, tone of voice—even the way they dress and the language they use—are situation-specific in accordance with social rules. We *expect* people to act differently in different situations—so much so that when people do not alter their behavior to fit the situation, we say, "They don't know how to behave." So it is not surprising if people alter their behavior in front of a documentary crew and camera. As we'll see, this is not really a problem.

People's Behavior Will Remain Consistent with Their Beliefs about Themselves and Their Place in the World

While we can expect situation-specific variations in behavior, it is the overall pattern that counts. If we have had a chance to observe someone's behavior in one situation fairly carefully, we should be able to make pretty good inferences about that person's beliefs about himself and his world. Therefore, we should be able to make fairly strong predictions about how he will behave in other situations. Naturally, the more we can see someone in different situations, the more powerful are the inferences about him that we can make.

Most People Are Unable to Maintain a Pose or Act Out a Role for Any Length of Time

Most people just aren't very good actors. In fact, many people may not have much of an idea of what their normal behavior is. They never see themselves as others see them, so they have no authentic baseline from which to alter their behavior.

Try to role-play a personality different from your own for an hour or so. To do so with any credibility—and without a script—without going out of character even once, requires intense concentration. Much more than people are willing to give just to fool a camera. And that is the point to this section: People's behavior in front of a camera will be consistent with their behavior elsewhere. Even if they start out playing a role, they'll soon fall back on their normal pattern of behavior.

It Is Hard for People to Be Themselves When They Have Nothing to Do

You can't just plop people down in front of a camera, tell them to be themselves, and start recording. What you'll get is people trying to remember how they act when they are being themselves.

The Presence of a Video or Film Crew Becomes a Factor in the Documentary Situation

The pretense that the camera is not there, which was so much a part of the traditional documentary, simply distorts the evidence that is recorded in a behavioral documentary. That's why I often include in a documentary at least one shot of the crew at work. It reminds the audience that what they are seeing took place in front of a camera and microphone, under lights, with one or more strangers tiptoeing around behind the scene.

If the people in the scene are busy doing familiar things, they'll get interested in what they are doing and let the camera take care of itself. Even in an interview, where people are essentially talking for the camera, most are able to overcome their camera-consciousness and talk directly to the interviewer. Certainly they are aware of the camera, but this awareness becomes a part of their behavior.

When I was shooting an interview with a self-described "mentally ill" patient, the first thing he asked after the camera rolled was, "Are we being on TV now?" In editing the film, I left in that statement. It showed he was aware not only of the fact that he was being filmed, but also of the intended use of the footage. It made his statements about himself which followed, even more powerful and credible.

But sometimes the camera gets in the way. For *Schools for Children* I wanted an interview with the principal of one of the schools in which we were filming. I hoped to use it as a narrative to tie the scenes in the school together. What he had told me in the preinterview was so in keeping with the philosophy underlying the film, and so well said, that I just knew he'd be great. Unfortunately, he wasn't. When the lights came on, he began talking for the record. His informal statements of the day before were transposed into the safe, polysyllabic jargon of an education text, and nothing I did as the interviewer could make him change.

The Behavior of the Production Crew Can and Will Affect the Behavior of the People in the Shooting Situation

This is most dramatically shown with the police captain in Wilkes-Barre. What you must strive for is to create an invisible wall between the production crew and the people in the scene. Hubert Smith, who shot 160,000 feet of film documenting the behavior of

Mayans in the Yucatán Peninsula, said that one of the hardest things he had to do was to convince his subjects that he and his crew were not guests in their homes, but were working.

It took incredible patience, he said, just to sit in a room and keep insisting, "whatever you do is interesting," without yielding to the temptation to suggest some activity. But that's what they did. They also refused all offers of refreshment during the shooting period, promising to come back later—after all the shooting was finished—to eat with the family. Eventually this would pay off, and the family would be able to go about its business in the presence of the film crew without attempting to include the documentarians in its activities.

In Order to Avoid Controlling the Behavior of the People in the Documentary, You Must Control Yourself and Your Production Crew

A good model for shooting a behavioral documentary is the live television coverage of a football game. The program documents an event in progress with the outcome in doubt. Shooting concentrates on the behavior of the subjects in the scene with a heavy emphasis—instant playback, isolated cameras, slow motion—on presenting evidence of that behavior.

There is a well-defined line of demarcation between the production crew and the subjects in the shooting situation. For instance, the camera operator cannot go out onto the playing field to get a better shot. Nor can the director ask the quarterback to run the play that resulted in a touchdown again—but this time at the other end of the field where the light is better, and with a three-beat pause before the pass is thrown.

All the director can do is prepare carefully, select the crew and equipment that will do the best job, give each person a specific assignment, try to be ready for anything, strive for excellence, and above all, forget a poor shot or missed opportunity as soon as the moment has passed.

Making a documentary is very much like that. You have to do

your homework. You have to know why you are going to this location to shoot. And you should have a good idea of the kind of visual evidence you are looking for. You have to make sure your equipment is in good working order and is appropriate to the job at hand. You have to brief the crew on what you expect from them—not just on what you want them to do. You also have to make clear precisely what you *don't* want them to do. You have to make certain that cameras and recorders are loaded appropriately. There's nothing worse than running out of tape or film right at the height of the action.

You Can't Worry About Behavior that Happens Off-camera

You have to be willing to shrug off a missed shot or the fact that an interesting piece of business happened off-camera, out of the lights, or while you were reloading. The best you can do is note it, remember it, and try to be ready if it happens again. Every documentarian knows that interesting behavior always seems to happen immediately after the camera has been turned off. I *expect* that I'll see something that I'm going to *wish* I had shot. That way I don't get depressed when it happens and begin to wonder if, just this once, I should intervene and try to get the people to re-create the scene. As the producer I say to myself, as the director, "If you don't have the footage, then as far as this documentary is concerned, it never happened. Don't worry about it. Work with the visual evidence you do have."

What Is Actually Recorded Comes as the Result of a Combination of Preparation and Luck

You have to know what you eventually want to show to an audience. This defines the purpose of the documentary. It may be quite vague, such as, "I want to show evidence of early learning in young children." Or it could be quite specific, for example, "I want to show the different ways in which husbands and wives talk to each other when they are angry."

Careful preparation should lead you and your crew to a location where you have a high probability of observing the behavior you want to record. And a sensitivity to the material you're looking for will increase the probability that you'll have the camera turned on when it does happen. But since you don't have control over what happens in front of the camera, there always remains an element of luck.

Maybe nothing interesting happens the day you're there. That's bad luck. Preparation, planning, and control of yourself and your crew can hold this to a minimum, but there will be times when you use up videotape or film with no apparent results. That's why the shooting ratio for a behavioral documentary is high. You just keep shooting and smiling, never letting the subjects know that you're not getting it.

There's also good luck. Sometimes you'll get a piece of behavior that is so much better than anything you could have dreamed up that you can hardly believe it happened. For instance, when I was shooting A *Young Child Is* . . . , I went to the home of a friend to record his thirteen-month-old son who was just beginning to walk and talk. For half a magazine of film, the kid just sat on a rug playing with his bottle. Then he did do some walking—which we shot—but no talking. It wasn't until weeks later, in the editing room, that I discovered a sequence of incredibly powerful learning going on while the baby was sitting on the rug doing *nothing*.

Shooting a Behavioral Documentary Is an Active Process of Selection and Decision Making

Cameras don't make movies—people do. There is absolutely nothing of the "passive observer" in the efforts of a behavioral documentarian. There is no way to avoid the responsibility for what is shot. Everything that is recorded is the result of a deliberate series of decisions:

To go here, and not there.
To take a camera along.
To load it.
To point it at something—this, and not that.
To shoot at eye level, floor level, or standing on a ladder.
To bring in lights, which may be distracting, or to shoot with available light.
To frame a medium shot rather than a close-up or long shot.
To turn the camera on.
To turn the camera off.

Even when the camera is locked off and you stand frozen, holding your breath to keep from intruding even minutely into the scene, there is an active, totally engaged, decision-making process going on below the surface. It began with the decision to make this documentary, and not some other. Then there were the decisions to be in this location at this time, to shoot this scene, and to do it with a locked-off camera rather than handheld and moving about, to turn the camera on at a certain time, and either to turn it off at some point or to let it go until you run out of videotape or film.

As the complexity of the shooting situation increases, the number of decisions to be made increases. Some of the things the documentarian must continually keep in mind are:

- the purpose of the film
- the kind of behavior he or she is trying to capture
- what is happening in the scene being shot
- the fact that the footage will be edited for presentation to an audience
- how what is being shot in this scene might go with what has been shot before and what is to follow
- how to get the best possible images and sound as visual evidence of the event being shot
- how far the crew can go with all this and still remain on their own side of the invisible wall

The process of editing the footage you've shot is, if anything, even more deliberate than shooting the documentary.

You start with an empty reel and fill it with images and sounds selected from the raw footage, choosing and organizing what the audience will see from what has been recorded.

In the end, there is nothing in the final version of your documentary that was not put there deliberately.

· ·

5

VISUAL EVIDENCE

There is no substitute for good footage.

Advances in film and video technology have given us the ability to record images from reality that would have been impossible just a few years ago.

Cameras attached to telescopes and cameras mounted on satellites look outward into space.

Cameras using fiber optics, cameras mounted on microscopes, and cameras and video repeaters hooked up to electron microscopes, fluoroscopes, and God knows what else, are examining inner space.

Cameras take pictures in the dark using infrared film or light-gathering lenses.

Cameras operating at high speed slow down events that occur too quickly for the eye to follow.

Time-lapse photography speeds up action that occurs over too long a time for the process of change to be noticeable.

In the area of re-creation, models and miniatures are used to abstract significant details from events that are too complex to be observed in full.

Computer animation systems create three-dimensional pictures as if a camera were moving around—inside or outside—structures that do not exist, presenting images of events that never happened.

Therefore, if you can think of an image, you, or someone, can make a picture of it.

But getting it shot is not all there is to making a documentary—not even when you are shooting events as they actually happen in the real world. Because it is not what *you* saw happening that counts. It's not even what you aimed the camera at that matters. It is the actual scene as it's recorded on film or videotape that has to provide the visual evidence for the audience of what occurred while you were there.

MISS DARLING AND THE
SCENE THAT WASN'T THERE

We were working on a documentary about open education in a classroom of third and fourth graders. The teacher was a beautiful young woman, very likable, very photogenic, who got along well with the kids. My crew immediately nicknamed her "Miss Darling."

One of Miss Darling's strong points as a teacher was that she related well to the boys in her class. Fourth grade boys can be difficult and some teachers have trouble with this. So I wanted to show what happened in Miss Darling's classroom.

We filmed a group of boys playing with dinosaurs in a diorama they had made until we used up the film in the camera. While Jack Behr, my cameraman on that film, reloaded the camera with a fresh four-hundred-foot magazine, I looked around for another bit of behavior to shoot. In a quiet place, away from the other children, a husky ten-year-old boy in a football jersey was sitting with Miss Darling, learning to knit.

I liked the look of the scene and motioned to Jack and the soundman to move in and shoot. At first, I didn't have much more in mind for the scene than a few shots of a young, would-be football player and an attractive teacher, sitting together and knitting. But as we started to shoot, I began to realize that they were carrying on a conversation in low voices. From where I was standing I couldn't hear what they were saying, but the scene was so poignant—the boy looking up with wide, trusting eyes, the teacher bent toward him with a tender look on her face, the quiet conversation—that I whispered to Jack, "I don't know what's going on, but I like it. Shoot the whole magazine."

I was convinced that we were capturing an intimate and personal moment in the relationship between a teacher and her student. It would serve as a shining example for teachers everywhere that (1) the classroom won't go to hell if you spend some quiet time with one student, and (2) boys, even rough-and-tumble boys in jock sweatshirts, can be interested in more than sports and all-male activities. Beyond that, it was such a charming scene that I was convinced it would enhance the documentary and please the audience. In my mind, I made space for as much as five minutes of this scene in the twenty-five-minute running length of the finished film.

Unfortunately, I neglected to tell any of this to Jack while he was shooting. He had started out concentrating on close-ups of the teacher and the boy and of their hands as they were knitting. From his point of view, through the viewfinder of the camera, he was too close to them to see what I felt was going on. As a result, the footage consisted of a set of related close-ups and two-shots that covered the process of learning to knit far more extensively than was needed, but barely hinted at the deeper, more personal sharing that I thought had been there. I spent three weeks trying to edit that footage to show what I wanted, and then gave up in defeat. No matter what had actually happened in that classroom during the eleven minutes we were filming, what we had on film was a rather prosaic sequence of a boy and his teacher knitting.

And that's all.

Although I remain convinced that the tender, almost loving, moment between Miss Darling and the boy actually occurred in the way I witnessed it, there was no way I could use the footage we had shot to communicate to an audience what I had seen and felt. Even describing it in narration wouldn't do. The evidence simply was not in the footage.

A Great Opening Scene

But, later, Jack found and photographed a scene that was so powerful that we used it as the opening shot to represent the theme of the documentary.

We were in the playground of a nursery school. The children had been tie-dyeing T-shirts, and one five-year-old boy was trying to hang his on a low clothesline to dry. He had the T-shirt in one hand and a clothespin in the other, with the clothesline bouncing up and down in front of him. The boy knew what he wanted to do. But he lacked the experience to hold the clothesline steady, drape the T-shirt over it, and secure it with the clothespin. He experimented with several different approaches, but always seemed to need one more hand than he had to complete the job. The more he tried, the more frustrated he became. This was such a clear example of the difference between knowing about something and having the skill and experience to do it, that we used the entire two minutes, uncut, as the opening scene of the film.

No audience has ever misunderstood that scene. At first they laugh at the child's difficulty, but after about thirty seconds, a large part of the audience is leaning forward as if to help him. Moreover, the scene is so powerful, visually, that it serves as a metaphor to help the audience understand the rest of the movie.

KEEP IT VISUAL

A documentary is existential. It has to stand on its own. You can't go along with the print and explain to the audience what you meant to show or shoot, or what a particular scene is supposed to mean. You simply have to shoot the best analog of the actual situation that you can manage and then edit the footage into a single, coherent print that will clearly communicate your intentions to the people who will see it.

Sound—narration, dialogue, interviews, and music—may help the audience to *interpret* the documentary. But it won't take the place of solid evidence in the form of concrete visual images.

Documentary Ground Rules

Here are some simple ground rules that I find helpful. They may seem obvious, but having them in mind can keep you out of trouble when you're on location in a hot shooting situation.

- A documentary is made to communicate to an audience.
- A documentary communicates through strong visual images organized in sequence to make a statement.
- Visual images can only be described with concrete nouns and action verbs.
- Editing is the heart of the process of communicating in a documentary.
- It's the documentary you show, not the footage you shot, that counts.

All filming, and especially documentary filming, is tentative because you can't know which footage will be used, or how the footage will be edited, until you see how the finished documentary goes together.

Even in a fully scripted motion picture, where each scene is carefully blueprinted well in advance, changes are frequently made in the cutting room to improve it. In documentary, where the script for a half-hour presentation may not be much more than a one- or two-page outline of possible shooting situations, the editing process is a critical step.

WHEN IS A FILM NOT A FILM?

If a film—or a video—isn't composed primarily of visual evidence, then even though you recorded it with a camera and show it on a screen, it really isn't a film. Try this sometime: Play back a video with the monitor blanked out or turned off. If you can follow what's going on, then too much of the information is coming in the audio channel and not enough through visual evidence. Or try watching TV news with the sound turned off. Usually you can only make a wild guess at what's happening. News people call their visuals "B-roll" and the reporter talking "A-roll." Guess which they consider more important?

I cringe whenever I hear documentary producers, directors, or writers talk about their documentaries in terms of recording interviews. Getting people to talk about the subject of the documentary is important, but mainly for research purposes. Yes, you always hope for a great sound bite that will drive home a point. But if all you have is people *telling* about the topic, you lack the visual evidence to make a documentary film.

Recognize that some ideas just aren't visual ideas. They belong in an article, or a pamphlet, or a speech, or a recording, or a wall poster. And there's nothing wrong with that. Unless you try to force them to become a documentary.

Concrete Nouns and Action Verbs

The more concretely you can describe your documentary idea in terms of visual images, the better your chance of communicating through film or video. Similarly, the more abstract or interpretive your idea is, the more important it becomes to build up evidence for the idea through specific, concrete images.

To be filmed, an image has to be solid, tangible, existential. For instance, there's no problem in filming the image-idea:

The boy runs toward the camera.

Just turn the camera on, yell "Action!" and shoot what happens.

But it gets trickier with the addition of adjectives. How would you film this image-idea in one shot?

The frightened *boy runs toward the camera.*

Probably you'd try to have the boy act frightened—his face contorted, breathing heavily, looking over his shoulder, bumping into things, and so on. You might also try to film in a situation that helps the audience infer fright from the boy's actions: At night on a dimly lit street. In a dark forest. On a battlefield.

Let's try one more. In one shot, how can you film this image-idea?

The intelligent boy runs toward the camera.

You can't.

You need two scenes in sequence. First a scene that establishes the boy's intelligence, and then the shot of the boy running.

You can't film abstractions, such as:

Economics is the dismal science.

Nor can you film the absence of something:

On Tuesday, the mail didn't come.

Yes, of course, you can film two actors talking. One says, "Happy Tuesday, did the mail come?" The other says, "No." You could also put the statement in narration. You just can't shoot a picture of it.

The best you can do, in either case, is to shoot and organize a sequence of concrete events from which you hope the audience will infer your meaning.

GATHERING EVIDENCE

The point to all this is that it's not enough to know what you want to shoot. It's not even enough to know what really is happening in the situation you shot. You have to have the evidence on film or video.

This has two important implications for the documentarian. First, during shooting, it's important to keep firmly in mind the fact that the documentary is going to be edited in order to organize it to communicate with an audience. And second, during editing, it's necessary to forget, for a while, what you intended to shoot and look at what you've actually recorded.

Seeing What Is There

Being able to see what you have actually recorded can be tough, even for an experienced professional. For instance, I wanted the footage of Miss Darling and the boy to be usable so badly that I worked at trying to edit it long past the point where I should have admitted to myself that the evidence simply wasn't there.

And for the person who is new to documentary, learning to see what is there can be especially hard. Most of our experience in looking at films and videos, from grade school on, has been in interpreting them. And I take the word *interpreting* quite literally to mean translating from visual imagery to some form of verbal response.

For example, I was working with a graduate class in the use of visual communication in education. I showed them *The Birth of Aphrodite*, a short, somewhat abstract and artistic film about the myth of Aphrodite rising from the sea. Then I asked, "What did you see?"

At first their responses were either generalities about beauty, art, mythology, and the human condition, or had to do with creative writing, the classics, and how to use film in the classroom.

"Yes," I said, "but what did you *see*? What is in the film? What happened within the frame? What was the first shot? What was the next shot?"

With a great deal of difficulty, and with everyone contributing, the students slowly were able to start re-creating and describing from memory the sequence of shots that made up the film.

As they worked on it, they got better. When they came to the last few shots, where we see the naked Aphrodite dancing in the moonlight at the edge of the sea, several people remembered that the "just-born" goddess had the white outline of a swimsuit on her otherwise beautifully tanned body.

We can only speculate as to whether the filmmakers noticed that flaw when they were putting the film together. Perhaps they did, and thought they could get away with it. They almost did. Or perhaps they didn't see it at all. It takes time, training, and experience to look at your own work and see it for what it is.

Communication with an audience through an existential, visual medium is far different from communication in a face-to-face or voice-to-voice situation. Audiences have the perverse habit of assuming that the way they think you are communicating is the way that you intended to communicate. As far as they are concerned, the message they get is the only message there is. And you have no opportunity to defend yourself—to revise, clarify, or explain what you actually meant.

BEHAVIOR AS VISUAL EVIDENCE

Making documentaries—and to me that means filming the behavior of people—gets you involved in trying to capture pieces of a process on film or videotape. People are seen in the middle of the process, between their history and their hopes. The documentarian can choose to trap them in roles—the manager at his desk, the housewife at the supermarket—or to explore them more fully as individuals.

It's not simply a matter of getting a lot of background footage of these people in other situations. That's the solution most often proposed by film students when they sense a caricature in the footage rather than a portrait. "If I could only see her at breakfast, or playing with her children," they say, "then I'd understand her better."

Could be. And I'm not opposed to fleshing out a portrait with anything you can get that works—if you've got the time and space in your documentary. But a cardboard background of a cardboard person will simply lend cardboard detail to the caricature.

When the visual evidence is well realized, however, you can get a sense of the situation in a flash. The fact is that we are all skilled at reading people. We attend not only to what is said but to the way it is said and the nonverbal behavior occurring in the situation.

While a documentary is not the same as face-to-face interaction, it is similar when we show a person talking with an interviewer or speaking directly to the audience. The difference is that there is no feedback channel for the audience to test their impressions of the person. They can't say, "You frowned when you said that. Are you angry about it?" What they see is all they've got. And that makes it all the more important for us, as documentarians, to record and show as accurately as we can the visual evidence in the scene.

RECORDING VISUAL EVIDENCE

It is important to think of the images that you shoot as visual evidence. The question is not whether you can argue the case for what your images mean. You'll never get the chance. The only real test is whether the images can stand on their own and argue the case themselves.

For instance, in a documentary about a protest march, there was a shot of a cold-looking police officer standing by a police barrier. Behind him was a completely empty street. The narrator said, "Twenty thousand people took to the street in protest . . ." but the visual evidence said *nobody was there.* Imagine if the voice had come from an interview rather than from the narrator. The use of this shot would have suggested to the audience that the person in the interview was not telling the truth.

Silent films were great on visual evidence, because that's all they had. Don't turn up your nose at them if you've seen movies from the silent era only on children's TV shows. Go back and get a look at some of the classics from the silent era. And be sure they are run at the proper speed. The main reason we laugh at silent films today is that they were shot at sixteen frames per second, and we play them back at twenty-four frames per second. Which is why everyone seems to bounce around and walk funny.

If you want to see good visual evidence, find a rerun of "Mission Impossible" and look at the opening montage. It foreshadows the entire show in a series of quick shots that show you interesting things about to happen—with just a musical background, no voice.

A recent winner in the International Documentary Association Awards is a beautiful short film, *89 mm from Europe*, which shows how trains arriving at the border between Poland and the former Soviet Union must have all their wheels changed to proceed because of an 89mm difference in the width of the rails. Shot like a silent film—although there is voice, natural sound, and music—it is *all* visual evidence.

The Interview Problem

Try not to rely on interviews to make your case. Even in court, where the interview—questions by an attorney, answers by a witness—is the way virtually all information is elicited, there are complex rules governing what information can and cannot be used. This is because the courts know that what people say is terribly unreliable. And yet many, many documentaries being made today are virtually created from interviews.

I was watching a documentary called *Natasha and the Wolf* on "Frontline" on PBS. Not only is all the information in this documentary carried in interviews, but the interviews are conducted in Russian with simultaneous translation into English, and what is shown visually often bears little relationship to what is talked about. I saw no convincing visual evidence. And without the ability to hear the way the person talks, because the voices were covered over by simultaneous translation, there was no way to use behavioral clues to evaluate the information. I turned it off.

Behavior Is Visual Evidence

Films of behavior have to be made up of visual evidence, because no one today is willing to settle for an illustrated lecture. For instance, *The War Room* shows the behavior of people working on the 1992 Clinton campaign. There are no interviews. There is no narration. It's all visual evidence.

On the other hand, *Baseball: A Film by Ken Burns* stops dead at regular intervals while people with only a tangential relationship to the sport are shot in an absolutely static situation, talking about what baseball, or some event in the history of baseball, meant to them. *No visual evidence.*

Shoot people doing what they do, even if you're mainly interested in what they have to say. Plan the location so that it becomes a part of the evidence of the scene. If you're filming an expert on juvenile delinquency who is proposing alternatives to putting adolescents in adult prisons, film her at the prison rather than in her office. You'll have the visual evidence that says this woman is talking about concrete reality, not just some theory she's concocted.

Words and Actions

Remembering that what is said and what is done should both be considered behavior, what happens when people's actions seem to contradict the words they are saying?

Here's a situation from a videotape of a counselor working with a husband and wife whose marriage was in trouble: If you simply had a transcript or an audio recording of the words being spoken, you could easily come away with the feeling that while all was not right with the marriage, at least the couple was trying. But if you looked carefully at the body posture and behavior of the husband and wife—with or without sound—you couldn't escape a quite different conclusion. The wife was eager to please the marriage counselor, trying to put a good face on things, quick to cooperate. The husband said little and did nothing.

At one point the counselor asked them to turn their chairs to face each other and talk to one another about their problems instead of talking to him. The wife immediately moved her chair. The husband didn't budge. He sat slumped down, hands in pockets, present—but not there. It was clear from the visual evidence of their behavior that she was living on hope, desperately clinging to the marriage, while he was already gone.

EDITING VISUAL EVIDENCE

Obviously, you can't show everything you've shot. In editing, you abstract visual evidence that will serve as an accurate analog of the events that were filmed. And you organize it into a statement that will communicate to your audience—honestly, directly, and forcefully—what you know about the event.

Clearly, you have to be careful, in editing, not to distort the evidence. And that can be hard. You were there when the footage was shot. You know everything that happened. It takes only a little bit of the footage to spark your memory of the entire event. But your audience wasn't there. So the footage you choose for the scene has to stand as an accurate analog for everything you remember.

Cutting the Part Where Nothing Happens

Suppose the marriage-counseling sequence had been edited into a scene in a documentary, ending with the marriage counselor giving a summary of the case. And suppose, as so often happens, it had been edited to keep what was being said flowing smoothly. The long pauses where the husband said nothing might be cut out because the editor found them uninteresting. And the scene in which the husband didn't move his chair might be eliminated because nothing's happening. The visual evidence would have been altered so that it seemed to support the verbal statements that everything was going to be okay.

Then it would unquestionably come as a shock to the audience for the marriage counselor to state—as he actually did to me—that there was very little chance of this marriage lasting, and that a divorce might be the best solution for both parties.

Good Mother—Bad Mother

Here's a problem that came up in one of my documentaries. I had separate sequences of two mothers and their two-year-old children, working and playing together. Let's call one the Bad Mother. Her own behavior was pretty neurotic, and she tended to see only her little boy's faults, never his good points. She couldn't understand what he was doing or make sense out of what he said.

The other was clearly a Good Mother. She talked freely with her daughter, paid attention to her, and encouraged her to do things on her own. She was a Scandinavian, and she liked everything clean and neat. I filmed her daughter helping her mix the batter for a cake.

In editing the documentary, I put the two mother-and-child sequences back to back, the Bad Mother first. Each sequence ran about four and a half minutes, cut down from nearly two hours of original footage.

In the sequence with the Bad Mother, I had focused on the little boy. It was his behavior I was interested in. I had sidestepped and cut around the mother's neurotic outbursts as much as possible, because I wanted the audience to watch the behavior of the boy and not waste time psychoanalyzing his mother.

In the Good Mother sequence I was especially interested in one point, where the daughter is handing eggs to her mother to crack and put into the mixing bowl. Then the daughter tries to crack an egg herself. The mother exclaims, "No! Please, dear! Let me do that." But the little girl persists, and finally does crack one egg. I had been concentrating on the talk between the two, leaving in as much as possible.

When I ran the two sequences, I realized I had made a big mistake. I had included almost all of the footage in which the Good Mother clucked about the mess, worried about neatness, and said "Don't . . ." to her daughter—a total of about a minute out of the forty-five minutes of original footage.

As a result, while I had neutralized the Bad Mother, I had inadvertently ended up making the Good Mother look pretty bad. Enough that, by the time the daughter tries to break an egg on her own, an audience was quite likely to miss the point that the mother could have stopped her, but didn't. I was afraid they might see it instead as just one more case of a fussy mother worrying about the mess. So I re-edited.

In the final version, the concern of the Good Mother for neatness is shown, but it doesn't overpower the important behavior of the child. And it doesn't turn a really good mother into a villain. The visual evidence of the sequence is in balance with what actually happened.

INTERVIEWS AS VISUAL EVIDENCE

You're shooting a documentary about a subject that has become controversial. One side makes charges. The other side denies them and makes countercharges. You shoot interviews with spokespersons for both sides. What evidence do you have?

The fact is that while an interview is prima facie evidence that the person shown said the words that were spoken, it carries no evidence whatsoever about the truth value of the statement the person makes. But an audience, like a jury, is not above using other cues to decide whether or not to believe a speaker. His or her dress and manner, as well as the logic of the statement, can have a powerful effect on them.

I once did an interview with two employees of a mental institution. Both of them were leaders of the committee to keep the institution from being closed down. One was a lay therapist who dressed in hippy chic, tilted his head at a crazy angle when he talked, and spoke in a mixture of street slang and social science jargon. He made several good points in favor of keeping the institution open. But in the course of an eleven-minute interview, he also made two or three really outlandish statements.

The other man was the union shop steward and a member of the janitorial crew. He had a full beard, neatly trimmed, and was wearing his working clothes. What he said wasn't elegant, but he spoke in an even voice and stated the facts as he knew them. Most important, his attitude and behavior indicated that he believed what he was saying.

This was a sponsored documentary, and the sponsor was trying to remain neutral but actually leaned toward closing the institution. So it would have been an easy thing to use the interview with the weird lay therapist. Most audiences would find him unlikable and difficult to believe, not so much because of what he said but because of the way he said it. Fortunately, the sponsor agreed with me that doing that would be stacking the deck. We chose to keep the visual evidence neutral and use the statement by the shop steward instead.

WHEN PICTURES CONTRADICT WHAT IS SAID

When I talk about visual evidence, I'm concerned primarily with the images that are an integral part of your documentary. Every documentarian knows he's got something going if he has evidence on film or video that contradicts what the speaker says. Suppose you're doing a documentary on industrial waste. The president of a chemical company says in an interview on camera that his company is not polluting the river. But you've got footage that shows raw chemicals being discharged from his plant directly into the river. You're going to use that footage, along with the company president's statement, to show that either he is lying or he doesn't know what he is talking about. That's an obvious situation, and needs no comment.

Contradiction in Narration

But what happens when the images and the narration are in conflict? These elements are both under the control of the documentarian. I mentioned the protest march film showing an empty street while the narration talked about a huge crowd. That was bad editing. The filmmaker had footage of the crowd. He just didn't use it to open the sequence.

But what if the documentarian has actually recorded images that don't belong? Before making my documentaries on kids and schools, I screened all the films I could find on early learning in children. Many of these films had obviously had the narration written before the film was shot, following the child development theories of whatever expert was the consultant to the film. Images of children had then been shot to illustrate the narration.

Quite often, unfortunately, the behavior shown was not the behavior described. The narration might say that at a certain age young boys join together in inseparable gangs. But what we actually saw on the screen was several boys on a playground—each playing by himself. They were playing beside each other, not playing together. There was no visual evidence to support the gang thesis. It was as if the filmmaker or the expert or both had decided that everyone knows that young boys gang together at a certain age, so it should be enough to show a bunch of boys—no matter what they were doing—for the audience to get the point.

Lying by Exception

Or let's take this situation from a public relations film made to recruit students for a famous university. Many of the strong points of the school are brought out in the film. But two scenes stick in my memory. The university is located in a cold, northern city with a long, bitter winter. But there are no shots of cold, snow, and wind in the film. None. There is, however, a rather idyllic sequence of students sunbathing and swimming at a lake which almost certainly was shot during summer school, not during the regular academic year. The narration explains that the students enjoy their outings at the lake, and adds, almost as an afterthought, "Of course it's not always like this. It can get pretty cold in winter."

In a sequence on the life of a student, the filmmakers chose to shoot an attractive female graduate student living with two other young women in an expensive townhouse close to the campus. Again the disclaimer in narration, "Of course not all students live like this," followed by a reference to the availability of student dormitories for most undergraduates—although these are never shown.

Such disclaimers in narration mean next to nothing. The visual evidence is that if you go to that university, you'll live in an expensive townhouse and enjoy sunny afternoons at the lake.

Because that is what is shown.

Misrepresentation

A documentarian was doing a social documentary on teenagers. He had done a highly successful documentary about the college protest movement and wanted to look at younger people of high school age to see if he could find the roots of protest in a suburb that sent most of its children to college.

The opening scene of the film, as I recall, showed a lot of sixteen-year-olds, dressed up, looking very somber. The boys looked sad, the girls seemed on the verge of tears. I think this was used without comment as the title background. Although nothing was said, certainly the visual evidence of the footage was that being a teenager at this place at this time was a pretty serious thing.

After the film was shown on TV, the charge was made by residents of the town that this scene had been filmed at the funeral of a classmate. I don't know whether that's true or not, and for my purpose it really doesn't matter. My point is, if a documentarian takes a scene like this out of context and uses it as evidence to give a false impression, that's lying on film.

Sure it's real; it really happened. But it's not the truth in the visual argument of the documentary.

UNREAL IMAGES

The modern documentarian has available a number of tools that simply didn't exist a few years ago. Or if they did exist, they were too expensive to use. But today, as mentioned in chapter three, it's a simple thing to rearrange the location of the pyramids by computer. Digital effects and computer animation make it possible to create images of *anything.*

I think this is wonderful, and the documentarian has every right to make use of these images, as long as they are used truthfully. That means labeling made-up images as simulations. It means not using digitally enhanced images as if they had been recorded in an actual situation.

Fiction Footage

One of the things documentarians making historical or biographical shows have started to do is to take footage from fiction films about their subject and use it to illustrate their topic. Again, I have no problem with this *as long as the audience knows what they're looking at.* But if scenes are taken from fiction and used as if they were actuality footage, so that the audience is led to believe that what they are witnessing really happened, then the documentarian has left the truth behind in order to serve some other purpose, such as keeping the story interesting. Unfortunately, that's what docudrama does, and why it is not nonfiction.

Reenactment

Reenactment has been a technique of documentary from its earliest days. It can be an extremely effective way of showing an event for which no documentary footage exists.

Colonial Williamsburg made and distributed an outstanding series of documentaries, which used reenactment to show life in colonial times.

In re-enactment as with any other footage not documenting real events, the documentarian must be honest with the audience.

VISUALS, EMPTY SHOTS, AND VISUAL EVIDENCE

To the best of my knowledge, the term *visuals* came in with television and was the direct result of transferring word people—writers and radio broadcasters—into a newly created visual medium that had no history and no traditions. These television people—and I'm talking about early practitioners in the '40s and '50s, not contemporary videomakers—used the word visuals as a reminder to themselves that without pictures, it wasn't TV. They'd say, "I've got some good visuals to go with the doctor scene." And that statement, taken literally, suggests that the "doctor scene" is the one in the script—words on paper—and not footage that's been shot. Whereas to a documentarian, there is no doctor scene until there is footage of a doctor.

All that is ancient history. But the notion of visuals continues to pop up from time to time. And it means, quite specifically, pictures used to illustrate a verbal point. It comes from thinking that the verbal statement is the most important thing. Which leads to believing that as far as the pictures are concerned, close enough is good enough.

And that brings us to the current usage in talk-talk documentaries of *empty shots*—neutral images used to provide filler to cover the continuation of an interview as voice-over, or used as cutaways to cover an edit in an interview. Outside, shots of trees and sky are favored. Or any nature scene—a stream, flowers, whatever. Inside you have the long tilt down a wall to arrive at nothing in particular, or furniture, books, whatever.

These scenes may be very pretty, even occasionally dramatic, but they are shot as filler—visual wallpaper—not as evidence to make a visual argument.

Another term for visuals or empty shots is *B-roll*, which stands for images that run while someone is talking.

As a documentarian, your job is to find, record, and organize visual evidence to make a powerful, dramatic statement on the screen. The minute you find yourself thinking about visuals or B-roll footage, an alarm should go off in your head to tell you that you lack the visual evidence you need and are relying on words to tell your story.

Talk is cheap.

6

· ·

VERISIMILITUDE
IN DOCUMENTARY

If you cannot rely on the objective reality of whatever you have recorded to convince an audience of the truth of your argument, then in recording and editing the documentary, you have to present the case so an audience will believe it. One way, as we've seen, is to find and record convincing visual evidence.

Making a documentary requires meticulous attention to what will ultimately be shown to an audience. The verifiable truth of a documentary depends on the honesty of the documentarian in presenting an accurate analog of the situation as he or she understands it. But that alone is no guarantee that the audience will accept the documentary as true—because a documentary, every bit as much as a Hollywood movie or a Broadway play, must work within the framework of audience beliefs, conventions, and expectations. The images on the screen may be both real and true, but if they lack the appearance of truth, the documentarian sets up a credibility gap with the audience that he or she may never overcome.

An audience comes to any film or video—including a documentary—bringing with it what in the theater is called the willing suspension of disbelief. Violate that and you may lose your audience—sometimes for good. In addition to good visual evidence, structured into a compelling argument, a documentary requires the appearance of truth. The term for this is *verisimilitude.*

In fiction, verisimilitude is generally taken to mean an attention to detail—and to the logic of human behavior—so that what is written or shown will have the appearance of truth. Fiction is unreal. It never happened. But it is expected to have an internal consistency called the logic of the piece. Truth *is* stranger than fiction, because fiction is bound by rules, whereas truth rests on the chaos of reality.

If you're filming a cold, winter scene in a studio and you take care that the actor's breath is visible, that's verisimilitude—in a fiction film *or a reenactment* documentary.

VERISIMILITUDE IN *THE WAR GAME*

One of the most unrelenting documentaries I know of, Peter Watkins's *The War Game*, is about an event that hasn't happened—a nuclear war. The major premise—that both sides engage in a saber-rattling game of bluffing and escalation from which they are unable to back down—is stated so simply, and is so consistent with what we have come to know about our governments and the people who run them, that it is accepted without a murmur. The remainder of the documentary—the implications of a nuclear attack on England worked out in human terms—is done with a gritty realism that is utterly believable.

For instance, there is a firestorm scene in which people are suddenly caught in the grip of a hundred-mile-an-hour wind and flung off their feet. This is what Watkins said about shooting the scene in an interview in Alan Rosenthal's book *The New Documentary in Action* (1971):

> We put a mattress down, and got the people to sort of run and pick themselves up off the mattress. . . . As you are running, you have to suddenly feel yourself caught and turned by an air current. To achieve this we started pulling them with wires, but finally decided not to do that, as we thought it would hurt them. We also thought it would look false. We also helped the effect by having

flares roaring in the background and putting two fans quite close to them to whip bits of shredded paper and flour across, so that you got the visual impression of a sudden whipping across of something. As they ran to a particular spot where their mattress was, the white bits of paper would whip across and catch them. That would be their cue for letting themselves be caught in it and turned. (p. 162)

That's verisimilitude—the appearance of truth, even in an unreal situation, to give it the look of realism.

Reenactment and Re-creation

Documentaries using reenactment and re-creation require the conscious use of the techniques of verisimilitude every bit as much as a fiction film does. Because you are reproducing people and events rather than recording them in actuality, you must do nothing to upset your audience's willing suspension of disbelief.

VERISIMILITUDE IN A DOCUMENTARY

Okay, verisimilitude is useful in a fictional setting or a re-creation, to provide a look of realism for a scene that might be the truth, but is not real, it's a reenactment. But what is the need for verisimilitude in a documentary where, it is hoped, truth and reality lie nestled in the same set of images?

Mood Music

Paying attention to the verisimilitude in a documentary could mean asking whether the use of background music enhances the mood of a scene or detracts from its believability. Since this is a convention from the fiction film, will the audience accept the music as belonging, or are they likely to infer that you are playing on their emotions, perhaps because your facts are thin?

Showing the Crew and Equipment

In a documentary of behavior, I often include in an early scene a shot of the documentary crew at work. It serves as a reminder to the audience that what they are seeing occurred in front of a camera, and that they should keep that in mind in evaluating the behavior they see.

But it also helps with what can become a sticky problem of verisimilitude later on. I've done a lot of documentaries with little kids, and when a little kid decides to move, he *goes*— sometimes right past the sound tech or the microphone or a light stand that everyone thought would be out of the way. Usually we're able to cut around that, and maintain the convention that the crew remains behind the camera and the documentary subjects in front of it.

But occasionally the behavior is unique, important, and never repeated. Having already shown the audience the documentary crew at work, there should be no problem with using the shot, even though the edge of a microphone shows in the picture or part of a light stand is clearly visible in the background.

Little Errors, Big Problems

Whenever you're dealing with a specialty or a technical area, it's important to get the details right. Because I'm a former navy pilot, I often get annoyed when I see a sequence aboard a carrier that purports to follow one airplane taxiing forward and taking off. Usually these scenes are edited from stock footage. And all too often the director and editor seem to assume that all blue airplanes with propellers are the same. So we see a World War II Corsair spread its wings, a Hellcat taxi forward, and a Korean War Skyraider take off.

In the footage I received for *Defenders of Midway*, there's an interview with a man in his sixties who was a marine dive-bomber pilot at Midway during the battle. In their defense, this was not a scene that the crew I was working with had shot. The director had gotten it from another producer who had shot it for a different documentary.

For some reason, the director shooting the scene had put this former marine pilot in an air force flight suit and had him wearing a navy officer's cap, but with no insignia on it. It made the man uncomfortable and it made no sense.

Compounding this idiocy, the director asked him not to call his former enemies "Japs," but to refer to them as "Japanese." And when the pilot said, "That's what I think of them as. I hated them. I wanted to kill them," the director replied, "But you don't now."

"Yes I do," mumbled the pilot, and they went on with the interview.

Why put a seventy-year-old man in a flight suit to talk about something he did when he was twenty? It's bad verisimilitude. But certainly, if you're going to do it, then the uniform should be correct.

Using verisimilitude in documentary means you can never assume that close enough is good enough.

Wrong Behavior

When I was shooting a documentary called *Light in Art* for Hawaii Public Television, I had a long sequence with photographer Brett Weston taking photographs of the work of his friend Henry Bianchini, a sculptor. A verisimilitude problem developed in that each time we would begin a shot, they would call each other by name at the start of the scene. It's a small thing, but, in our culture, friends working alone together over a period of time do not normally use each other's name frequently as they talk. They know who they are and whom they are talking to.

I think they fell into the use of this for two reasons. First, there were others in the room, and while we were behind the video camera, we *were* there. Social rule says you may need to address someone by name to distinguish him from the others who are also there. Second, what we were videotaping was a scene that had been set up for our documentary. So it felt to them like a somewhat formal presentation. And social rule says that you may call the other by name at the start of a formal presentation. The problem there was that they treated each take as the start of a new presentation.

I knew that if this continued, when we edited the takes into a sequence, we would have them calling each other Brett and Henry far too often to seem natural. Bad verisimilitude. I asked them to stop using each other's names.

We shot this sequence like a reenactment, not like a behavioral documentary. If I had been shooting a documentary about their behavior, where we would go in and observe whatever they did and said, I would have given no such direction. But I also would not have been shooting in short, slated takes.

More Bad Talk

In the many hours of the PBS presentation *An American Family*, there's a scene of Pat Loud visiting her hometown, and driving around the community with her mother as they talk about the way things were and the way things are now. As I watched it, I felt that something didn't ring quite true. And as I listened a little longer, I realized it was what they were saying.

Pat and her mother were overexplaining. Two people simply don't go into such detail about events that both of them are thoroughly familiar with *unless* there is a third person in the scene—a stranger who otherwise wouldn't know what they were talking about. And of course there was. The sequence was shot from the backseat of the car. At a minimum there were sound and camera people back there, and possibly the director or producer as well. And that's who Pat and her mother were talking to—not to each other.

For a scene that pretended to be a private conversation between mother and daughter, the verisimilitude—in words and behavior—was wrong. In this case, as in many others in this series, the invisible wall between subjects and crew was down, or had never been put up in the first place.

"Repeat the Question"

What about asking an interview subject to repeat the question before answering it? Obviously, after my experience with the police captain in Wilkes-Barre, I'm against it. In documentary it puts a burden on the subject, which is not his or her responsibility. But beyond that, it makes the behavior wrong. People don't repeat questions before they answer them. They just don't do it. Period.

Bad verisimilitude.

Solving Problems

Suppose you're shooting on location. Off camera there's a machine making a continuous noise, loud enough to be heard on the sound track, but not so loud that it interferes with the voices of your subjects. And it can't be shut off while you're shooting.

For verisimilitude, you might want to include the machine in a shot, so that the noise is explained and your audience can immediately disregard it. Otherwise, that noise may become a question mark that grows in the minds of the audience until they not only stop concentrating on the scene but also may start to question your skill as a documentarian. And when that happens, you're in deep trouble.

Ambient Sound

Verisimilitude is the reason I record ambient sound on everything I shoot, even obviously silent footage. Suppose I have a scene of people sitting in a room, talking and drinking coffee. Perhaps the importance of the scene is just to show that they are all together and to provide a visual space in the documentary for some essential narration. I still record sound.

Even though I have the narration track to cover the entire scene, which prevents the sound track from going dead, I can also lay in the ambient sound and keep its level very low. Even when the narrator is speaking, the almost subliminal click of a coffee mug against the table and the low murmur of voices in the background increase the believability of the scene. It becomes much more than a visual. It comes to life. Verisimilitude!

VERISIMILITUDE AND EDITING

Using verisimilitude in editing can mean trying to get into the heads of your audience to see how a sequence will appear to them. Here's where a knowledge of film conventions, and of human belief systems, can help you. It's not only important to communicate the message that you intend, it is equally important *not* to communicate a message that you *don't* intend. What is selected in editing to be shown to the audience is usually a small segment of a much larger hunk of footage. It is abstracted from the event that was recorded and is edited to suggest as much as possible about all that happened in the event itself.

You were there. Your audience wasn't. As you look at the footage, you might recall everything that happened. But your audience knows nothing about the event except what you select to show them from all the footage and sound available. It, alone, has to communicate to the audience what you consider to be important. And it is not enough that it was shot in a real situation. It has to be presented to your audience with the ring of truth. And that means paying attention to verisimilitude.

7

ETHICS IN MAKING
A DOCUMENTARY

Who owns my image?

That, in brief, is a question you should give some thought to as you set about the business of producing a documentary.

If (you might ask) this documentary were being produced by strangers—people about whom I knew little or nothing at all—and if I were a subject in it, just how much freedom would I give them to use the images of me that they record?

Never mind about what *you* plan to do with, for, and to the subjects of *your* documentary. Naturally, you are honest, honorable, benevolent, a seeker after truth, and one who intends harm to no one. But how much slack would you allow the other guys to use your image in any way they please if *they* were documenting *you?*

Today, anyone with access to a little bit of video equipment can make a "documentary" of virtually anything he decides to point a camera at. The documentary of behavior poses new ethical problems simply because it is *the people themselves* who are the subjects of the documentary. Unlike other artists and communicators, behavioral documentarians *require* the spontaneous and personal behavior of their subjects in order to do their work.

Therefore, what is—or should be—the relationship of the documentarian to the people whose behavior is being recorded? What is—or should be—the responsibility of the documentarian to these people?

Frankly, until I met Cal Pryluck at a conference of the Society for the Anthropology of Visual Communication some time ago, I felt it was enough to get a release in advance and to tell the truth as I understood it. Professor Calvin Pryluck is one of a handful of documentarians and communications scholars concerned with questions of image ethics.

THE QUESTION OF RELEASES

Until now, the question of the rights of the people who appear in a documentary has been resolved through the expedient of getting a signed release from the subjects that grants all rights—or limited rights—to all recordings of the image and voice of the subject either to the documentarian or to the sponsor of the documentary.

As far as I know, the legality of such a release has never been fully tested. Television news crews, and even some television documentary crews, often don't bother to obtain releases on the grounds that they are reporting newsworthy events and are therefore protected under the First Amendment right to a free press. In ambush situations, like some of those on "60 Minutes," the probability of getting signed releases is remote.

Producers who hope to earn money from a documentary in theatrical release usually get signed release forms from everyone who is recognizable in the footage. But this is usually a matter of economics, not ethics. The people in a theatrical documentary are the talent in the film, and as such are entitled to compensation. In the absence of a signed release form, a court would probably award compensation not lower than minimum scale for the Screen Actors Guild or the Screen Extras Guild. Not only will few documentary budgets tolerate that rate of pay, but the time and expense involved in a court case would usually be prohibitive. I doubt, however, that for *Roger & Me*, Michael Moore even tried to get releases for his ambush interviews at the offices and plants of General Motors. His closing credits list nine names under the heading *Legal*.

As for the remainder of documentarians—those making films or videotapes with neither television backing nor the hope of theatrical profits—the signed release is their insurance policy. It protects them from nuisance suits by people appearing in the film who either hope for additional compensation or who decide, after the fact, that their privacy has been invaded.

If You Don't Want to Be Filmed, Leave

In lieu of releases, some documentarians record the subject's verbal consent at the start of shooting. With the camera running, they briefly explain the purpose of the production and ask the subjects if they are willing to be recorded. Or, at the start of a meeting or other group event, the documentarian will record himself announcing to the audience that the meeting is being recorded for use in a documentary. He briefly explains the purpose of the documentary, and then states, "Your continued presence here indicates your consent and willingness to be recorded as part of the documentary."

In essence, under this system, the only way an individual can guarantee the protection of his or her rights is to refuse to appear in the documentary. If people don't want to give someone else control over the use of their images, they can refuse to have them recorded. They can refuse to sign a release. They can refuse, on camera, to give their consent. They can get up and leave a meeting or other event—even though they may sincerely want to attend—if to remain is to give implied consent to be a part of the documentary being made. They need not complain that their privacy has been invaded if they have refused to participate. And that, in general, is the answer to the legal question of the rights of subjects.

But it doesn't come close to resolving any of the ethical questions. Nor does it absolve us as documentarians of our responsibility toward the subjects who appear in our productions.

THE NEED FOR A DOCUMENTARY ETHIC

While people who are potential documentary subjects may protect themselves from unwarranted invasion of privacy by refusing to appear on camera, few of them actually do so. The only refusals I have ever had came from people who had a vested interest in one side of a conflict and who, I think, felt there was a chance that their position might not be presented fairly. In other words, they were people with a fairly sophisticated awareness of the risks of giving up control of their images to an outsider.

Most people, however, are not nearly so sophisticated. Or perhaps they just don't care. The question most often heard by a documentary producer is not "How will you use the footage?" but rather "When will this be on TV?" Many people seem to be more than willing to trade their dignity for their fifteen minutes of celebrity—at least before the fact. Again, most documentarians report that the people in the documentary love it when they see it—until the reviews come in.

My own experience is that most people will do almost anything to *appear* on camera. Some examples:

A production company was shooting a commercial for a bank, which centered on a young couple having their first baby. And they needed a baby. They were shooting in a hospital, and it took less than ten minutes to convince the parents of a newborn infant, just six hours old, to permit their baby to be taken from the newborn nursery to a nearby room to appear on camera. Yes, the filmmakers kept the baby in a newborn isolette except for the few seconds it was on camera in each take. And yes, they had a nurse in full-time attendance. And yes, they explained all this to the parents. But the parents gave their consent without any hesitation and with only minimal consideration for any potential risks.

A friend of mine had no problem finding couples willing to appear in a medical school–sponsored behavioral documentary entitled *Sexual Intercourse*. The behavior to be filmed, of course, was sexual intercourse.

When such is the situation, one is tempted to question whether documentarians have any ethical responsibility at all toward the subjects who appear in their films. But the fact is that most people who agree to appear in a documentary are not involved in anything nearly so dramatic as the examples above. And few people who give their consent to appear on camera have any notion of the potential that exists for a damaging portrayal.

In chapter four I gave some examples of potential image victims: the policeman in Wilkes-Barre whose interview went badly, the school principal who babbled bureaucratese about his program, and the Good Mother and Bad Mother in A *Young Child Is.* . . . They willingly consented to my use of images of themselves that could have proven highly unfavorable and not at all what they had expected. And those were all situations in which I was operating with the best of intentions.

In an article entitled "Ultimately We Are All Outsiders: The Ethics of Documentary Filming," which first appeared in the *Journal of the University Film Association* (Winter 1976) and is reprinted in *New Challenges to Documentary* edited by Alan Rosenthal, Calvin Pryluck cites several examples from the literature of documentary in which the intentions of the documentarian may have been less than 100 percent aboveboard. He quotes Marcel Ophuls *(The Sorrow and the Pity):* "If you have moderate gifts as a fast talker or a diplomat or if you appear moderately sincere, you should be able to get cooperation. . . . It's a con game to a certain extent."

Pryluck continues:

> Regardless of whether consent is flawed on such grounds as intimidation or deceit, a fundamental ethical difficulty in direct cinema is that when we use people in a sequence we put them at risk without sufficiently informing them of potential hazards. We may not even know the hazards ourselves. Filmmakers cannot know which of their actions are apt to hurt other people: it is presumptuous of them to act as if they do. (p. 23)

What Is a Documentarian to Do?

What, then, is the documentarian to do? Part of the documentarian's responsibility, as I see it, is to *do no one harm unintentionally.* I state the case that way because, clearly, there are times when the very purpose of the documentary under production is to get the goods on some person, organization, or institution with malice aforethought.

But most of the time, especially in the behavioral documentary, the purpose is to show real people as they are, not as someone or other might think they should be.

In the same article, Pryluck writes:

> In one important respect the ethical problems of actuality filmmakers are identical to those faced by research physicians, sociologists, psychologists, and so on: scientific experiments and direct cinema depend for their success on subjects who have little or nothing to gain from participation. The use of people for our advantage is an ethically questionable undertaking; in its extreme it is exploitation in the literal sense. (p. 24)

In effect, the documentary of behavior has moved away from journalistic protection under the First Amendment and placed itself within the canons of social science and medical research. These documentaries carry with them a potential for the abuse and exploitation of the people who appear in them for which few ethical models exist. Even in the social documentaries of the recent past, the people shown were there less as individuals than as representations of the effects of social problems on specific human beings.

There is a distinct difference between the migrant workers who permitted themselves to be interviewed about working conditions for the Murrow-Friendly documentary *Harvest of Shame* and the members of the Loud family as they consented to be filmed for *An American Family*. The migrants knew the risks they were running. They knew that in telling about their plight as migrant workers they risked the possibility of brutal retaliation, and that the loss of their jobs might be the least of their worries. But they went ahead in full knowledge of the potential consequences.

The Loud family, on the other hand, had no idea what they were getting into, clearly did not understand the process as they were being filmed, and were unprepared for the impact the documentary had on their lives when it was released.

It would probably be fair to say that the producers of *Harvest of Shame* were well aware of the risks they were asking the subjects of their documentary to assume. The same cannot necessarily be said of the producer of a behavioral documentary. Quite often he or she has no way of foreseeing the way the film will come out, let alone what the risks to the participants might be. How, then, does the documentarian go about seeking consent from people he or she would like to have appear in the documentary?

INFORMED CONSENT

Informed consent in scientific and medical research depends on at least three elements:

- the absence of coercion and deception
- thorough explanation of the procedure and its anticipated effects
- competence of the subject to give consent

In the quest for consent, should the producer detail all of the horrible possibilities, from obscene phone calls to public ridicule, that might conceivably occur, and take a chance that the potential participant will say no?

Or is that more than is required? In order to get a signed release, should the documentarian downplay the possible risks to the participant in order to go ahead and make the movie? And if he does, is that really informed consent? In research, consent is flawed when it is obtained through the omission of any fact that might influence the giving or withholding of permission.

That sounds clear-cut, but it isn't. What is a fact that might influence the giving or withholding of permission? Do you have to tell every potential participant that "Some people have found that their neighbors laughed at them after they appeared in a documentary"?

At the other extreme, isn't requiring someone either to give implied consent or to leave a public meeting a form of coercion?

THE EYE OF THE BEHOLDER

One year my friend Chris Speeth and I both made sponsored documentaries about two different educational programs in two different cities for two different clients. Each documentary featured an administrator who was responsible for the educational programs shown in the film.

What I remember about Chris's film is that his man was always on the go. Chris showed him riding in every available type of transportation. When he was afoot, he walked briskly. And as he traveled around, he talked about his hopes and plans for the educational programs of his city. He often used the language of overstatement common to people who operate in a political arena. At one point he expressed the belief that his city's tax-supported college could become "the Sorbonne of the Midwest."

The educator in my film operated in a smaller arena, administering several grant-supported programs within a single high school. In style he was solemn and super sincere. His commentary on the program was an uncomfortable mixture of student slang and pedagoguese, with an overlay of the mechanistic psychobabble of special education.

When film students at The Annenberg School of Communications saw these documentaries, they found it hard to believe that Chris and I had been able to "get away with showing" the administrators as we did. To them, the educators came across as pompous bureaucrats talking nonsense, and the students interpreted each film as a put-down of the man in charge. They couldn't believe that we had gotten approval from our clients for films such as those.

But—and this is the important part—in each case, the administrator was quite pleased with the way he was shown in the film. The man in Chris's film saw himself as a forceful, active person getting the job done. The one in mine thought he came across as a well-informed expert who cared about young people. Remember, these were sponsored films, which had been reviewed by the clients, including these administrators, before they were completed.

I don't know how Chris felt about the administrator in his film. I didn't much care for the man in mine. But I would argue that the behavior shown in each film was an accurate and honest analog of the everyday behavior of those two men in similar situations.

Proof within the Frame

That a segment of the audience finds the way an individual is presented within a documentary unflattering may indicate that the documentarian is not a Pollyanna, finding the best in every situation. But it is certainly not proof of unethical conduct. There is usually no evidence within a documentary to prove whatever a critic may think reflects an ethical problem.

Suppose I had left the Good Mother and Bad Mother sequences as they were originally edited, with the Bad Mother neutralized but the Good Mother looking pretty bad. In my opinion it would have made the film dishonest, a less-than-accurate analog. *But no audience would have known that.*

On the other hand, suppose that I had concentrated on the neurotic behavior and negative attitude of the Bad Mother toward her son. The film was a documentary about the way children learn. And, certainly, the relationship between mother and child is a factor in early learning in young children. In my opinion, to have done so would not have made the film dishonest—it would have been showing the mother as she was—but it *would* have been unethical. It would have been changing the intent of the film as I had originally conceived it—and, more important, as I had explained it to the parents in seeking their permission to film them and their children—in order to take a cheap shot at a target of opportunity. The film was not a psychological study of the interactions between mothers and their children. Since it wasn't, the behavior of the mother had, in a limited sense, come under my protection. But, again, no audience would know any of this from watching the film.

AREAS OF CONFUSION

I suspect that much of the criticism on ethical grounds of the behavioral documentary comes from a confusion over such concepts as *objectivity, reality,* and *truth.* To be fair, this confusion isn't at all limited to critics. There are a lot of documentarians who are equally confused about how these concepts relate to the films and videotapes they shoot and eventually show.

Confusion about Objectivity

The very notion of objectivity in documentary is a fairly recent development in the history of the genre. It is an outgrowth of the peculiar rules governing American network television and a basic misunderstanding of both the requirements of journalistic objectivity and of the nature of scientific objectivity.

Certainly the pioneers of documentary made no pretense of using a journalistic approach in their films, and would have found any discussion of journalistic "objectivity" totally irrelevant. They unashamedly used the documentary to make as powerful a statement as they could manage about something they considered important. And this continues among contemporary documentarians who take up a specific social or political point of view. They are not objective; they are advocates. But so long as their work adequately documents their position, they remain documentarians.

Scientific Objectivity. Objectivity in science means that a scientific investigation can be verified independently. If it is an experiment, the results can be replicated by another scientist using the same procedures and materials.

Journalistic Objectivity. Objectivity in journalism came about as a reaction to the highly opinionated, politically positional press of the eighteenth and nineteenth centuries. It seeks to separate fact from opinion, assumption, and evaluation, and to make clear which is which. News reports are expected to be founded in fact and capable of independent verification. Opinion, conclusion, evaluation, interpretation, speculation, and so on are dealt with in editorials, signed opinion columns, and bylined feature stories. In areas of controversy, TV journalists try to present "both sides of the story" and attempt to give equal weight to each. The television documentary evolved within this tradition.

Cinema verité and direct cinema are, if anything, a reaction to the journalistically objective television documentary.

Confusion of Actuality with Reality *In comparison to feature films.*

A behavioral documentary is shot in an actual situation, not on a staged set, with actual people, not actors, doing whatever it is that they actually do, not acting out a script. The resulting documentary can have such immediacy that both documentarians and the audiences who view their work have often made the erroneous assumption that the documentary showed reality.

This assumption is simply not valid. The best you get is bits and pieces of whatever happened, filtered through the eyes, ears, and minds of a documentary crew and the recording capabilities of their equipment. When we are present, and everything is right, we can record the image and sound of the behavior that takes place in front of the camera. We do not penetrate to the thoughts, instincts, history, social conditioning, and all the other complex elements that underlie behavior. We do not even record the taste, feel, or smell of the situation. At best we try to imply these. Often we ignore them.

Imagine, for example, a documentary interview in which

- the person being interviewed is from a culture that prefers a fairly close social distance for conversation and
- has incredibly bad breath, while
- the interviewer prefers a wider social distance and
- has an extremely sensitive nose.

Such a situation might well produce visual images of a dance of approach-avoidance on the part of the interviewee and interviewer quite unrelated to the subject matter of the interview. How do you handle that? That's actuality, but are the images that result *reality?*

Confusion about Truth and Honesty

Such a scene would certainly be an interesting—and true—piece of behavior. But the next bothersome question is: Does it belong in the documentary? If the implication of the scene is that the interviewer does not care for the person being interviewed when in fact the interviewer simply doesn't want to stand as close as the interviewee prefers, what is the honest thing for the documentarian to do? Probably the director has to find some solution that won't give the wrong impression—either a fix in editing, such as use of the interview as voice-over, leaving out pictures of the interview altogether, or, if it is crucial to the documentary, shooting it again in a way that avoids the problem.

MAKING OUR OWN ETHICAL JUDGMENTS

In other words, resolution of the ethical questions, like that of all the other questions pertaining to the production of a documentary, lies with the documentarian.

There can be no help for it. The documentarian must take the responsibility for that which is shown. The ethical milieu surrounding the production of a documentary of human behavior is the product of the integrity of the person or persons responsible for the production.

There will be abuses, as there have been in the past. And there will be brilliant documentaries made by thoroughly honorable people. Sometimes subjects will become collaborators in the organization and editing of the material, and sometimes they'll be locked out of the editing room.

Ultimately the responsibility for the accuracy, validity, honesty, and truth of the analog that is a documentary, and for the ethical milieu in which it is produced, rests solely with the documentarian in charge of the production.

What I hope is that, as you go about the planning, production, editing, and presentation of any documentary, you will do so with a heightened awareness that your actions have ethical implications.

In the last analysis, you will have to make your own ethical judgments.

There is no other way to practice our craft.

PART II

PREPRODUCTION

It is not the will to win that's important.
It's the will to prepare to win that
really separates those who wish and dream
from those who make it happen.

. . . .

—Coach Dick Tomey

8

STEPS IN PRODUCING

A DOCUMENTARY

In the previous chapters it has been convenient to assume that we all know, in general, how a documentary film or videotape gets made. There have been references to the film idea, to shooting, to editing, and to showing the final print to an audience.

But a lot happens in between coming up with an idea for a documentary and the day you wait in a darkened room while an audience views your finished product. With current technology, the entire process could take just a few days. Or with a documentary such as *Hoop Dreams*, it could take several years. It can cost a few hundred dollars or hundreds of thousands. It can be a wonderful experience or a terrible one—and you never know in advance which it will be.

So let's see what has to be done to make a documentary happen.

PREPRODUCTION

The preproduction period is crucial to the success of a documentary. Failure here sends you out on the wide ocean in a leaky boat with no charts and few provisions.

Concept

The *concept* is the documentary idea. It tells why you want to make the documentary, what it will be about, and what effect you hope it will have on an audience. In general, you should be able to state the concept in not more than a hundred words. Be specific, but don't get bogged down in details. These belong in the treatment or script.

More on the documentary idea in chapter nine.

Treatment and Script Preparation and Approval

The *treatment* for a film is often called an outline, but it really should be thought of as an explanation of the documentary you intend to make. It tells what is to be shot and why, and how the documentary will be organized to make a statement to an audience. Because it sets the visual approach to the documentary, the treatment should be written by a film- or videomaker or by a writer with a good film sense.

The problems with the Midway documentary began with the lack of a proper treatment. All that existed were several pages of the hopes and dreams of the producers—who were not filmmakers.

Approval of the treatment is approval of the concept and approach set forth in the treatment.

For many documentaries, the treatment is the basic shooting document. For some, a *script* will also be written. The script is a blueprint of the documentary, as detailed as possible, for shooting and editing. For each scene it tells what is shot, how it is shot, who is in the scene, and what is said. You would have a script for a historical documentary or a re-creation, while you would expect to go with a treatment for a documentary of a unique event or a behavioral documentary.

A good script may seem a little thin on paper. That's because, as my son Greg has said, the scriptwriter should tell what goes into the documentary, not write "a manual on how to make my movie." It's the director's job to bring the script to life and the editor's job to organize the footage into a film. The director and editor should be allowed some leeway in shooting and editing the film, if for no other reason than because an idea that reads well on paper may not work on the screen.

More on writing the documentary in chapter ten.

Budget

The budget details the cost of the documentary and is usually developed along with the treatment. Sometimes the budget will have a strong influence on the treatment, for instance when there is a specific amount of money available to produce the documentary. Then, unfortunately, you have to tailor the treatment to the budget.

There is no truth whatever to the notion that a film or video should cost so many dollars per minute. The cost of a documentary depends entirely on what is to be shot, how many days it will take to shoot it, how large a crew is required, the equipment that will be used, and all the other things that may go into a production, such as the cost of actors, props, makeup, special effects, and special items such as original music. Only the cost of film printing is related to the running length of the finished print.

It's a good idea to develop a budgeting checklist to be sure all costs are accounted for. And once you've developed a budget, be sure to allow 10 to 15 percent extra for unforeseen contingencies.

More on budgeting a documentary in chapter fifteen.

Scouting and Preproduction Planning

With the script and budget approved, the real work begins—getting ready to shoot.

Scouting. Scouting is necessary if the documentary is to be shot on location. The director and camera operator need to know about the places they'll be shooting in—what they look like, what the light and sound levels will be, and whether there are going to be any constraints on shooting.

More on scouting in chapter eleven.

Casting. If actors will be used, the director needs to audition them. Similarly, the director may need to meet and talk with any people who are not actors who will be appearing in the documentary, to select those who will look and sound good on camera and who won't freeze up when the lights come on.

More on working with people who are not actors in chapter nineteen and on casting in chapter twenty.

Scheduling. A production schedule has to be worked out, which will make the most efficient and effective use of time, money, people, and equipment.

Scheduling is covered in chapter fourteen.

Crew. A production crew has to be selected. While it is possible to shoot a documentary with just a camera operator and sound recordist, the normal minimum crew for a nonfiction film will also include a director and a production assistant or camera assistant. More complex films will require additional people.

More on crew selection in chapter twelve.

Film or Video? The decision as to whether you will be recording on film or videotape has to be made. In general, film gives better quality, but video offers greater economy. Film should probably be used if you have any idea of releasing the documentary to theaters. For all other uses, video will probably suffice.

Equipment and Supplies. The appropriate equipment has to be chosen and reserved or rented. The appropriate film stock or videotape has to be ordered. If the documentary is to be shot on film, arrangements need to be made with a processing lab.

More on equipment and supplies in chapter thirteen.

PRODUCTION

Then the documentary goes into production.

Filming and Recording

There can be no documentary until footage has been recorded. Shooting film or recording videotape for your documentary can occur in quite limited time and space or may require months or years in many different locations.

Shooting Ratio. Normally, far more footage is shot than can be used in the final version. This allows for retakes, changes in camera angle or position, and some risk taking—filming of scenes or events that could be great if they work out, or could be nothing. The relationship of the amount of footage shot to that used in the final print is the shooting ratio. Most documentaries will require a shooting ratio of at least 10:1. Others may go 20:1, or even 50:1 or 100:1. It all depends on what is being shot. Recording video permits a much higher shooting ratio than using film, since videotape is much cheaper to buy than film and requires no processing.

Film Processing and Sound Transfer

If your documentary is being shot on film, the film is sent off to a processing laboratory to be developed. At the same time, the sound that has been recorded on audiotape is transferred at a sound laboratory to magnetic film. This is a film stock base that has been coated with a magnetic emulsion for recording. The *mag film* is used in editing and postproduction.

The camera original is carefully stored until it is needed to make the final print of the film—either at the vault at the lab or in a safe place where you are—and a copy is made for you to work with. Until recently, this would have been a film work print, which is a low-cost print from the original for use in editing. Today, however, the film will most likely be transferred to videotape for viewing and editing on a video editing system.

Viewing Videotape Footage

If you have been shooting on videotape, you don't have to deal with laboratory processing and sound transfer since videotape is ready for playback immediately after recording. But even though videotape can tolerate much more handling than film original, most documentarians will make copies of all the camera tapes to work with. The originals go in the vault for protection until the last step in video postproduction—on-line editing.

POSTPRODUCTION

Preproduction is full of hopes and dreams. Production is all potential. But it is in postproduction that you have to deal with reality. This is where you discover what you really have in the footage as opposed to what you think you shot. Editing is the heart of the documentary process. This is where you shape the material you've recorded into a coherent visual statement for presentation to an audience.

Look and Log

The first thing to do is to find out what you've got. Everything that was shot must be viewed and logged for later reference. A written log is essential, because as the footage piles up—and in a documentary this can mean hours and hours of film or tape—it's impossible to remember what reel each shot is on. Both film and video come with reference numbers which can be used in preparing the log.

More on this in chapter twenty-three.

Editing

Rough Cut. The good takes are organized into a rough cut, which is the first edited version of the documentary. The rough cut is edited to see how things go together. Since the editing may not be much more than splicing the takes together, the rough cut will usually be longer than the intended final length of the print. Such refinements as music, narration, titles, and optical effects may only be suggested.

Fine Cut. In essence, the rough cut teaches you what your footage is like, while editing to fine cut may be a slow process of seeing what scenes go together in what order to make the documentary statement. Getting to a fine cut usually involves a series of successive approximations, each of which gets closer to the documentary lurking in your imagination. This may be a long, slow process.

Titles, Music, and Narration. These visual and sound elements are added during postproduction. Music, if it is to be used, is composed or selected and scored to the fine cut. If there is to be a narration, it should be written (or rewritten), recorded, and transferred at this point.

More on editing in chapter twenty-four.

Review and Approval of Off-line or Interlock

When the fine cut is completed, there is usually a formal step at which the documentary is reviewed in its current state and approved for completion. If it has been edited on film, this step requires an *interlock*, which is the showing of the fine cut with all the picture and sound in its proper place. This is a critical formal step in film production, because following approval at interlock, the filmmaker will cut the original, mix the sound, and have a print made—all of which are expensive. Interlock is, therefore, the last point at which changes can be made inexpensively.

If the fine cut has been done on videotape, this stage simply involves viewing the video off-line edit. And, again, approval moves the production to on-line editing, which can be expensive.

Finishing on Film

The process of completing the documentary is different with film than it is with video.

The Sound Mix. The filmmaker takes the edited work print and all the various edited sound tracks (there may be several) to a sound lab for a sound mix. The tracks are skillfully blended into a single composite sound track in perfect sync with the picture.

Conforming the Camera Original. The camera original is taken out of the vault and sent with the edited work print to a conforming editor. This is the most critical technical step in post-production, since it involves cutting and splicing the original to match the work print frame for frame.

Laboratory Printing of an Answer Print. Next the preprint materials—the conformed original, the composite sound track, the edited work print, and a scene-by-scene log of the work print—go to the processing laboratory. The original is timed, which means estimating the correct printing exposure for each scene, and color-corrected, which means determining the color composition of the light on the printer to give each scene the best color.

Timing and color correction are estimates, although pretty accurate ones at most labs. The real test lies in the first print made: the *answer print*, which answers the question "How close did we get?" The answer print is also sometimes called a check print. It is for internal use for checking and correcting. It is not a print to be shown to the public.

Corrections and Printing of the Release Print. The filmmaker checks the timing and color correction of the answer print and the synchronization of the sound track with the picture, and necessary corrections are noted. The answer print is returned to the lab, the changes are made, and a *release print* is struck. This should be the first perfect print of the film, and is the one shown to the public.

Manufacture of a Printing Negative. A *printing negative* is usually made to protect the conformed original. This is a single strand of negative from which prints in quantity can be struck. An internegative is made from reversal (positive) film. In making the printing negative, the film can be blown up from 16mm to 35mm for theater use.

Film-to-Tape Transfer. If the film is to be released on videotape or videocassette, a video master will be made from a clean release print, which may be interlocked with the composite magnetic track for the best possible sound.

Finishing on Videotape

Video is edited by rerecording rather than splicing. Therefore each approximation—or edited version—is, in a sense, a finished product. The video equivalent to cutting and splicing the film work print is the off-line edit. This is done in a small—and usually inexpensive—editing suite that can handle the normal editing functions but may lack effects, graphics, and other expensive support found in an on-line editing studio.

Sound Sweetening. Videotape offers only two to four sound tracks on the tape itself. Therefore, in order to have the kind of sound complexity in video production that film editors have long taken for granted, video editors have developed the process of *sound sweetening.* Once the video is frozen, either as an off-line template for on-line editing or as a completed on-line, it is taken into a sound studio, where multiple tracks are synchronized with the picture and layers of sound can be added as needed.

On-line Editing. The final editing stage is the on-line edit, in which the edited master tape for the finished documentary is created with all of its components—picture, graphics, narration, titles, and sweetened sound—in place.

Duplicate Master. A duplicate video master may be made from the edited master videotape if copies in quantity are desired. Its purpose is the same as that of the printing negative with film: to protect the original from being worn out by repeatedly passing through the equipment as copies are made.

Tape-to-Film Transfer. It is possible to do a tape-to-film transfer from videotape, resulting in a printing negative and sound track from which prints on motion picture film can be made. This is an expensive process and the quality of the film print made from videotape will usually not be as good as a print made from original film stock.

More on finishing the documentary in chapter twenty-five.

Distribution

This is the last step in the process—getting a usable print of the film or copy of the videotape in the hands of the intended audience.

And that's the process—all the steps that have to be gone through to take a film or tape from idea to audience. Some of the steps are more fun, more interesting, or just plain more like filmmaking than others. Some involve a great deal of skill and creativity. Some are more or less mechanical. And some are mainly administrative. But each step is important to the full realization of the finished documentary.

9

THE DOCUMENTARY IDEA

Planning a documentary begins with the documentary idea. And the documentary idea may begin with nothing more than a vague urge in some direction. For instance, I've noticed that some of the pedestrian WALK lights in my city are on for no longer than four seconds. The other day, as I tried to walk across a seven-lane boulevard on a four-second light, three cars—one right after the other—made a right turn on red without stopping, keeping me from even trying to cross while I had that oh-so-brief WALK light. And the thought flashed across my mind, "I wish I had that on videotape. I'd like to show it to the county council."

Maybe that urge will grow until it becomes forceful enough to result in a documentary on pedestrian safety, or dumb traffic engineering, or bad driving. And maybe it won't. Making a documentary requires time, energy, and money. So the documentary idea has to be important enough to you for you to put in the time and energy to gather the money and do the work.

WHAT IS THE CONCEPT?

A documentary idea is some sort of notion of what the film will be about. As the idea evolves, it will come to determine, more and more, what will be shown on the screen in the final print of the film.

My idea about videotaping what happens at a traffic light could result in several different documentaries. Because I'm interested in behavior, I'd probably state the idea initially in terms of filming the behavior of pedestrians and motorists at traffic lights. But then there's the business of that four-second WALK light. I'd want to find out why that was permitted—it's too short to do any good—and what the rationale was.

It might turn out that the people responsible don't even realize that the WALK light is on for so short a time. They may be working from some formula that says the steady, red DON'T WALK light must be on for so many seconds for each lane of traffic, and before that the flashing, red DON'T WALK light must be on for a specified period of time, and all that is left is four seconds of WALK time. If that were the case, then the documentary idea and the resulting film might lurch in the direction of exploring bureaucratic rules that don't accomplish their purpose.

It might be that in the course of researching and filming the traffic light idea, a community group—senior citizens, perhaps— would try to call this to the attention of responsible lawmakers in order to have the situation corrected. In my experience, calling government's attention to something silly that it is doing rarely results in immediate rectification of the error. So the documentary might look at the process of trying to get a stupid situation corrected when government agencies are involved.

At this point, what started as a random thought about documenting a stupid situation has begun to evolve into the kind of film I like—a documentary of human behavior with the outcome in doubt.

Why Do You Want to Make This Documentary?

At the International Documentary Association Documentary Workshop in late 1994, Mitchell Block, a University of Southern California professor and head of Direct Cinema, Ltd., spoke about the documentary idea. "I submit that all works," he said, "whether they are fiction or nonfiction, are made for one of two reasons— either to do good or to make money."

What is your reason?

The best documentaries are undoubtedly made because the documentarian had a driving desire to deal with the topic. Still, there's nothing wrong with making money. It's just that if you approach making your documentary primarily from the point of view of making money, you're faced with one set of questions:

- What is the market for this kind of documentary?
- What is this market buying?
- How can I make my project attractive to this market?

Whereas if you approach your documentary with a burning desire to get it made, the important questions are somewhat different:

- What do I want to show?
- What do I need to show?
- What will it cost to do this?
- How can I raise enough money to get this documentary made?

The Things We Do for Love

My own bias is always to go for the documentary you burn to make. There are plenty of good reasons, and the first is that those projects I have taken on just for the money have never been satisfactory, either artistically or financially. But those I have done because I really wanted to do them have paid off in many unexpected ways

It takes an enormous amount of time and a substantial amount of money to make any film or video—even a very bad one. So why invest your creative force in something you're not in love with? The annals of filmmaking are stuffed with examples of projects no one wanted except the filmmaker—until they were finished. But nobody either counts or reports on the dull, mediocre, and sometimes unfinished projects that were taken on to make a buck.

I'm distinguishing here between serious documentaries and commercial videos. I write, and sometimes produce and direct, sales and corporate videos as my day job. And I invest very little of myself in these other than my demonstrated *skill* at getting such projects made. If the client wants changes, I don't argue; I make them. Unless, of course, they are absolutely stupid. In which case I point out that these changes will be bad for the final product. Even so, if the client insists, I make the stupid changes, because this is not *my* project, it's the client's.

But when I'm making a documentary, I'm in charge, and it has to be done my way. And no one brings that kind of passion to a project undertaken just to make money. The story is that *Woodstock*, the movie—which was a tour de force documentary project about Woodstock, the event —almost didn't get made. With time running out before the concert, negotiations almost broke down between the promoters and Michael Wadleigh, who directed the film. At the last moment, the filmmakers managed to explain that Wadleigh wasn't asking for a bigger piece or more money, "He just wants creative control." With that agreed to, the film was made, and it became a part of documentary history.

At the IDA Documentary Workshop, the experts kept repeating that it's going to take three years to get funding. Who wants to spend that kind of time and money for anything less than a project you believe in?

Building a Body of Work

Mitchell Block went on to say at the workshop that he thought it was important to design a work "that you can build on. So if you want to make films dealing with women's issues, make sure your first work is dealing with women." In other words, your body of work begins with your first project.

Like it or not, to the outside world—especially sponsors, underwriters, and funding agencies—you are what you do. And each documentary is a learning experience. So it's important to be learning the things that let you demonstrate that you are able to do the kind of work you *want* to do.

Can You State the Concept in a Few Words?

Sol Worth would ask his film students to begin the process of planning their documentaries by writing a short statement that began, "I want to make a film about . . ." Sol always asked for it in a hundred words or less. That was good discipline, especially for graduate students who were more accustomed to writing several pages than one paragraph. But it's also realistic. You should be able to describe the bones of a workable documentary idea in two or three sentences—something a little longer than the blurb in *TV Guide* but somewhat shorter than a letter to a friend.

Try it. If you have an idea for a documentary, see if you can state it in a hundred words or less.

Here's mine: I want to do a documentary about . . .

. . . why my town has four-second WALK lights when it takes twenty seconds to cross the street. Public figures are alarmed by a rise in pedestrian fatalities, which wouldn't happen, they say, if people would use the WALK lights. We'll show that WALK lights on many wide avenues are on for just four seconds! We'll show that drivers making turns often don't check for pedestrians, so intersections may be the most dangerous place to cross. Then we'll explore who knew about the short WALK lights, why the situation has persisted, and whether government helps or resists common sense change.

That's ninety-nine words. The statement tells what I am thinking about and what the thrust of the documentary will be. Each sentence evokes additional ideas for amplification and suggests images that could be recorded to make up the visual evidence of the documentary. But it's only a first draft. As the concept evolves through research, thought, discussion, and the process of getting it down on paper, it is bound to change.

Here's another. My documentary *A Young Child Is* . . . was to be a film about learning in children too young to go to school. I had absolutely no idea how the final film would begin or end, or what it would look like. But I had a statement of what the film was about, and what it was supposed to do:

> The film will show the tremendous amount of learning that children do on their own, long before they ever get near a school. It will demonstrate to teachers and school administrators (the intended audience) that children are not born on the steps of the kindergarten at the age of five.

Note that these short statements are for the documentarian's use. They are the concept from which everything else that goes into the documentary will eventually flow. They are not what you would write for a fund-raising proposal. That might begin with the details of one of the pedestrian fatalities or with an example of out-of-school learning in small children. Nor are they treatments—although they might be the start of a treatment. The actual treatment for A *Young Child Is* . . . is included in chapter ten.

Does the Concept Lead to Concrete Images That Can Be Recorded on Video or Film?

The documentary idea should help you to develop a shot list for your documentary. It should suggest where you have to go and who and what you need to shoot to record the visual evidence you need. This should lead you to imagine the kinds of concrete images that would serve as evidence of what you want to show.

When I was teaching documentary filmmaking with Sol Worth, this was the point at which the students would normally ask, "How can I do that? It will all depend on what happens when I get there."

That's when Sol would say, "Make it up. Make up a list of ideal scenes that would show exactly what you want." This is, of course, actually a process of fine-tuning yourself as an observing and decision-making instrument. It is not that you will try to shoot the scenes that you have made up. But the exercise of listing possible scenes will help you be ready to recognize the kinds of images you should be looking for when they happen.

If you can't make up a complete hypothetical shot list based on your documentary idea, the idea isn't good enough.

CONVENTIONAL CONCEPTS

I think there's a Hollywood way of looking at documentary, which often is to see it as a stepping stone to doing feature films. Which means making a documentary with big-screen production values. Certainly, having a big-screen look was a consideration for Theodore Thomas in making *Frank and Ollie*, about two of Disney's foremost animators. Because he wanted to use clips from the Disney library as part of the documentary, he felt any new documentary footage he would shoot had to be done with enough production value to be able to intercut with the Disney animation without jarring the viewer.

There has certainly been a PBS way, which is to deal with certain themes and ignore others, to concentrate heavily on interviews, and to mix in a little academic art or humanity to improve funding.

I'm sure there's a cable TV way, as seen on The Discovery Channel, A & E, The History Channel, The Learning Channel, and so on. Their documentaries tend to deal with biographical figures, historical events, and gadgets —including the weapons of war and Hollywood special effects—possibly just because there's interesting footage available of gadgets at work.

Then there are reality videos—made by putting a camera crew in the back of a cop car or in an emergency room or anywhere else that interesting and exploitable footage may be recorded.

Documentary Categories

In the worlds of network and cable TV, where the way you describe an "original" idea is to name the other films it is *like*, and where you can't get a script read unless you are willing to sign a release which acknowledges that there are no new ideas, you are going to be asked to fit your documentary into a precast set of categories— historical, biographical, social commentary, unusual events, travel, nature, or behind-the-scenes, for example. At the IDA Documentary Workshop, Mitchell Block suggested that all documentaries fit into one of the four Ps: *portrait, performance, place,* and *poetry.* To which I would add *process,* to include the documentary of a unique event with the end in doubt, although I think Block might include that under his category of performance.

But I'm also convinced that in documentary—just as in feature films, book writing, painting, music, and drama—there are the exciting and unexpected results that come from dedicated artists immersed in impossible projects that seem totally reasonable to them. And these aren't easy to categorize.

One of the reasons that a series like *FDR* is able to raise over two million dollars in funding is that it's easy to categorize. That makes it easy for underwriters to know what they are putting money into and what they can expect to see when it's done.

It certainly took a lot more courage for the Michigan Council for the Arts to put money into *Roger & Me* than for any funder to give money to *FDR.*

Terry Zwigoff had great difficulty in raising money from conventional sources for his offbeat documentary *Crumb.* He said every now and then he'd put together a short sample tape and travel from San Francisco to L.A. looking for money. And it was available—if he were willing to change the concept to a more conventional portrait of an unconventional artist. Which he wouldn't do.

Overdone Ideas

In spite of the voracious appetite of cable TV and the willingness of PBS to fund bad documentaries, it is very hard to get funding for, or to license the distribution of, a documentary on a subject that has already been covered. At least not until a lot of years have passed since the first film was made.

AIDS awareness, problems of the homeless, environmental pollution, and many other subjects are certainly worthwhile, and a
righteous way for a documentarian to spend his or her time, except . . . they've already been done! And done to death!

If your documentary idea is about a hot topic that is getting a
lot of coverage in the newspapers and popular magazines, you're
too late. You can be sure there are documentaries—or proposals for
documentaries—on that topic already in the works. And if the
topic is so hot that you saw something about it on TV, forget it; it's
already old and done.

On the other hand, if you have a truly original slant on an old
topic, then it becomes new again, and you may be able to get both
funding and distribution.

The point is that for conventional support, your idea has to be
conventional enough to be understood but different enough that it
hasn't been done before.

Unconventional Concepts

Crumb got made and has enjoyed decent success in theatrical release. It's a dark, moody, revealing story of three brothers from a
very strange family. Zwigoff's concept for the film is so much
stronger than any conventional biography would be that he was
right to wait it out, even though it took seven years to complete the
film.

Roger & Me is a brilliant satire on corporate public relations and
municipal mismanagement.

Woodstock became a legend in its own time.

If you want it badly enough, you'll find a way to get it made.
And if your documentary idea is good, your filming is honest and
effective, and the editing skillfully organizes your footage to present the idea clearly to an audience, you'll have a documentary you
can be proud of. And if you've gone that far, then either this documentary—or the next one—will make you some money.

PLANNING

With a good documentary idea, you should have a lot of confidence that you will be able to find good images—good visual evidence—with which to tell your story. But it still requires planning to be in the right place at the right time with the camera on and in focus. Look, if it were easy, everyone could do it.

You have to plan:

- what kinds of events will be shot
- where you'll go to shoot them
- who—or what types of people—will be included
- what sort of behavior you are looking for
- what you need for background or for establishing shots
- what kinds of statements—either from behavioral footage or from interviews—will help you present the documentary idea

A *Planless Documentary*

Without a good documentary idea and the requisite planning step, you're just like the cops and robbers in a bad TV show—going out and shooting all over the place without hitting anything. Sad to say, a lot of documentaries get made that way.

Much of the next chapter, Writing a Documentary, is adapted from my book *Video Scriptwriting*. Here is a story I tell in that book about a documentary that lost its way:

I got a call from a good friend, a producer-director, who said his company had shot a lot of video documenting a unique event. A chain of restaurants had opened several new locations and had added some new items to their menu. They decided to make a special day out of officially opening, or reopening, five of their restaurants. They had the restaurants blessed by a minister—which is a tradition in Hawaii—and they offered live music, balloons, prizes, and freebies at each of the five locations. Customers were encouraged to visit all five restaurants that day and get a special "passport" stamped to win a prize.

Members of the company's executive staff traveled from location to location accompanied by a Dixieland band and my client's video crew. My friend (and client) told me that the public relations firm which handled the restaurants was originally going to write the script, but now they wanted him to bring in a writer.

I found out why as soon as I got a look at the footage. In spite of the fact that there were two camera crews in operation all the time, and that the same procedure was gone through at each of the five restaurants, the footage was woefully incomplete. For instance, it didn't contain a complete sequence of a blessing, a complete statement of the purpose of the event by someone from management, or even a complete song from the Dixieland band. It just showed the same set of mistakes being made five times.

Along with the footage, I got some written information about what this special day was supposed to be, including the PR firm's own game plan for the event. So I had a pretty good idea of what was missing. These are excerpts from a letter I sent to my client about the footage:

> There are no shots whatsoever of the special passports (500 to be given out at each restaurant). No shots of anyone receiving a passport. No shots of anyone explaining the passport. No shots of a passport getting stamped at a store.
>
> Although six different radio stations participated, there is only limited footage of two radio DJs, and no radio broadcast audio.
>
> There is only one shot of a drawing for a door prize (which is also one of the two shots of the DJs).
>
> Too much camera time is spent on people from the PR firm riding the bus.
>
> No close-up of an employee wearing the Celebration Day button.
>
> I don't see in the footage any evidence that "each restaurant will be decorated professionally" as indicated in the game plan.

There is . . . no systematic coverage of the new menu items. There is one shot of the menu, close-up of the word NEW, and no return to what is NEW.

There is no complete coverage—establishing shot, MS, CU while the sound continues—of the country and western band at Westridge Shopping Center or the Hawaiian music group at Windward City Shopping Center.

No footage of the 20 × 30 posters announcing Celebration Day.

We have no interviews or statements from (company executives) such as:

"This is an important marketing test for use on the mainland."

"We're introducing a new image, brighter more complete restaurants, rather than takeout places, and a new menu."

"This is going to be great for business."

I want to stress that this footage was not shot by a bunch of amateur wannabes who went out with their camcorders and got into trouble. The work was done by a highly regarded film and video production company in Honolulu. The production involved a director and a cameraman who had created many award-winning commercials, but who had no experience with unscripted productions, especially a documentary of a unique event. They obviously had gone off to shoot an actuality situation with little or no planning in the belief that all they had to do was be there and reality would jump right into their cameras.

They had never developed a clear documentary idea, and therefore had not made a plan, a shot list, or even a *guess* list of what to shoot.

Focus on Showing, Not Shooting

It is almost impossible to go into production without a plan when the documentarian is focused on the film or video that will be *shown* rather than the one that will be *shot*. There are documentarians who can see the final print in their mind's eye long before they have exposed a single frame. And there are those who have no idea what the final print will look like when they start out, but who know what they want the documentary to communicate, and who have a strong notion of what they are trying to get as raw material from which to edit the program.

DOCUMENTING BEHAVIOR OR A UNIQUE EVENT

A documentary idea—especially one that involves filming human behavior or documenting a unique event—is a plan. It can never be a script. The script for a documentary of a unique event, if there is one, will be written in the editing room.

Overplanning

A friend of mine was hired as a sound recordist for a documentary about auto racing at Daytona. Even though a race is a unique event with the end in doubt, the director, who was also the camera operator, had carefully worked out every shot, down to the camera angle, time of day, and height of the sun.

For one of the scenes, the camera was carefully placed to aim up the track and catch the cars coming out of a turn. Suddenly, behind the camera, there was a multicar accident, with lots of crunching, grinding, flames, and smoke. My friend heard it on his earphones and turned to look.

"Quick! Turn the camera!" he shouted. "There's a hell of an accident just behind us. We'll get everything."

"I don't plan to shoot an accident," said the filmmaker, and he went on shooting race cars coming out of the corner and speeding past the camera.

Maybe he was right.

And maybe the cameraman in Rome in the story in chapter two was right, also.

Obviously, you'll never get a film made if your camera is at the mercy of every stray event that blows in on the breeze.

But I think they were overzealous.

In Rome, an inflexible attitude toward film technology prevented the filming of a unique event. At Daytona, although there were no technical reasons not to shoot, rigid adherence to the script took control, and a unique opportunity was lost.

Planning for A Young Child Is . . .

Based on the documentary idea, and my research, I had some rough ideas about the kinds of learning that might be demonstrated at various ages. I wanted to show on film that young children learn from their direct experience with the world around them, and that verbal interaction plays a relatively small part in their learning. I believed that small children actually learn from failure, without being defeated by it. I wanted to show that they can fail at what they are trying to do without getting a sense of failure. That they are self-correcting.

I wanted to use normal, healthy children from babies up to kids about four and a half years old. I wanted a mixture of boys and girls, white and black. I knew that I wanted a child who was young enough to be completely dependent on others, another who was learning to walk and talk, a "body bright" child who was gaining experience from direct physical contact with the world, another child gaining experience with language, and so on.

In short, I had a strong notion of the kind of behavior I was looking for and how to recognize it when it happened. And I had a pretty good idea of what the finished film should do, even though I had not the least idea of the images that would eventually be included.

Partly in preparation for this film, I had screened a large number of films on early childhood. Virtually all of them suffered from the same flaw: a script had been written that told some expert's opinion of what children should be like at various ages. Then children had been filmed doing whatever the expert said they would do, to illustrate the script.

I wanted to start with the real behavior of some normal children and then put a film together that would let an audience observe that behavior.

Accepting What Is There

In this way we captured on film some truly unique elements of early learning in children. For instance, we found a thirteen-month-old boy who was just starting to walk and just beginning to experiment with making sounds in the pattern of English sentences. Since these were both things that I wanted for the film, we went to his house and filmed him playing on the floor.

At one point he was playing alone with some toys—occasionally taking a drink from his bottle. It seemed like a good establishing shot, even though I couldn't see that anything we were looking for was happening. But behavior is behavior, and besides, I thought that at any moment he might start to do something important, like talk. So we kept the camera on him and running. In a couple of minutes he crawled over to his mother, then stood up and tried to walk. Great! Just what we'd come for!

Much later, I began trying to edit this sequence. On about the fifth or sixth time through the footage, I began to realize that something truly important was going on in that "establishing shot." The child was engaged in behavior that I was convinced—from watching my own kids—was the key to learning in young children, but had never before been able to prove.

Here's what he was doing:

While he was playing alone, he kept rubbing a wet spot on the rug. Then he picked up his bottle, lying near the spot, and sucked on it. He put the bottle down and touched the wet spot. Then he picked up the bottle and shook it until some drops fell out onto the rug. Finally, he rubbed the spot he had just made.

As far as I was concerned, that thirteen-month-old baby had formed a hypothesis about how the wet spot got on the rug, had tested it empirically with his bottle, and had satisfied himself as to the results of his experiment. And when he was done, he crawled off to play with his mom.

This became the opening of the film. I had the original footage duplicated so I could run it twice. The first time, I said to the audience in narration, "Here's a baby playing on the floor. What do you see?" The second time, I explained my interpretation, step by step, as we watched the child's behavior.

In effect, this scene became the topic sentence for the rest of the film. An audience could disagree with my interpretation. What they couldn't do was ignore the behavior that they had seen.

That behavior came from the child, spontaneously.

But the conceptual framework, and the preparedness to recognize what was happening in a simple establishing scene, came from the film idea.

. . . .

10

WRITING A DOCUMENTARY

The modern documentary quite often will run from beginning to end without a word of narration or dialogue and without anyone acting out a written scenario. And so it should. A large part of the fascination of doing documentary is this: What happens in the real world is often far more interesting—and usually more exciting and astonishing—than anything that could be made up by a scriptwriter.

So what's to write?

Quite a bit. The writing phase may extend from preproduction all the way to the final stages of postproduction. The writing may be done by the producer, the director—sometimes even the editor—or by a designated scriptwriter. It expands the documentary idea into a plan for shooting and, at the very least, a theory for editing.

WHAT DOES THE WRITER DO?

So what does a screenwriter do in documentary?

The answer depends on the kind of documentary. If it's a historical documentary, a biography, or a re-creation or reenactment of some event, the writer's work will be very similar to writing a feature film. The writer must gather and organize the information and then write a screenplay containing a well-structured series of scenes that can be created on film or video. If archival footage exists, reviewing it becomes part of the research process.

On the other hand, if the production is a spontaneous documentary of some kind of behavior or of a unique event, there may never be a script in the sense of a screenplay, because no one knows ahead of time exactly what is going to happen. In writing a spontaneous documentary, the emphasis is on visualization and organization, not on writing narration or dialogue. This is what I call the art of writing without words.

Unfortunately, it is also true with a spontaneous documentary that the writer may not be brought into the production until the last minute. After all the footage has been shot and edited, the director may show the cut to a writer and indicate what needs to be written for narration. In which case the writer is nothing more than a translator, turning the director's notes into a narration script.

Or, as happened to me with the restaurant documentary, the writer is brought in after shooting and before editing to try to organize the footage into a coherent entity.

Which means that unless the writer is a hyphenate—a producer-writer or director-writer—his or her role in a documentary production often ranges from ambiguous to nonexistent.

THE WRITER'S GIFTS TO THE PRODUCTION

When the writer's involvement is limited to doing a polished draft of the words to be said, the production uses less than a fourth of the talent an experienced screenwriter potentially brings to a documentary. These are the things that documentary scriptwriters do:

- research and planning
- visualization
- organizing a structure for the documentary
- writing the words

Research and Planning

Good images don't just happen. You have to plan for them. You have to be ready to recognize them and, even more important, be ready to record them on film or tape when they do occur. Then you have to select and organize them to present a visual argument to an audience.

Making a documentary is an exercise in model building, creating an analog of some event. And a scriptwriter is a film architect. Which is why, if a writer is to be used at all, it's important that he or she come into the process as early as possible.

Someone has to do the same kind of research for a documentary that a writer would do for a magazine article. Visit the location, talk to the people, and get the facts—the who, what, when, where, why, and how of the event to be documented. Out of this should come, at a minimum, an outline of the information, a list of copy or story points, and a shot list of people, places, and events that should be filmed.

If no one does this, the result is a body of video with no head, like the documentary about the restaurant openings in Honolulu.

In that situation, I came in after the fact, with the mistakes already recorded on tape and the production budget spent. I wrote an editing script that organized the chaos of the footage into a reasonable presentation of information, wrote some new scenes, which could be shot inexpensively in the studio to cover the missing pieces. And I got us all out alive.

The thing is, prior to shooting, *any* competent scriptwriter—or any experienced documentarian—could have spent less than an hour with nothing more than the written background information I received and written a treatment that would have eliminated *all* of the problems listed in my memo to the producer.

And a really good scriptwriter might well have spent a little longer and come up with some suggestions of concept and coverage that would have made this into an exceptional piece.

Visualization

The writer's research should be focused not just on the facts of the documentary topic but also on ways to show it clearly to an audience. What will be shown? What will make up the visual evidence for the argument presented in the documentary?

Some documentarians actually think in terms of recording a lot of interviews, having them transcribed, and then organizing the script by pasting together pieces of transcript. That may be a good start toward writing an article, but it won't make a very good documentary. And as a former magazine journalist, I can tell you that it usually won't even make a good article. You need a lot more than just people *telling* about the topic. Certainly in documentary, if you can show a picture of the topic, you can cut down substantially on the words that must be spoken. The audience wants and needs to see it, to experience it on the screen through images that are powerful and unarguable.

If you're doing an environmental documentary, you could go and interview an environmentalist who says a chemical plant is polluting the river. Then you could interview an official from the chemical plant who says they're not. That's a standoff. It's what you get on local TV news. And it is what we see far too much of, for instance, in the documentaries on PBS. Talking about a problem is not documenting the problem, it's documenting what people have to say about the problem.

But if you've got footage of ugly stuff pouring out of a pipe into the river, you're beginning to *show* the problem, not just talk about it. And if you can get some neutral party to test the ugly stuff on camera and demonstrate through the tests that it either is or isn't pollution, you're building a chain of visual evidence.

I've said it elsewhere and I'll say it here again: *There is no substitute for good footage.*

Organizing a Structure for the Documentary

Structure is one of the most important—and least understood—aspects of production. Bad structure is worse than bad writing, bad cinematography, and bad acting. It can lose you your audience almost before you start. And you will *never* know why.

A documentary normally does not have the three-act structure familiar to feature film screenwriters, with turning points, barriers, and other structural elements designed to advance the plot. But it does face the same structural need, which is to keep the audience interested from the beginning through the long development of the middle to the resolution and closure at the end.

In a creative writing class at the University of Pennsylvania, Dr. Bruce Olsen explained beginning, middle, and end this way:

The beginning is the point in your work before which nothing needs to be said. The end is the point beyond which nothing needs to be said. And the middle runs in between.

Beginning: The Point Before Which Nothing Needs to Be Said. The beginning states the theme, asks a question, or shows something new or unexpected. It gets the documentary started and raises the expectations of the audience.

Defining the beginning this way eliminates the problem of having two or three opening scenes, one right after another, which plagues so many documentaries and information videos. Does the audience have to know this? No? Then leave it out.

Within or following the beginning, you weave in a brief presentation of the theme of the documentary, the problem it deals with, the main people involved—whatever the viewer needs to know for the documentary to go forward. Keep this short! Trust your audience and limit this section to the absolutely essential information, without which the audience won't understand the documentary.

Inexperienced documentarians have a tendency to stop the documentary *dead* right after the opening titles and try to explain everything. If you don't get caught up in the idea that you have to impose an order on your documentary based on some sort of exterior logic—first you have to know this, then you have to know that—you'll find that this sort of exposition will take care of itself. Let essential information come in when it is needed and relevant. You may play hell with chronology, but your documentary will flow smoothly from point to point. And that, I'm convinced, is the key to good understanding and retention on the part of the audience. Audiences, I believe, can handle a lot more ambiguity and uncertainty than most documentary producers can.

Middle: The Presentation of Evidence. You've gotten the audience interested. You've given them a notion of what the documentary is about. Now you need to present some hard information to keep them interested. The middle explores conflicting elements of the situation by showing visual evidence in support of and in opposition to the theme.

Evidence related to the theme may be evidence that supports the theme (or some part of it) or it could be evidence that appears to contradict the theme you've established.

Then go to opposing evidence. If what you presented first was positive, this is negative, or vice versa.

Note that this sequence of presenting one kind of evidence followed by evidence opposing it may be repeated several times as you explore a variety of subthemes. Similarly, both sides could be presented simultaneously, as when the voice-over seems to contradict what is being shown.

The purpose of this is to introduce something like dramatic conflict into the structure of the documentary. Dramatic conflict doesn't mean some kind of encounter situation with adversaries yelling at one another. It is a structural tension that keeps the outcome of the documentary somewhat in doubt—and keeps the audience interested.

For instance, in *The War Room,* we see Gennifer Flowers holding a press conference saying she was Bill Clinton's lover, and later we see the Clinton campaign's response.

You can also provide dramatic conflict without playing opposing scenes against each other if the evidence you are presenting runs counter to the expectations or experience of the audience. In documentaries of human behavior and documentaries of unique events, the outcome is often sufficiently in doubt that there is tension built into the documentary from the nature of the event itself.

A documentary is expected to explore conflicting elements of the situation. This doesn't mean that it has to be passively neutral. But even when it takes a strong position in its theme, it should be able to acknowledge that this position isn't universally accepted. If it were, there would be little reason to make the documentary. One of the differences between information and propaganda is the willingness of the former to acknowledge that other points of view may legitimately exist, even if they are considered wrong.

Sometimes, of course, this kind of dialectic approach won't work. In a documentary of behavior, it's the behavior that is important. But even here, you may be playing actual behavior against audience expectations. In *A Young Child Is . . .* , I show Stevie, a little boy a year-and-a-half old, amusing himself for a long time by climbing over a low brick wall, getting a handful of sand, climbing back over the wall, throwing the sand in the lake, and then repeating the process again and again and again. The narrator says:

> You've probably heard it said that young children have a short attention span. We've come to doubt whether the concept of attention span has much meaning when the child initiates his own activities. We think attention span only refers to how long a child will tolerate doing something someone else wants him to do. If you don't believe us, believe Stevie . . . This went on all afternoon.

In a documentary of a unique event, it is the process that counts. *The War Room*, for instance, is about an election campaign, a unique event with the end in doubt. Dramatic conflict comes through problems that occur and the way they are overcome as well as by finding other points of tension within the event.

Ending: Resolving the Conflict. The ending shows the outcome—which up to now may have been somewhat in doubt—in which the conflicting elements are handled and resolved. It is really the point to the documentary, toward which all the evidence has been leading. If the documentary is about a scientific experiment, the resolution would be the point at which the theory is confirmed—or if the experiment failed, the explanation of why.

The ending is a final sequence within or after the resolution that ties up the loose ends, drives home the theme, and completes the documentary for the audience.

PROPOSAL WRITING

Documentary films and videotapes are usually made with other people's money. And those people want an idea of what they'll be getting before they sign the check. So getting started usually takes a written proposal.

The proposal is a selling document. Documentaries are expensive to produce. The organizations putting up the money have to be convinced that the benefits of producing a documentary justify the cost, either in profitable distribution or by doing good in some way. You may be interested mainly in the content of the documentary and the production techniques that will be used to achieve that content. But content and technique are not likely to be the sponsor's hot buttons. And as the old salesman used to say, "You don't sell the steak. Sell the sizzle!"

You'll probably find that the funding organization has a standard format for a proposal. But regardless of whether it is written to format, done as a letter, or written as a report, in a few pages the proposal has to engage the fantasy life of the sponsor, stress the benefits of making the documentary, and shake loose the money. The proposal has to convince the people putting up the money that

- there are good reasons why this documentary should be made,
- you know exactly the kind of documentary that is needed, and
- your production unit is the only one that can possibly do justice to the documentary.

Demonstrate why this new documentary is needed.

Push the sponsor's hot button, whatever it is. Stress the direct and indirect benefits of producing the documentary. Show how the new production will fit into the existing body of work.

How long is a proposal? The best rule is to be as brief as you can, but be complete. Keep the proposal short, and save the details for the treatment.

Keep in mind that there's an enormous difference between a neat idea in your head and a workable plan for a production. Somehow, what seems so pure and simple in your imagination, gets a lot tougher to describe when you begin writing about the way the documentary will actually be made. So it's good practice to do a proposal even if you're doing the documentary all by yourself with your own money. Getting it down on paper can be a big help.

And, of course, if you're trying to raise money, a proposal is essential.

TREATMENT

Part of the planning process for a documentary is the treatment, which sets forth the idea of the documentary comprehensively enough to be understood, but with enough flexibility to allow for chance, change, and the occasional flash of creativity. A treatment is often referred to as an outline for a documentary. But it's more than that. It's really an explanation of the documentary. It describes the content of the documentary and the style in which it will be shot. What it is about. What will be included. How it will be shot. And what it will look like. It includes all the elements—the people, places, things, and events—which must be a part of the documentary. And it tells how the documentary will be organized to communicate with an audience.

How long is a treatment? As long as it takes to do the job. Most documentaries can be handled with a few pages of specific information, giving the purpose of the documentary, the approach you expect to take in filming and editing, and the expected content, including a list of possible shots. The treatment should be complete enough that it can be used as the basis for developing a preliminary budget for the documentary.

A Treatment Instead of a Script

In writing a behavioral documentary, the emphasis is on organization and visualization, not on writing narration or dialogue. For a behavioral documentary or a documentary of a unique event, a comprehensive treatment often will take the place of a script. The treatment will show that you know what to look for and how to use it in the documentary you are planning, and that the documentary crew is well organized to cover whatever happens.

A *Young Child Is* . . . was planned as a documentary of behavior, in which the images that would make up the documentary would be found in the behavior of the people we filmed. The treatment had to deal with the fact that while we didn't know specifically what would be filmed, we had a strong concept of both what the documentary would be about and how it would look.

Here is a major part of the treatment:

FILM TREATMENT: *A YOUNG CHILD IS* . . .

· ·

Purpose of the Film
1. To focus on young children from birth to the age at which they begin school.
2. To show the tremendous amount of learning accomplished by these very young children before they ever come in contact with schools and teachers.
3. To foster an attitude of respect for the learning ability, and the accomplishments of young children.
4. To show some of the processes young children use in learning on their own, which differ from the processes schools use to "teach" children.

5. To show the ways in which young children grow and develop.
6. To include on the agenda of learning not only that which is abstract, cognitive, and "school-like," but also that which is emotional, social, and decisional.
7. To explore the validity of concepts such as "attention span" and "failure" in the context of preschool learning.
8. To promote respect for the young child as a human being, a person, and an individual. To lay a foundation for the second film *(Schools for Children)*, which will take the approach of seeking educational programs that match the way children actually are.

Approach to the Film

The approach to filming will be open and documentary in style. We wish to observe the behavior of very young children, recording it on color film with synchronous sound. We wish to explore and document what children actually do, including, if appropriate, what they do in the presence of cameras. Little or no attempt will be made to direct the children's activities, and, in no case, will children be asked or encouraged to "act out" some preconceived activity to illustrate what children are supposed to do.

What we get is what you see.

Content of the Film

Filming situations will include, but not be limited to:

1. The behavior of babies less than a year old.* We shall be looking for the development of language—patterning sentences, experimentation with words, feedback and re-

---

* I think I had in mind that the paragraph headings I used in describing content might become divisions within the documentary. It didn't work out that way in editing. Nevertheless, in this treatment I have developed a possible organization of the material, through these headings, without being unalterably committed to it.

ward—the development of motor ability, trial-and-error efforts toward walking and crawling, and the emotional environment of the very young child.

2. The behavior of toddlers. We shall be looking for concrete examples of exploratory learning, of "play" which gains the child a familiarity with the object or task, and gets him "ready" to use it. We shall also be looking at attention span, and the ways in which these very young children learn from failure, without being defeated by it.

3. The trusting environment. As we film babies and toddlers, we shall be looking for examples of "trust" built into their environment, and the ways in which these children develop a sense of trust.

4. Two-year-olds and the sense of autonomy. In filming children roughly two years old, we shall be looking for the ways in which these children attempt to separate themselves from the background—to define themselves as unique, as individuals—to use as examples of the ways children develop a sense of autonomy. At the same time we shall be looking for examples of sophisticated development of verbal behavior, the self-correcting mechanism that turns "baby talk" into a reasonable facsimile of adult speech.

5. The Age of "Why?" Here we're dealing with two-, three-, and four-year-olds, looking for some replacement of trial-and-error learning with verbal interaction. Let us be clear about what we expect to find: We do not expect that every "why?" is a reasoned request for information. But, as in patterning sentences before the child has words to fill them with meaning, we do expect to find a new emphasis on verbal behavior—practicing, playing with it—so that he will have the form ready when he wants to fill it with content.

6. Curiosity. This exists at all age levels, and we want to capitalize on it wherever we find it. We want to look for curiosity as it develops, to see how it develops and how it is turned off.

7. Creativity. Again, one can find examples, perhaps, at all age levels. We shall be looking for them. By "creativity" we do

not mean merely artwork, or singing, or anything particularly related to the creative arts. We shall be looking for evidence of children taking what they know and reformulating it into something new, the creative solution to a problem, the development of a "new" word of precise meaning out of two old words, etc.

8. The Age of Initiative. Here we are looking for examples to show that the child has learned to trust his environment and has gained a sufficient sense of himself that he can now try on other roles. He can begin to accept others and interact with them. He can play with other children instead of alongside others.

9. Verbal behavior of five-year-olds. We want to observe five-year-olds talking with each other and with adults. Our premise is that their verbal behavior can be quite sophisticated, and is a necessary part of the readiness in communication which will lead them naturally into other communication skills such as reading and writing.

10. Decision-making. At all levels we shall be looking for evidence of very young children making decisions on their own, guiding and directing their own behavior.

11. Repetition, familiarity, mastery. We want to show the ways in which young children approach novelty. If they don't like it, they have "a short attention span." But if they do like it, they want it repeated, and repeated, until it becomes familiar and they have a feeling of mastery over it. Examples might be a parent reading a story, and when he has finished the child says, "Read it again," perhaps preferring it to a new story he hasn't heard. Or a young child going down a sliding board. As soon as he has convinced himself he won't be hurt, he wants to slide again, and again, and again.*

This is the way you indicate the kinds of images you'll be looking for. It doesn't mean you will use these exact images. As it happens, we never even tried to film a parent reading a story. We did shoot in a playground, where we got some film of kids going down slides. But I didn't use it in the finished film.

12. The effects of frustration on young children. In our film-
    ing, we expect to find instances where a child finds him-
    self frustrated at what he intends to do. We want to
    observe this, to see how children deal with frustration.
13. Abstract learning—the learning of colors, numbers, let-
    ters, etc. How does a child learn these concepts? What
    does it mean to say, "He knows the alphabet," or "He
    knows how to count"? What is evidence that he does,
    and what is evidence that he doesn't?
14. Learning vs. "Right Answers." Again, we shall be looking
    for evidence of the difference between learning some-
    thing, and learning how to give right answers about it. As
    an example of what we shall be looking for, we have a film
    clip, five minutes in length, shot in a classroom this past
    summer. In it, a teacher is working with two seven-year-
    olds, trying to teach the concept: "$2 + 3 = 5$." She has a
    filmstrip projector with a picture of two red chickens and
    three white chickens on it and a box of blocks set before
    the children. At the beginning of the clip, she points to
    the two red chickens and asks Johnny (his name, *really!*),
    "How many chickens do you see?" Johnny answers,
    "Five." He has solved the problem, but she doesn't know
    it. She is looking for the answer, "Two," which is the right
    answer as far as she is concerned. She says, "No. How
    many do you see here?" She then goes through the entire
    process, counting two red chickens, counting three white
    chickens, counting blocks for red chickens, "1-2," count-
    ing blocks for white chickens, "1-2-3," counting all the
    chickens, "1-2-3-4-5," counting all the blocks,
    "1-2-3-4-5." She then says, "So, two plus three equals how
    much, Johnny?" And Johnny answers, "Four!" He has
    learned to look for "right answers" and has lost the ability
    to solve the problem.

Where appropriate, the treatment might go on to discuss the
kind of music, if any, that will be used, the lighting, the mood to

be evoked, the editing style to be used, and so on. It might also include a shot list and a production schedule covering both filming and postproduction.

THE SCRIPT

For documentaries that do not record spontaneous behavior or the unfolding process of a unique event, a complete script will probably be required. This then becomes the basic production document for the documentary.

A script starts at the beginning of the documentary and runs in a continuous progression of scenes to the end. It is written in master scenes that describe all the action and speech that occur at a specific location at a given point in time. You start a new scene whenever you change the time or place.

The script will include dialogue for actors. But where real people will portray themselves, it may simply suggest what they can be expected to say.

It is not necessary to detail camera movement, camera angles, close-ups, long shots, and so on, unless the camera work is essential to the script. A master scene simply describes what happens in that scene and leaves it up to the director to decide how to photograph it. A simple device is to begin descriptive passages with the words, "We see . . ." and then tell what the audience will see on the screen.

Obviously, when the sense of the scene demands it, camera directions should be written into the script—for example, "Close-up of an empty boot." The point is, don't get bogged down in worrying about camera directions, changing angles, reverse shots, and so on. Just tell the story.

Script Formats

There are two basic formats for scripts—the classic screenplay format and the television two-column format—and it doesn't really matter very much which you use, or even whether, for some reason, you invent your own, as long as you and the others involved

Figure 10.1

DISSOLVE TO:

170. SSGT. Hicks talks about counterattack.

SSGT. HICKS
(To recruits)
Now once Bravo Team has cleared out
the bottom of the building we now own
the building. The only problem is,
you've just taken this building away
from the enemy, is that correct?

RECRUITS
Hoo-ah.

SSGT. HICKS
Whenever you do that, the longer you
are in this building, the more familiar
you are going to be able to become
with that building, or that piece of
terrain, for that matter, the better you
are going to be able to fortify it, and
the longer you are going to be able to
defend it. So the enemy wants to try to
come back on you and kick you off of
this piece of terrain as quickly as
possible. That's called a counterattack.

171. Recruits listening.

SSGT. HICKS
(Continues off camera)
A counterattack will normally occur
between ten and thirty minutes after
you initially take possession of
whatever piece of terrain or building
we're talking about.

Figure 10.2

Video	Audio
19. DISSOLVE TO: Tony Milici takes large sheet of glass from stack near the wall, carries it to the cutting table and lays it down.	NARRATOR: Experimentation with light has led artists in new directions. Las Vegas light artist Tony Milici (Meel-EE-chee) has found his challenge in creating light sculptures out of sheets of plate glass. SOUND: (Tony carrying glass to table)
20. CU hand clamps edge of glass to table, Tony moves back out of frame.	NARRATOR: Working with these, he cuts the
21. MS cutting 2" strip of glass.	NARRATOR: glass into narrow strips
22. MS breaks off a strip.	NARRATOR: of different lengths . . .
23. CU cuts a triangle from a rectangle, puts the two triangles together, and adds others to make a set.	NARRATOR: and into various other shapes and sizes . . . to meet the needs of the sculpture on which he is working.

in the production agree that it's the right way to script this documentary.

The Classic Screenplay Format. The screenplay format used for a theatrical or feature film is typed in "tombstone" fashion—straight down the page. Figure 10.1 is an example of the classic screenplay format from the documentary *Basic Training: The Making of a Warrior.*

The TV Two-Column Format. This format splits apart audio and video much more completely than the screenplay format does. It is the standard format in live television because the director can easily keep track of both picture and sound. And it's the format normally used for television commercials.

The example in figure 10.2 is from a half-hour documentary, *Light in Art,* which I wrote for Hawaii Public Television. As you can see, in the TV two-column format, picture information goes on the left, audio information on the right. In some ad agencies the audio side is typed in all capital letters. This was done originally for use on a TelePrompTer. I don't do this for the simple reason that it's harder for a narrator or actor to read all caps than to read copy in uppercase and lowercase letters.

With either format, the script sets the scene, tells who is in it, and describes what is seen and what is heard. For more details on script formatting, see *Video Scriptwriting* or the books on formatting by Reichman and by Haag and Cole listed in the bibliography.

WRITING THE WORDS THAT ARE SAID

It's helpful to remember that cameras and word processors don't always coexist peacefully. That's because filmmakers create with images, and writers create with words. Words are sometimes easier to understand—and to get approved when that's important—than a string of images written down in sequence. But it's the images that will make the documentary. The same skill with words that can turn out a sizzling proposal may result in a script that is overwritten, dull, and talky, if the writer fails to make the shift from words to pictures in creating the script.

In a documentary script, words are used to describe what will be shown and to explain the thrust of the documentary. Be very careful about the use of words in narration and dialogue. Always let the pictures carry all the meaning they can. I can't say this often enough: *When language is used in narration to evoke images, it can get in the way of the images you are showing on the screen.*

Narration

The purpose of narration is to tell the audience the things they need to know and may not be able to pick up from the footage alone. Its purpose is *not* to fill the sound track with meaningless words like the three guys in the booth on "Monday Night Football."

My preferred way to handle narration in documentary has been, wherever possible, not to have any. Life doesn't come with narration or music—or a laugh track, for that matter. Therefore, I reasoned, a documentary that observes life shouldn't either. Through several documentaries I stood on principle and avoided narration completely.

The problem is that life also doesn't come with a limited running time, but documentaries do. And a few words of well-chosen narration can often cover what would otherwise take several minutes of footage to explain. So when running time gets short, and the documentary material is rich, even the most committed cinema verité documentarian may type out a narration script.

If the footage is good, the narration can be straightforward, in simple, easy-to-understand English. What belongs in narration? The things the audience needs to know to understand your documentary, that are not covered by the documentary itself. And nothing more. Honest. *Nothing more.*

Always write narration as late in the process as possible. Sponsors, clients, even producers love to read the narration ahead of time. It's the one part of the script they feel they truly understand.

But the documentary producer who writes the narration before editing picture is borrowing trouble.

In the first place, the lazy person inside all of us is likely to look at a well- but prematurely-written narration and just select pictures to illustrate it. Visuals. In the second place, your images are the visual evidence of your documentary. They have to be able to stand on their own.

Dialogue

The problem of dialogue in a documentary can usually be decided on the basis of whether real actors will be used. If they will, you can write dialogue just as you would in a feature film. If not, don't write dialogue.

For instance, if you have a scientist playing herself and telling about an experiment she's done, don't write dialogue. It won't work. Most people will be themselves on camera if you'll let them. But if you try to turn them into actors when they're not trained for it, what you'll get is bad acting and an unacceptable performance. Where real people are used in a documentary, I simply suggest what they can be expected to say and leave it up to the director to elicit the information from them.

The Difference Between Conversation and Dialogue

Conversation maintains contact among two or more people and sometimes carries information. It is made up of incomplete ideas and fragments of sentences. The parties feel free to interrupt each other, to talk at the same time, and to change the subject capriciously. Dialogue, on the other hand, takes place among two or more characters for the purpose of informing a third party—the audience.

Dialogue is artificial speech which must be accepted by an audience as believable. You have to write dialogue the way people *think* they are talking and not the way they actually speak. But remember that it never happens in real life that two people who share the

same information recite it to each other. That happens only in bad
radio commercials.

Storyboards

For some productions, a storyboard may be prepared. In its simplest form, a storyboard contains a sketch of what will be seen
along with a written description of all the sounds that will be
heard. Each frame of the storyboard shows a different piece of the
action of the documentary. In a sense, a storyboard is almost like a
slide show about the documentary.

The reasons to use storyboards are:

- to explain visually a scene which is difficult to understand
  from words alone
- to help visualize how a scene or sequence should be shot
- to help get approval or financing from a sponsor, funding
  source, or client

If you are an artist, or have access to one, you can make finished
storyboards like ad agencies use to show for approval. But don't be
put off from storyboarding because you're no artist. My stick-figure
storyboards cause artists to break out in uncontrollable giggling.
But they do the job for me.

When I'm storyboarding, I try to do it with sketches alone, without writing in any narration or dialogue. If I can do a series of
images that tell the story without any written description, I'm confident that what I've got is a film and not something else.

SUGGESTIONS FOR
DOCUMENTARY SCRIPTWRITERS

For heaven's sake, if you're new to documentary, look at documentaries and information videos. And look with a critical eye.
Documentaries, like any other creative form, range from excellent

to lousy. Try to find the ones that appeal to you and analyze what it is you like about them. Do the same with the documentaries you dislike. You can learn a great deal by analyzing what it is about the way the documentary is made that turns you off.

Think Pictures, Not Writing

Writing the script for a documentary film or video means thinking in pictures. And that can mean placing yourself mentally in a theater seat looking at a screen, instead of at your desk facing a word processor. If you can't see it, you can't film it. If you are a writer trying to get a handle on how to do a script, remember that the hardest thing to do for a writer beginning to work in documentary is to stop relying on words.

Show the Research as Well as the Results

Take some time to absorb what you've learned and to think about the way in which you learned it. Your problem is to abstract from all that material a sequence of visual events that will show the audience, in a very short time, what you have learned over a period of days or weeks. Take the audience through a process of discovery that is similar to your own. Show the good and the bad. If you have the screen time, you can even take the audience down a few false trails. You may know everything that is going to happen in the documentary, but you didn't when you started your research. Don't deprive your audience of that delicious uncertainty.

Don't Write a Novel When You Only Have Room for a Short Story

It's better to develop one theme completely in a short documentary than to try to cram in too much and lose your audience. Resist the pressure to try to make a single documentary that will be all things to all people. Such a documentary ends up meaning nothing to anyone.

Be Careful of Interviews

Interviews are an important part of documentary and nonfiction films, but they can get awfully dull and they slow up a documentary. A person talking can only say one hundred to two hundred words per minute. But in the same minute, you can show six to ten different images, if you want to, at a comfortable pace. Resist, as you would the devil, the temptation to create the structure of your documentary by stringing together excerpts from the transcripts of interviews. Build the structure visually.

Film and Video Are Always Right Here, Right Now

In creating a documentary, you have to have concrete images to show. But documentary doesn't have to be literal. A woman can walk out her office door and be anywhere—on the moon, in the fourteenth century, or across the country. You can cut from one location to another without a transition, as long as the difference is clearly evident. When I started writing for films, I asked a documentary writer-director the best way to get from one scene to another. "That's easy," he said. "Hit the space bar on your typewriter twice."

You Can Hardly Go Wrong if You Write
Narration as If You Were Being Fined $10 a Word

Keep it to the bare essentials. Don't talk it to death. As a writer, I've always looked askance at the statement "A picture is worth a thousand words." As a documentarian, however, I take it literally.

11

SCOUTING

It can be lovely to shoot in a studio with soundproof walls, a level floor for dollying, and lots of electricity available for lights—but I've rarely had the chance. The modern documentary gets shot where the action is. And except for those "documentaries" that intercut a lot of static studio interviews with stock footage, the action is out there, in someone else's home, office, factory, or backyard.

In return for a shot at the good stuff, you give up the home court advantage. And this sets up some problems you should be aware of.

When you shoot in a studio, you have total technical control. Lights can be set exactly where you want them. A path is cleared for camera moves. The people stand where you tell them. Phones are turned off, and no interruptions are permitted. On location you give up a great deal of control.

Everything and everybody that you will need to do the shoot must be brought to the location. If cost were no object, that might mean that you could bring every piece of equipment you can think of, and everyone you know who might be helpful, just in case. But there are few films where cost is no object. If you are renting equipment, you usually pay for what you take along, whether you use it or not. And you can run up a big bill in a hurry with expensive items that you might like to have but don't actually need. As to people, crew costs are the single biggest item in any documentary budget. Most producers have a strong aversion to paying, feeding, housing, and transporting crew members who are just standing around doing nothing. And most documentary directors would rather trade off the cost of an unneeded crew member for additional days of shooting or editing.

Making a documentary on location means that you'll be shooting real people, doing real things—and you have to work with the people who are available. So it's a good idea to find out ahead of time who they are, what they can do, and what they are willing to do.

All of which means you should do some scouting, if at all possible, before you pack up the equipment, gather your crew, and go on location to shoot.

If you need a particular kind of location, such as a prison or hospital, you'll have to find it. For *Dialogues with Madwomen*, Allie Light needed to re-create her own experience in a mental hospital. She found a hospital, built and equipped but not open, which she could rent by the day. Other scenes were re-created in her veterinarian's examining room, after hours.

More commonly, the documentary requires you to work in a specific location, because that is where the people or events that will make up your documentary are to be found. Some direct cinema documentarians insist on going in cold. They work with a minimum of equipment, use natural light, and feel that any scouting visit will contaminate the situation for filming.

But for most documentary situations, it's better to find out what the location you'll be working in is like. Here are some of the things to look for on a scouting trip.

LIGHTING

A film or video is made with light. You have to have a certain minimum amount of light, or you won't get any picture. But the type, location, and quality of the light can be equally important.

Interior Lighting

What kind of light does the location have? Most interiors in offices, factories, and public buildings are lit with fluorescent lights, which can pose a problem if you will be shooting film. Fluorescents do not behave at all like the theoretical black body tungsten light for which most film is balanced. There are filters available to compensate for fluorescent light, but to use them effectively you have to know what kind of fluorescent light tubes are in use. Check it out. If possible, shoot tests. My own solution for problems with fluorescent lights is to turn them off, if I can, and bring in my own lights.

Does the room have a lot of windows letting in sunlight? Sunlight doesn't mix well with artificial light. Will it be better to gel the windows to convert the light coming in to tungsten color balance, or will you do better to filter your light source with dichroic filters or blue gels to bring it to a daylight color balance?

How large an area must be included in the scenes you'll be shooting? It's not a big problem to bring in enough lights to shoot comfortably in anything up to the size of a standard school classroom. But if you are trying to film in a gymnasium, a sports arena, a large factory, or any other fairly huge space, it's probably better to think of using fast film, or increasing the exposure index of the film you've got, and, if necessary, using fast prime lenses on the camera in order to be able to shoot with available light.

If you are shooting video, you should be able to white balance your camera to match the light sources. But if there is any question about the quality of mixed-light sources, or the amount of light available, you may want to bring in a camera and shoot tests.

Remember that even though your video camera or high-speed film stock may be capable of recording an image in very low light, lens depth of field is inversely related to the amount of light available. In very low light, you may have a problem keeping what you want to shoot in focus.

If you decide to bring in lights, check the availability of electric power. How many circuits are now available? What's their capacity? Where is the fuse box or circuit breaker panel located? Will there be an electrician available to help you, or should you plan to hire one as part of your crew?

Exterior Lighting

If you'll be shooting outdoors, what will the light be like at the time of day when you'll be shooting? Direct sunlight? Shadow? Or a combination? Should you plan on bringing in reflectors or some floodlights to fill in the shadow areas? Remember that on a bright sunny day with a clear sky, you can have a difference in exposure of five f-stops between direct sunlight and shadow.

Where will the sun be at the time you'll be shooting?

Shoot Tests Wherever You Can

When I'm scouting for a film shoot, I carry a 35mm still camera with me, loaded with film similar to the motion picture film I'll be using. This gives me a quick way of testing the look of the available light. And it also is a way of keeping a record of what the location looks like. For video, you may be able to use an inexpensive camcorder for tests, or you may need to bring in a production camera.

Write It Down

Keep notes on everything you shoot: where, time of day, exposure information, what the picture is about, and who is in it.

And make diagrams as you go. What are the approximate dimensions of the area, including the height of the ceiling? What color are the walls, ceiling, and floor? Show the location of furniture, doors, windows, electrical outlets, and anything else that may be important.

SOUND

What are the acoustics like? Are the rooms lively or dead? What about background noise—not only right where you'll be filming, but other noises, the kind you normally tune out, but a recorder won't. Are there airplanes flying overhead? Is there a lot of traffic noise from the street? Is there piped-in music, and if so, can it be turned off? How about the copy machine in the next room, the refrigerator, nearby bathrooms, people noise in hallways?

What kind of microphones will you need? Do you need to record one person at a time, or many people? Should you plan on a boom mike or shotgun, or will you be better off with one or more lavalieres? Will you need a microphone mixer? Do you need wireless microphones?

PEOPLE AND THINGS

You are planning to film at the location for a reason. What is it? What must be shown in the film? Are there important people who must be interviewed—or at least seen? Who are they? When are they available? What will make a visually interesting setting to film them in? Should you do a preinterview while you are scouting? Can you?

Who are the other people you would like to include? People who will look good and talk well on camera? Are there people with an interesting story to tell, or who are doing an interesting piece of work?

What things have to be included at this location? It may be that the location itself is the thing of interest. Or there may be equipment, facilities, or a process that you must document. Investigate it. Plan out the shots you'll need. Find out if you'll be able to film whenever you wish or if you will be limited to certain times of the day or night.

FEES, PERMITS, AND MINDERS

The use of certain locations may require getting a license or paying a fee. When you take over someone's home to shoot in, you'll normally have to pay them a location fee for the inconvenience, and you'll want to be sure that your liability insurance covers any inadvertent damage that might occur.

If you are working on the street, in most cities you'll need to get a shooting permit (with a fee attached), and you may be required—or feel it's a good idea—to hire an off-duty police officer to accompany the crew. State and national parks may hit you with a usage fee or license requirement and may also require you to pay for a park guard or other employee to baby-sit the production.

Part of scouting is to check out these costs and to be sure that you have covered all jurisdictions. In some locations you may need separate city, county, and state permits to shoot.

CONVENIENCE

How easy or how difficult will it be to film at this location? How much cooperation can you expect? How close can you park to unload equipment? Is there good security for equipment left overnight? Will you have a guide or liaison person with you when you are working?

Can you work at your own pace or must you schedule around other activities, which might mean setting up and breaking down equipment several times? Will you have to shoot at unconventional times, such as at night, in the early morning, or during the lunch hour?

CREW COMFORT

What about motels and meals? I once did a shoot in a remote location and didn't bother getting an advance motel reservation for the crew. We got there to discover it was something of a resort area, and all the motels within twenty miles were booked solid.

Is there a place at the location where you can get a meal, snacks, coffee, and cold drinks for the crew, or should you plan on bringing these essential items with you? A hungry or thirsty crew is an unhappy crew.

OUT-OF-TOWN LOCATIONS

If you'll be shooting at an out-of-town location, what is the availability of rental equipment and freelance crew people? Unless the location is in a major metropolitan area where you are already familiar with the quality of the equipment and people available, you will probably want to bring your own gear and key crew members. But it's nice to know whether there are good rental facilities available in case you need extra lights, lenses, or mikes, or for backup if a piece of equipment goes down. And if you normally rent equipment anyway, the ability to rent on the spot can save you shipping costs and rental fees for the time the equipment would be in transit.

Similarly, you may be able to save travel and per diem costs by hiring production assistants at the location. When I'm filming in a strange town, I like to have at least one local person on the crew whom I can use as a driver, guide, and informant on local customs.

What about buying film stock or videotape at the location rather than taking a chance on having it pass through airport X rays? And what about shipping exposed film to your lab? Is there an air freight or express office near the location? What does shipping cost? Can you pay for it by purchase order or check, or will you need cash?

LOCATION COSTS

Going on location usually means some out-of-pocket expense. That's obvious when you're headed for an out-of-town location— you know there will be travel expense, hotels and meals, shipping costs, rental cars, tips, and so on.

Producers who travel regularly are considered good customers by the travel industry and can usually get discounts for motel rooms and rental cars, and possibly for some of their other expenses. Check this out. Also check with the city or state film commission to see what they may have to offer that can save you money.

Even if the location is close to home base, you want to be prepared for normal costs and have a reserve for unanticipated expense. Normal costs would include crew meals, gasoline for vehicles, phone calls, snacks, soft drinks or juice, coffee, and so on. I carry a cooler with me on location and make sure that my driver or one of the production assistants has petty cash to keep it filled with ice and canned drinks.

Unanticipated expenses could range from buying replacement batteries for a recorder that has gone dead, to repair, rental, or even replacement of an essential piece of equipment that has gone down. How you run your budget is your own business. But if I have a crew and equipment in the field, costing hundreds, maybe thousands of dollars a day, I'd rather spend some money to be able to keep shooting and get finished than have to schedule an additional day at the location.

GENERAL CONSIDERATIONS

In general, scout the location at the same time of day, and under the same conditions, as when you plan to shoot. You can't tell how much of a hassle shooting will be unless you see the place in operation. This will also let you see how the sunlight comes through the windows and hear how much noise there is.

In addition to bringing along a still camera or camcorder for lighting tests and to record the look of the location, you might want to carry a decent audio recorder to record research interviews. This might yield some interesting voice-over that you can use. Audio interviews also serve as an audition device—you can find out in advance who's going to freeze up, and who drones on and on without ever getting to the point.

PLANNING FOR SPONTANEITY

There is nothing like a brilliant spontaneous moment captured by the camera to make a documentary come to life. Just remember that it takes a lot of planning and preparation to have the camera in the right position with the right lighting, and a microphone where it needs to be, in order to capture that spontaneous moment on film or videotape.

Location scouting is an integral part of that preparation.

12

THE DOCUMENTARY CREW

What about crew members? Who will you need to make your documentary, and what do all these people do?

The crew for a behavioral documentary is usually three or four people, depending on the equipment and the requirements of the production. If the location you'll be working in is good sized and you have a lot of different setups to shoot, a larger crew may be justified by the time it will save. But if you are shooting in someone's home or in a small office or store, you don't want to bring a crowd. More than three or four in the crew and you may intimidate the people you're filming and get in each other's way in small spaces. It's a lot easier to maintain the invisible wall between crew and subjects when the crew is small.

Fewer than three or four, however, and you may not have the bodies you need to get the job done. To get something recorded on film or videotape, you need at least two people—one to run the camera and one to record the sound. Getting decent, legible images and audio is simply too much for one person to handle alone.

Other kinds of productions, such as a historical reenactment, may require a much larger crew.

WHO DOES WHAT ON A PRODUCTION

These are some of the people who are likely to be involved with your production. The nucleus of a production crew will be the people who get the stuff recorded: the camera operator, the sound recordist, and the director. Surrounding them may be a lot of other people who contribute to getting the images and sound recorded on film or videotape.

Producer

The producer is the person who assembles the financing for a project, pays the bills, and handles administrative details from preproduction through to distribution. The producer may hire all or part of the crew. The role of the producer in the creative process varies. Some producers will be intimately involved with the director, crew, and editor at every stage of production; others will leave the creative realization of the production to the people they have hired.

In documentary, the producer will often be a hyphenate—producer-director or producer-writer—directly involved in both the business details of the production and the creative process of bringing it to the screen.

Director

The director is the person in creative control of the documentary—the creative decision maker. He or she decides when, where, and what to shoot and, in consultation with the camera operator or director of photography, how to shoot it. The director of a documentary will normally stay with the production from preproduction planning through the completion of postproduction. He or she will select the narrator or spokesperson, supervise recording of narration and music, and work with the editor in organizing the elements of the documentary for presentation to an audience.

In many cases the director will "own" the idea for the documentary. In that situation, he or she may elect to be a producer-director, or may direct the documentary but hire a producer to handle the business details of the production. The larger the production—and the production budget—the more likely it is that the functions of director and producer will be handled by different people.

Scriptwriter

The scriptwriter researches the content of the documentary and organizes it into a visual argument. For a behavioral documentary or a documentary of a unique event, the scriptwriter may only write a treatment or a shot list prior to production and then may write any necessary narration during postproduction. For a historical documentary or reenactment, you need a finished screenplay, and this requires a professional writer. In many documentaries, the writer is also the producer or director.

Director of Photography or Cinematographer

The director of photography has responsibility for the overall look of the production. In consultation with the director, he or she sets the lighting, frames the shot, selects the lenses and film stock to be used, and instructs the camera operator. On a large production, the director of photography does not actually operate the camera. On a small crew documentary, the functions of director of photography and camera operator will probably be handled by the same person.

Camera Operator

This person used to be called the *cameraman*, and has always been one of the most important people on a documentary crew. Gender equality required replacing -*man* with *operator*. Unfortunately this new usage connotes that the person looking through the viewfinder is something of a button pusher, which fails to do justice to the hardworking and highly creative women and men who capture the images that make up a documentary. In any hot situation, the camera operator functions as codirector, making crucial decisions about what to shoot and how to shoot it.

My partner says she thinks we should replace all -*man* suffices with -*mun* and agree that this means a person of either gender. So a production would have a cameramun, a soundmun, perhaps an assistant cameramun, and so on.

The camera operator must have a professional understanding of the equipment that will record the documentary images. And he or she must know how the lighting in use—whether available light or a lighting setup—will affect the images you are recording. If the documentary is shot on film, the camera operator should know exactly what the footage will look like when the film is developed. Shooting on video—even though there may be a monitor available on which to check the shot—does not make this sort of professional expertise any less important. In a hot documentary situation, there is no possibility of a retake. You have to get it while it happens.

Camera Assistant

On a film shoot, the camera assistant or assistant camera operator looks after the camera—keeps it clean, loads and changes magazines, changes lenses, and watches like a hawk to be sure no emulsion has scraped off the film, which can cause a "hair in the gate." On any shoot, the camera assistant will look after the camera between setups, keep the camera log, and generally handle the heavy lifting and detail work so the camera operator is free to be creative. A small documentary crew may not have a camera assistant, although I think this is an extremely important person on the crew. A camera assistant should be included wherever possible, especially when you are shooting on film and whenever you are documenting a unique event.

Sound Recordist

This used to be the soundman. It is the person who records audio during filming and also records wild track or natural sound, when needed, and any interviews done without the camera. Recording excellent sound for a documentary is a technical skill that requires both professional knowledge and experience. Your sound person has to be able to record voices in a noisy situation so that they are well separated from the background noise. He or she must know where the camera is pointed at all times and must be sure to record sound that goes with the picture. In certain situations, the sound recordist may be receiving audio from several microphone sources, and must be able to record each source cleanly or to mix the sources so that the important sound at any time is clear. Just as the director of photography or camera operator will select the lenses and stock appropriate to the documentary, the sound recordist will choose microphones, recorders, and even tape to suit the production.

Sound Assistant

Sometimes there is a person to help the sound recordist. With a simple one-camera, one-microphone shoot, there is usually no need for a sound assistant. But as the number of audio inputs increases, the sound recordist may need some help. A sound assistant may operate a microphone boom or fish pole to get the microphone close to the people who are speaking.

Video Engineer

In an earlier time, when cameras were less sensitive and tape machines were large and hard to use, location video was shot just like studio video, by taking the studio to the location in a van or trailer. In those days, the person ultimately responsible for the video product was the video engineer. Along came truly portable tape equipment using three-quarter-inch U-matic recorders or one-inch reel-to-reel recorders which could be carried around by one person, and the video engineer became a tape operator. Today's video documentary crew will probably use a camera with an onboard recorder, and responsibility for the quality of the video image passes to the director of photography or camera operator, just as it is in film.

If you have a multiple-camera shoot, however, with video feeds coming back to monitors at a single location, or for some reason are shooting switched video, you may require a video engineer.

Electrician or Gaffer

The gaffer is the chief electrician on a film production. The gaffer works under the direction of the director of photography and is responsible for the mechanics of lighting—from providing a power source when necessary to setting and relamping the lighting instruments—and for meeting any other electrical requirements on the production. Most documentary crews will not need an electrician. But if the power requirements are tricky or involve tapping into a breaker box or other electrical source, an electrician should be used.

Grips

The grips on a production are the heavy lifters. They move and set lights, set up equipment and scenery, lay dolly rails when needed, and push the dolly. Most documentary shoots need at least one grip who may function as a camera assistant and gofer as well. Any production requiring much in the way of lighting, the use of a dolly, or moving furniture out of the way to shoot and putting it back when you are done, should have some grips along. Otherwise the producer, director, camera operator, and sound recordist will have to set the lights and move the furniture. And that is not only a waste of their time and talent, but also is tiring work, which will take energy they need for more creative endeavors.

Production Manager

A large production will have a person responsible for the business arrangements related to shooting. The production manager, sometimes called the unit manager, will often do the detailed budgeting for the production. He or she breaks down the day's shooting schedule to make the most economical use of crew, cast, locations, and equipment. On a small-crew documentary, all of this will be handled by the producer or a production assistant.

Production Assistant

On a documentary, a production assistant is a person who handles detail work, from arranging for the use of a location and getting the appropriate licenses to making sure that releases are signed. In a sense, a production assistant is a white-collar grip, relieving the producer and director of administrative detail. A production may have none, one, or several.

Location Coordinator

A location coordinator is a special kind of production assistant who is highly knowledgeable about the location in which you will be shooting. The location coordinator knows where you can find a log cabin or a waterfall, how much it will cost to rent, and what permits you will need. Think of a location coordinator as a casting director for places to shoot.

Casting Director

For historical documentaries, reenactments, and other productions in which you will use actors, a casting director can help you find and hire the people you need. More on casting in chapter twenty.

Makeup Artist

Applying makeup for the camera is an art, and the person who does it is a makeup artist. For a direct cinema documentary, you would not use a makeup artist, as that would be breaching the invisible wall. In a documentary with extensive interviews, you might want to have a makeup artist available to help your subjects look their best. In a reenactment or other documentary with actors, you'll need one or more makeup artists.

Someone to Look after Wardrobe and Props

In a historical documentary involving reenactment, you will have extensive wardrobe and property needs. Unless you have someone to keep track of the wardrobe and props, you're likely to get on location and discover that Abraham Lincoln forgot his top hat and John Wilkes Booth assumed someone else was bringing the pistol. An experienced wardrobe person can help you find the costume items you need and will know how many duplicates of each item of clothing you may need to keep on hand.

TelePrompTer Operator

If you use an on-camera narrator, host, or spokesperson, you may need to provide a TelePrompTer for them as well as an operator to run it. Today's TelePrompTers are computer-based rather than mechanical. The operator loads the script into the computer and sets up the TelePrompTer. During production, he or she runs the TelePrompTer so that the right words are visible as the talent needs to read them.

Postproduction Personnel

In postproduction, you'll become involved with another group of specialists who will help you complete your documentary. These include the creative editor, assistant editor, music director, composer, narrator, and others.

WHO WILL DO WHAT
ON YOUR PRODUCTION?

I made my first documentary with a borrowed 16mm camera on my shoulder and a friend with absolutely no film experience recording sound. The film was strong on content and well edited—editing is my strong point—but it was a technical nightmare. I knew *nothing* about shooting color film. And by the time the footage, shot on high-speed reversal color film, went through the several generations to a release print, the scenes shot in available light had become muddy and hard to see, and the scenes shot in sunlight, which seemed so sharp and clear in the rushes, had become contrasty and bizarre, like the colors in a comic book. Most of the location audio was terrible. We simply didn't know enough to do the job right.

Camera and Sound

In my opinion, it is best if the two critical people in the production phase of a documentary—the camera operator and the sound recordist—are people who practice their craft every day and know exactly what they are doing. This doesn't mean that any professional camera operator can shoot a documentary. In addition to technical skill, it takes a kind of sixth sense for when and where things will happen, an eye for real visual evidence, and an optimistic tolerance for the times when the camera is on and nothing seems to be happening.

As for audio, documentaries are often shot in hectic, noisy situations, where it is difficult to understand anything. A true documentary sound recordist finds a way to get legible sound, even under atrocious conditions, while keeping the microphone out of the shot. The collaboration between sound and camera often requires balletlike coordination.

Your Job on the Crew

If this is your project, then you are—like it or not—some kind of a producer. It may be executive producer with a host of professionals hired to do the work. It may be line producer, overseeing the task of getting the documentary made. Or it may be producer with a hyphen, as you take on one or more of the technical, professional tasks involved in making a documentary.

When I was a documentary film student, *everyone* wanted to run camera. That was the sexy job. And you may be tempted to say, okay, I'm not very experienced at shooting, but I'll know what I want when I see it.

Maybe. What I know is that it is easier to see what is going on all over the shooting situation when you are not trying to view it through the narrow angle of a camera viewfinder. In order to keep the crew small and the shooting situation intimate, sometimes the person functioning as producer or producer-director will run sound. But if you lack the technical experience to run camera or sound well and the expertise to direct, then hire people who know what they are doing until you've had a chance to gain the knowledge and experience yourself.

Directing

Today everyone wants to be a director. Will you direct the documentary yourself, hire a director, or do without? Again, it depends on what your documentary requires and what *you* bring to the project.

I think the best documentary directors start as editors, because one of the most important contributions the editor brings to the production is the sense of how the elements go together and what it takes to make a finished program.

In making a behavioral or direct-cinema documentary, I have a mental checklist of essential elements. So I am always on the lookout for an opening, an ending, and any visual evidence related to the themes of the documentary. Without these elements there is no documentary. During the course of shooting, I'm constantly revising my mental elements list. We may shoot something that will make a *better* opening or a better ending than the scene I previously had in mind. That's good. And, of course, in the editing room I may decide to use a different scene entirely.

If you are making a historical documentary or reenactment, you probably need a director who is experienced in working with actors.

Friends and Relatives

Low-budget productions often get made with friends and relatives, and that's the way it is. But the more amateurs you have on the crew, the more problems you may encounter. Just getting a documentary made is a difficult enough task.

FINDING AND CHOOSING
A PRODUCTION CREW

How do you find the production people you'll need? One way is to go to a film or video production company. You'll find them listed by the dozen in the Yellow Pages of any metropolitan phone book. Almost all of them will tell you that yes, they can do *whatever* it is that you need. They're in business, after all. But, as we saw in chapter one, that doesn't mean that they can make a documentary.

Another is to look in the directories of organizations such as the International Documentary Association or the International Television Association.

Another way is to look at lots of documentaries. Get into the habit of writing down the production credits when you see a documentary you like. Then contact the person or the production company.

The Selection Process

It's quite possible that early in your search you may find a producer, production company, or individual crew members who can do exactly what you want. If so, sign them up. You would probably end up hiring them anyway. Otherwise narrow your list as quickly as possible to a small number of candidates.

Don't Hold a Competition. In dealing with production companies, I *do not* recommend holding a competition or sending out a request for proposals (RFP) as a first step. You are likely to eliminate the very people you would most like to talk with, because many excellent filmmakers and videomakers avoid this kind of competition, for several reasons:

- They feel that an important part of their job is to understand and interpret the needs of your project. This requires the kind of personal contact that is generally eliminated by an RFP.
- They regard a competition involving a large number of production companies as little more than a lottery. It requires a lot of work for which they will not be paid unless they win.
- The best people, once they have established a reputation and a body of films and videos that show what they can do, are unwilling to do any creative work on speculation. And that is essentially what an RFP usually asks for.

Good people are certainly willing to present themselves and their work for your inspection. And they *will* make a proposal and discuss costs when they feel they will be judged on the quality of their existing work, not on how well they guess what you want from an RFP.

Do Look at Their Work. If you are talking with a production company, be sure to find out if the person you are dealing with is in sales or production. Withhold judgment until you've met the production people and seen their work. The best way to find the people you need is to look at the films and videos they've made, because their skill and the nature and quality of their work are the *only things that count.*

Look at complete productions; a composite reel of highlights or best shots tells you nothing about the ability of the crew to sustain a quality effort over a complete production. If you are planning a long documentary of an hour, two hours, or more, you won't learn much by looking at samples of short works. The planning, pacing, and editing of a long documentary is quite different from that of a short production.

Look at the Technical Quality of the Work. If the color is off or the sound is bad, don't accept an explanation such as this is an answer print or an off-line edit and all the flaws were corrected in the final version. After all, they are choosing to show you this print and not the final version. And be very leery of anyone who tries to tell you that you have to expect some technical problems in shooting a documentary. That may have been true some time ago, but it is far less true today. Bad picture, bad sound, or bad editing are most likely evidence of a bad production company. Look elsewhere.

When you see a documentary you like, find out:

· How much it cost in current dollars.
· Who directed, shot, and edited it. Are these people still working there? Will they be available for your production? Can you see other work they've done?

Contracting with a production company is one way to find the crew for your documentary. Another is to build the crew yourself, by locating the key individuals you need. You might find a director or camera operator whose work you like and ask him or her to recommend other people to fill out the crew. In general, good people choose to work with other good people. So finding one key player may lead you to everyone else you need. Nevertheless, look at their work, ask for their credits, and check their references.

. . . .

13

EQUIPMENT

If you've decided to work with a production company, then the question of where your equipment will come from is solved—the production company will provide it. But you may have some critical decisions to make about what sorts of equipment they should bring.

FILM OR VIDEO?

The first decision will affect everything else you do. Are you going to make your documentary on film or videotape? In general, film will give you better quality, while videotape yields better economy and versatility.

Theatrical Release

You should probably plan on shooting film if you have any thought at all about releasing the documentary in theaters. Yes, *Hoop Dreams* was shot on video because it was planned as a television production. And, yes, the producers did manage to transfer from video to film for theatrical release. But no one is pretending that those were theatrical production values up on the screen. I've seen *Hoop Dreams* in a theater and on television, and it looks a lot better on TV. It is far easier and better, at least at the present time, to go from 16mm film to 35mm for theatrical release than to go from any sort of standard video to film for theaters.

But the state of the art in video continues to change rapidly. Either digital video or high-definition television will undoubtedly approach—or even exceed—film in sharpness, color, and resolution in the very near future.

Television Release

For all other uses, video is probably the better medium. If you will distribute on television or as a retail video, then there is probably no real reason not to shoot on videotape.

If, however, you have any thought of distributing in Europe, where the higher-definition PAL format is the standard, you may want to consider shooting on film. With the technology available as I write this, you will get a better product by transferring from film to PAL video than by converting the American NTSC format to European PAL.

Reusing Recording Stock

Film stock, once exposed, is used up. For economy, the director may decide not to develop a specific roll of film if there is nothing usable on it. And some cost saving is possible by printing only those takes considered good. That's an option in a reenactment, where you have total control. It's less likely to happen in a behavioral documentary. The director will want to view everything that was shot.

Videotape can be erased and reused. But don't be misled into thinking that this will somehow permit a lower shooting ratio than film. It is a rare and brave videomaker who will erase field tapes before having a chance to view them.

The advantage to videotape is a much lower cost per minute for shooting than film. And this allows the documentarian a higher shooting ratio on tape at a lower cost than film.

CAMERA EQUIPMENT

Once you've made the film or video decision, you'll need a camera. Most film documentaries are shot on 16mm film. Most videotape documentaries—as I write this—are shot with a Betacam camera, which records on professional-grade half-inch videotape. But some documentarians now shoot on high-band 8mm videotape and transfer up to Betacam or digital videotape for editing. And digital recording to a computer hard drive, already out in prototype, may be generally available by the time you read this.

Camera and Lenses

So you need a professional camera in the format you'll be using.

The camera should have a relatively fast, high-quality zoom lens with focal lengths from moderate wide angle to a medium-long lens. For a 16mm or Betacam camera this would be in the range of 10mm to 100mm. You'll need a variety of filters that fit the lens.

In today's documentary world, the video recorder will be a part of the camera. You may also want to have a separate, backup video recorder.

If you're shooting 16mm, you'll want a camera with a four-hundred-foot magazine capable of double system sync sound. You'll want several spare magazines, which you can keep loaded with film. A four-hundred-foot load of 16mm film has a total running time of just eleven minutes and six seconds. Then you have to change magazines.

In some cases you might have need for a small camera such as a "lipstick" video camera. This camera is small enough and light enough that it can be set on a bookcase or hung from a lamp or a picture frame, and can literally be placed in the middle of a scene without being noticed.

Whatever kind of camera you're using, you'll need spare batteries—plenty of them—and a battery charger.

Be sure you have spare parts, including battery and connecting cables for *everything*. It can be extremely frustrating to watch a high-priced crew sitting around doing nothing because a twenty-five-dollar cable has malfunctioned.

Support

You need a good, solid, heavy tripod with a fluid head.

Yes, a lot of documentary footage is shot handheld. But certain critical shots must not be. When you shoot an establishing shot of the exterior of a building, it needs to be shot from a tripod. An audience will accept a little shakiness in the handheld footage of people doing things, but they expect inanimate objects to be steady.

You may need or want a stabilizer system, especially if you'll be doing a lot of handheld or traveling shots. There are two kinds of these—those that hold the camera or the lens steady and those that stabilize the video image digitally.

While you will probably never use it in a behavioral documentary, if you are doing a reenactment you may need a dolly or a small crane or jib arm. These let you make smooth camera moves.

SOUND EQUIPMENT

Basically, you need a recorder and a microphone. But with today's technology, that covers a lot of ground. When you think of a documentary crew, the sound recordist is the person wearing earphones, with a Nagra recorder slung over one shoulder, holding a shotgun microphone wrapped in a windscreen on the end of a fish pole mike holder. And that's still the way a lot of documentaries get made.

But the sound recordist could also be the person sitting at a console, watching the dials on a sixteen-track recorder as sound comes in from wireless microphones all over the shooting area.

These are the things you need to know:

- The audio recorder can be synchronized to either a film or video camera by recording a control track or time code on one channel. This can later be matched to the running speed of the film camera or the time code of the video camera to sync the audio to picture. This means you can use any kind of recorder capable of recording a time code track. It also means you can put several of them together.

· The video recorder, whether separate or on board the camera, has just two audio tracks. These each accept a different input. You can use a microphone mixer to meld several inputs onto one track. But it is always better to isolate inputs if possible by giving each its own track. So if you anticipate complex sound, you may need an additional audio recorder giving you anywhere from three to fifteen additional tracks of audio.

· A shotgun or parabolic mike can reach out and isolate sounds from whatever area it is pointed at. It can also sometimes pick up sounds from behind the person you want, even from the other side of the wall.

· The cleanest situation *usually* is to hang a lavaliere microphone connected to a wireless transmitter on each person you want to record. But this is neither always possible nor desirable. And wireless transmitters sometimes will find themselves in conflict with taxi signals, CB radios, and other radio sources.

· You need lots of spare batteries. Lots! More than you think.

· You need a good, basic backup dynamic microphone that always works when everything else fails. And you need a nice, long mike cable to go with it.

· You get the best sound by getting a good microphone close to the person speaking.

· Never, ever record audio using automatic gain control.

· Pick a sound recordist with very good ears, and make sure that he or she wears a good set of headphones.

· Set audio levels manually and visually, using the VU meter on the recorder.

LIGHTING AND GRIP EQUIPMENT

A film is made with light. It's not that you necessarily need a lot of light, but you need the right kind of light in the right place. Lighting a documentary depends entirely on the style of the film or video you're making.

Reenactment Lighting

A historical reenactment will be shot like a feature, with all the lighting the budget will tolerate. If this is what you are doing, hire a good cinematographer or lighting director and let him or her go over the script and tell you what you need. Probably you'll do a certain amount of shooting in a studio, where a full lighting array is available. And when you go on location, you'll take along a well-equipped grip truck and generator.

Behavioral Documentary Lighting

If you're doing a behavioral documentary, you'll try to work with available light and use as little additional light as possible.

Hard, specular lights require careful lighting and total control of the situation. Otherwise they give a "lit" look to the scene, with shadows spilling everywhere, so that the people you are filming will seem to move from hot spots to deep shadows in a room in which the audience would expect the lighting to be fairly even. Therefore they are not much use in behavioral documentary situations, other than as bounce lights off the ceiling or to provide a certain look in a static interview situation.

I like to have a couple of soft lights or lights with umbrella reflectors that can be used to increase the overall illumination when necessary without creating a lot of shadow problems.

You should have some correcting gels or dichroic filters to help balance your artificial lights with the lighting in the situation.

You'll need some grip stands to hold the lights and gels and flags when required.

A documentarian should always have along a couple of battery lights to use where no electricity is available. And that means bringing spare batteries and a battery charger.

If you'll be filming outdoors, you should have some shiny boards or reflectors that can bounce sunlight into the scene to provide fill light.

MISCELLANEOUS

There are some other things that you may or may not want as part of your equipment.

Monitor and Video Assist

It's your call whether you are going to want to have a video monitor for the director to look at. It's easy enough to install video assist on a film camera to send a video feed from the camera viewing system to a TV monitor. A video camera, of course, provides a video signal, which can be run to a monitor.

This requires wiring the camera to a fixed location. No problem when you have control, as in a reenactment. But it could be a big problem if you're filming the behavior of a two-year-old who suddenly decides to leave the room or go from the front yard to the back of the house, and you have to follow.

What you certainly want is the ability to view what you've shot as soon as possible after you've finished shooting. So you'd like to have decent video playback and an adequate monitor available on location.

TelePrompTer

In some situations you may need a TelePrompTer. This lets your host or spokesperson handle a lengthy explanation or introduction without having to memorize it. As far as I'm concerned, a Tele-PrompTer can cause as many problems as it alleviates. For me, it is a last resort and should be used only with experienced professional talent who know how to read from one.

Two-way Radios and Cellular Phones

When the camera is at the bottom of the hill and the people you are shooting are at the top of the hill, you need some way to communicate with them.

Cars and Trucks

You need to get around from location to location. It's best if you can do it comfortably. At a minimum you need a lockable van for the equipment. It's good to have a separate car with seats for everyone in the crew, which can be used to run errands, pick up talent, whatever, while the van is on the shoot.

SHOULD YOU RENT OR BUY EQUIPMENT?

I'm a firm believer in renting equipment, unless you are in production several days a week—every week. Here's why:

- Production technology changes rapidly. This year's new, hot camera may be obsolescent in twelve to eighteen months and totally obsolete in two or three years. But you're still stuck with the payments.
- My friends who signed six-figure notes to get new equipment to work with soon found themselves working to support the equipment rather than the other way around.
- By renting, you can always work with the latest equipment.
- Even if you eventually want to buy your own equipment, renting is a good way to try before you buy.
- The rental payment and insurance is part of the production budget, and when you're done, you return the equipment to the rental house, pay the bill, and walk away clean.

On the other hand, if you have a long project with a lot of production time, it may be cost-effective to buy the equipment you need, use it for the production, and sell it when the project is over. In essence, you are renting from yourself. And if you really like the equipment, maybe you'll keep it.

BE SURE YOU HAVE AN EQUIPMENT MEISTER

If possible, you should have someone on the production crew who is really good with equipment. This should be a person who knows a lot about the technology of camera and sound equipment in general and knows the specific equipment you are using. This is the person who will know six good things to try when the camera won't run or the sound won't record.

14

SCHEDULING

Preproduction planning, or the lack of it, has been the ruination of more films and videotapes than the combined problems of equipment failure, processing errors, poor lighting, missed cues, and bad acting all put together.

Overplanning squeezes the life out of a film—deprives it of the possibility of spontaneity, the little unplanned touches that add to the documentary's humanity and believability.

Underplanning, on the other hand, carries spontaneity to the point of winging it, which may contribute to grabbing some exciting moments but more often results in a documentary that is incoherent, lacks essential elements, suffers from technical inadequacy, and is very likely to run over budget.

To schedule a production, include all the necessary steps as outlined in chapter eight. If you have a tight delivery schedule, you must work backwards from the delivery date. Never cut corners on processes that are not under your control. You may be able to save a day in shooting or editing, but don't count on the film-processing lab to deliver in less than its usual time or the video post house to have off-line and on-line facilities available exactly when you need them.

Allow time for things to go wrong. They will. Expect it, and don't be thrown by it. If they don't, consider it a gift.

Above all, when the numbers just don't work, be prepared to say to a client or sponsor, firmly, in a clear voice, "It can't be done."

PREPRODUCTION

Occasionally a documentary must go into production on a moment's notice because a unique event is about to take place and you must either cover it as it happens or forget about it. But most documentaries will go into production only after a long period of gestation and fund-raising—the preproduction process.

Research

It takes time to do the research that will result in a well-documented, interesting, and informative documentary. And documentary research goes beyond gathering factual information. It often includes finding the interesting, articulate, and necessary people who will appear on camera as well as the locations you'll need to shoot in.

How much time will it take? *Longer than you think.* Make your best guess as to research time and then double the number. Or at the very least add another 50 percent. You'll need it. Honest. You will.

Concept and Treatment

Out of the research you'll refine the documentary idea, which will lead to a treatment for filming or at least a shot list of visual evidence. You must be prepared for the concept to evolve as you learn more about the topic. And as the concept changes, the scenes you plan to shoot and the way you plan to shoot them will change also.

Scripting

If you are doing a scripted documentary—a biography or reenact-ment of an event—you need time to develop a finished script. It has always amazed me that a director who requires two days to shoot a three-minute scene somehow believes a writer can do thirty minutes of finished script in the same time.

Allow enough time for the writer to do a decent first draft, for the producer and director to read and digest it, for some discussion, and for revisions as needed.

Planning

It takes a lot of phone calls and a lot of scheduling—and revision—before you'll be ready to go into production. You can't assume you'll be able to shoot at a given location whenever you're ready; you need to pin down a time. And if your crew members are free-lancers with other commitments, you have to make sure they will be available at the time you want to shoot.

Don't forget equipment checkout, casting as necessary, and re-hearsal time.

PRODUCTION

The shooting schedule presents another set of decisions. Everyone knows that a film is shot out of sequence, but in what sequence?

Actuality Situations

In a behavioral documentary, you have to follow the behavior as it unfolds. If you are doing a documentary of a unique event, you have to cover the event. In each of these cases, people and events beyond your control will affect how you schedule production time. And for the visual evidence to be complete and to make sense, these events or this behavior probably has to be shot in the order in which it occurs. Not only is it considered cheating to do a reenactment in a behavioral documentary, it just doesn't work. The behavior won't ring true.

But you can distinguish between discretionary scenes and actuality events. You have to shoot behavior and unique events when they are happening rather than when it's convenient. But not everything that goes into an actuality documentary is a hot happening. There are establishing shots, for instance, and background interviews, which you can shoot on a quiet day, or use for backup if the hot stuff doesn't happen when it's supposed to and you already have the crew scheduled.

Reenactments, Profiles, Places

For more conventional documentary projects, more conventional scheduling strategies can be used.

Schedule critical elements first—the hard-to-get people and hard-to-get locations. You have to take them when they are available.

Schedule exterior filming before interiors, but try to have a backup interior location available if bad weather makes it impossible to work outside.

If a studio will be used at any point in the production, you may have to schedule around studio availability. Studio time often has to be scheduled well in advance, so check on this early. In scheduling studio time, don't forget to allow time to construct sets, and time to tear them down. Also, you might as well decide in advance what you are going to do with the set once you are finished with it. The choices are:

- store it
- sell it or give it away
- destroy it

Schedule for economy. Take advantage of discounts for continuous use of rental equipment. Plan for minimum days for freelance crews and for actors.

If the film will take you to several out-of-town locations, try to travel a circular route rather than going back and forth to home base.

Allow for slippage. Everything takes longer than you think it will. Have time to solve problems that arise. If you can, allow time for retakes and cleanup shooting.

LOCATION SHOOTING

Basic to this approach to making a documentary is to plan and organize yourself and your crew so that you will disturb the environment you are shooting in as little as possible. Make no mistake about it: your very presence is a major disturbance in any location. It may be a welcome distraction or it may be at best an annoyance to those who live or work there.

Your goal, like that of the wildlife photographer, is to become accepted as part of the environment as quickly as possible so that your presence can be more or less ignored by the people in it.

Good location scouting will help you to plan the shoot so that there is a minimum of disturbance and confusion when you arrive with the crew. Allow plenty of time for each setup. You may get what you want in a half hour or less. But you may run into problems and have to take considerably longer. The worst situation you can get into is to start falling behind schedule so that you are still shooting at setup number one when you should be at setup number two, and you are beginning to wonder if you will be able to arrive at setup number three before the total time scheduled there has passed, and if you will be able to squeeze in setup number four at all. When you get into that situation, you have created a major disturbance in the environment that no amount of excuses and explanation can undo.

Be Honest

Be honest with yourself about how long each scene or setup will take. Then add a little extra time to give yourself a fudge factor.

Be honest with the people at the locations about how long you will take. There is a tendency among producers to minimize the time shooting will take and the disturbance the production crew will cause. Their belief seems to be that if they tell the truth, they won't get permission to shoot. All they are really doing is creating problems for themselves when they get to the location.

I still recall a documentary—never finished—that I spent one day on as a volunteer lighting director. The members of the congregation of a church came out at nine o'clock on a Saturday morning for what the producer-director had led them to believe would be "about an hour's shooting." And they were still standing in place, grumbling and hungry, long after lunchtime. The producer-director had made two mistakes. He'd asked the members of the congregation to come at the same time as the crew call, perhaps anticipating that many of them would be late. But they weren't. So they had to stand around with nothing to do while we set lights, laid dolly tracks, and got set to shoot. And he hadn't been truthful with himself or with the congregation about how long shooting the sequence would take. It was a very unhappy shoot.

ONE DAY IN A HOSPITAL

Here's the story of a montage we shot in one day in a hospital, using volunteers, for a video on patient education. The script called for nine scenes, in the following order:

1. A child being treated in the emergency room.
2. An exterior long shot identifying the hospital and showing several people coming to it to attend health education classes.
3. A reverse shot of the people entering the hospital.
4. A medium shot of a person on hospital scales illustrating the weight management program.
5. A medium close-up of a man filling in a heart disease risk factor questionnaire.

6. A close-up of a cigarette being stubbed out, illustrating a program to stop smoking.
7. A medium shot of a person eating, to illustrate the hospital's better nutrition program.
8. A wide shot of several people and an instructor in a classroom during a health education class.
9. A shot of a patient in a hospital bed, being attended by a nurse.

Planning the Shooting Sequence

We were shooting on a school day, so the child for scene 1 wouldn't be available until late afternoon. The emergency room changed shifts at 3:00 P.M., and we wanted to give the new shift time to take over, so we decided that about the earliest we could shoot scene 1 would be 3:30.

Shooting scene 9 was going to depend on the hospital census for the day of the shoot. If all the rooms were full, we'd have to either create a hospital bedroom somewhere or go to an alternative. This could be shot in a corridor, showing a patient on a rolling stretcher being wheeled into a room—without actually showing the room—so that any corridor and any doorway could be used.

The hospital had a large, multipurpose room in which classes were held. It was the proper place to shoot scene 8, but we felt we could also create small sets for scenes 4 through 7 in that same room. And since it had convenient access to a loading ramp at the rear of the hospital, it would make a good base of operations. We asked that it be reserved for us for the entire day.

We needed morning light for the two exterior shots, scenes 2 and 3, as that was when the sun would be behind the camera in the long shot, giving the best illumination on the entrance to the hospital building. So we decided those would be our first shots of the day. We also felt we could use the same volunteers who were extras in scenes 2 and 3 as the students in the classroom for scene 8.

Therefore, we decided that these three scenes—2, 3, and 8—plus one other scene would make up our morning schedule. They required the most set-up time, they were the least controllable, and they would let us shoot our large party of volunteers in their three scenes, back-to-back, and then release them for the rest of the day. Also, since morning rain showers were not uncommon, it let us follow the rule of shooting exteriors first with an interior backup in case of bad weather. If it were raining, we could start with scene 8 and then, if the rain stopped later in the morning, go outside for scenes 2 and 3.

The production schedule looked like this:

7:45 A.M.	Crew call at the hospital. Set up for scenes 2 and 3.
8:30 A.M.	Volunteers for scenes 2, 3, and 8 meet in the classroom.
9:00 A.M.	Shoot scene 2 in the parking lot.
9:45 A.M.	Shoot scene 3 at the hospital entrance.
10:30 A.M.	Move to the classroom, set up for scene 8.
11:00 A.M.	Shoot scene 8 in the classroom.
11:30 A.M.	Release people for scenes 2, 3, and 8. Set up for scene 6 in the classroom. Call for "person" for scene 6.
12:00 noon	Shoot scene 6 in the classroom.
12:30 P.M.	Lunch.
1:00 P.M.	Set up for scenes 4, 5, and 7 in the classroom.
1:30 P.M.	Call for "persons" for scenes 4, 5, and 7.
2:00 P.M.	Shoot scene 4, in the classroom.
2:20 P.M.	Shoot scene 5, in the classroom.
2:40 P.M.	Shoot scene 7, in the classroom.
3:00 P.M.	Set up for scene 1 in the emergency room.
3:15 P.M.	Location call for child for scene 1.
4:00 P.M.	Shoot scene 1.
4:30 P.M.	Set up for scene 9 (hospital room), wherever the hospital directs.
5:15 P.M.	Shoot scene 9.
6:00 P.M.	Shooting complete.

We set the crew call for 7:45 A.M. on location to give us adequate time to unload and check out the equipment, and get set to roll tape on scene 2 at 9:00 A.M. I asked that the volunteers be available at 8:30 A.M. and plan to stay until noon. This gave me some leeway first thing in the morning, since volunteers are notorious for showing up late or not at all. And it gave the volunteers a realistic picture of how long I'd need them, so they could plan the rest of their day.

Sure enough, the production crew was delayed and didn't show up until a few minutes after 8:00. And by 8:45 it was clear that we were going to be short on volunteers due to no-shows. But the hospital development office had provided a marvelous liaison person named Hanna, who rustled up some extra extras in a hurry and became one herself. And since I had actually scheduled more check-out and set-up time than was absolutely necessary, the crew was still ready to go on time. We rolled tape on scene 2, take 1, at two minutes before 9:00.

The point is: If we had made the schedule based on minimum set-up time and had given ourselves a tight shooting schedule to get the scenes done, we would have been running a half hour late before we even taped our first shot.

Even with the delays, we were able to spend about an hour and forty-five minutes shooting the exteriors, including considerable time spent experimenting with a dolly shot that never quite looked right and eventually was not used. Then we went inside and set up and shot the classroom scene in less than an hour. By 11:45 we were finished with the morning's shooting, in spite of delays, and were ahead of schedule. The volunteers remained cheerful and helpful throughout the morning, and we were able to release them ahead of time. We had a comfortable amount of time for lunch, too, which always helps crew morale.

In the afternoon, everything went well and we continued to pick up time on the schedule. This meant we could approach each setup in an unhurried fashion, with plenty of time to think and to make changes or try different approaches if we didn't like what we were getting. We were better than a half hour ahead of schedule when we came to the next-to-the-last setup, the child in the emergency room.

And then we ran into problems. There were several emergency cases in the emergency room, and there was no way the hospital could spare the space or the staff for us to shoot there for the next hour or so.

Our agreement was that shooting would not interfere with hospital needs. Under different circumstances I would have tried to schedule the emergency room scene for earlier in the day, so that if problems like this developed, we could come back to it later. But that hadn't been possible in this case.

Nevertheless, because we were ahead of schedule and the child who was to be in the scene had not yet arrived, we moved on to the last setup, scene 9, in the hope that by the time we had finished it, the emergency room would be available. Scene 9 went smoothly, and we were ready to do the emergency room scene just fifteen minutes later than the time we had originally scheduled. Unfortunately, business in the emergency room was even brisker than before, and it would still be an hour or more before we could possibly get in there—and even that estimate was contingent on no more emergency cases coming in.

I had budgeted for a ten-hour shoot, so we could have waited another hour without going over budget. But by this time the child who was to be in the scene had arrived and had been waiting for close to half an hour. I was afraid that if we had another hour or more of delay, the little boy would be bored, tired, and cranky when we went to shoot.

Fortunately, our liaison person had an alternative for us—an outpatient surgical room that looked quite similar to the emergency room, and which was not in use. We set up and shot the scene in forty-five minutes, sent the child and his parents home on time, and finished the day's shooting an hour and a half ahead of time in a triumph of planning and contingency scheduling.

THEN THERE ARE THOSE OTHER DAYS

Then there are days when everything seems to go wrong, and no matter how much time you've allowed, you seem to be constantly slipping behind schedule. If time and budget will allow it, try to reschedule some of the scenes planned for the day to a later time, to take some pressure off you and your crew. If you can't do that, then at least alert everyone who needs to know that you are running behind and will probably get to their scenes later than originally planned. Then try to get back on schedule.

Make Haste Slowly

The only advice I can give, when you're playing catch-up, is to make haste slowly. If anything, slow down what you are doing. It's when you begin to feel the pressure of time running out that you tend to make mistakes that can cost you even more time, sometimes money, and sometimes even footage that is already shot. Before I learned to hurry up by slowing down, I got into one of these situations and, in the rush to change a magazine of film, I opened the wrong side before putting the magazine into the changing bag, thereby ruining four hundred feet of film that had just been shot.

So slow down. Do everything carefully and deliberately. Even call a break for everyone if you think it will help. It may just be that you'll soon find yourself back on schedule.

Staying on schedule is important, not only because you have a job to do and a budget to hold to, but also because you're the stranger in the other fellow's place. You want to keep the inconvenience you cause to a minimum, and you don't want any hard feelings to develop because of your presence.

SCHEDULING POSTPRODUCTION

The biggest variable in postproduction is creative editing. If you've shot to a script and will follow the script in editing, then you should be able to get a reasonable time estimate from the editor and director.

But if you've been shooting an actuality documentary whose structure and content will be found in the editing room, it can be hard to estimate how long it will take to put together a decent off-line or rough cut.

Here are things that have to be done to complete a documentary after it has been shot.

- Develop film and make a work print or video transfer, or if you've used video, make a windowprint dub for review.
- Review and log all footage. Eliminate bad shots and identify probable keepers.
- Make a tentative editing plan.
- Off-line or rough-cut editing.
- Create titles, graphics, and special effects.
- Record narration, music, and sound effects as needed.
- On-line or fine-cut editing.
- Sound mix or sound sweetening.
- Negative cutting and making an answer print for film.
- Audio layback for video.
- Complete video edit master or film release print.

The important thing in scheduling postproduction is to plan for the sequence in which things must be done and to allow enough time to get them done. Again, allow for slippage. Sometimes what seems like a good idea just won't work in editing. Sometimes equipment goes down. Sometimes the editor gets the flu.

In fact, production scheduling is really the art of getting done on time, even when things go wrong.

15

HOW MUCH WILL IT COST?

For the longest time there was a belief that a nonfiction film or video should somehow, magically, cost about a thousand dollars a minute. I've been hearing that number all of my professional life, during which the cost of film cameras, stock, and processing has increased exponentially while nonfiction video has gone from industrial-grade three-quarter-inch cameras, recorders, and editing systems to Beta-SP with nonlinear off-line and digital on-line.

In today's documentary world, just buying a minute of stock footage can cost a documentarian anywhere from fifteen hundred to six thousand dollars. And when a four-hour series comes in at $2 million, that's an average of more than eight thousand dollars a minute.

I once wrote an article on the cost of documentaries based on a survey of sponsored nontheatrical films that had won awards at a major festival. This wasn't a scientific survey, it was more the kind of information you might get from talking with friends. Also, it was possible that films which win awards may cost more (or might cost less) than films that don't. The point was that the average cost per minute for all those films was $1,785.28. They ranged from $416 per minute for a low-budget in-house production to a high of $3,846 per minute. And that was in the '70s! Nothing in production costs has gotten cheaper since then.

It also turns out that people have been quoting that thousand-dollar-a-minute figure since the 1930s, when during the Great Depression you could get your film shot and finished on 35mm for whatever the going rate might have been.

The fact is that there is almost no direct relationship between running time and the total cost of a production. It all depends on who and what have to be shot, where, when, and over what period of time. Even postproduction, which would seem to have some relationship with running time, actually depends more on how many shots there are, what effects are used, and how intricate the sound and picture editing is.

The one tendency I found is that shorter documentaries will probably cost more per minute than longer ones, simply because there are some fairly fixed start-up and administrative costs that are amortized over the total production. So the longer the documentary, the less these costs will average per minute.

FACTORS AFFECTING THE BUDGET

A number of considerations go into creating a budget for a documentary.

Who Is Paying?

The first consideration is who is paying to get the documentary made. If this is strictly your project and you are paying the bills, then what you are concerned with is the out-of-pocket cost. If you have your own camera equipment and editing facilities, you don't need to budget for these—or for your time, either—except to determine what the actual cost or fair value of the documentary might be.

On the other hand, if you have either a sponsor, a client, or a funding agency, then *everything* becomes a cost, including your time and the use of your equipment. You budget to be sure you don't spend more than you'll receive.

Small Crew or Large Production?

Almost all of my experience is in making behavioral documentaries with a crew of three or four people. And the production budget is basically so much per day for crew, equipment, film or tape, steaks, sodas, and mileage.

But if you are undertaking a reenactment, a historical documentary, or a biography with re-creation of events, you'll need to budget like a feature film. The only way to do this is to get an experienced production manager to do your budget for you, once you have a completed script.

Union or Nonunion?

Unless you are doing a large reenactment or are locked into a union contract through other work that you've done, your first documentary will probably be nonunion.

A union shoot will cost more due to union work rules. You may be required to hire more people than you would use in a nonunion, independent production. And you'll have to pay for travel time, meals, and overtime, as well as union benefits such as health and welfare. But if you are locked into a union production, you undoubtedly already know this.

If you are nonunion and independent, then the cost of everything is the best cost you can negotiate.

Live or Archive?

Where will the footage come from that will be used in your documentary? Will you be shooting it live? Or will it mostly be archival footage? Live productions mean shooting days, followed by review of footage, followed by editing. Productions based on archival footage replace shooting days with the costs of finding, duplicating, and licensing the footage that will be used.

In today's documentary milieu, it can cost far more to make a documentary out of old footage, when you have to buy rights to it, than to go out and shoot everything brand new. Which is one of the reasons *FDR* cost so much.

ABOVE- AND BELOW-THE-LINE COSTS

The budgets for feature films and for some other productions are divided into above-the-line and below-the-line costs. People accustomed to using this system of budgeting tend to think in these terms. It won't be important in planning a documentary unless a funder or sponsor asks you for an above-the-line and below-the-line break-out of your budget.

Above-the-line costs are generally contractual expenses that are negotiated on a run-of-the-production basis. These include the purchase of the script and property rights and the salaries of the producer, director, and cast.

Below-the-line costs are all those costs associated with the production that are calculated on the basis of use. This includes salaries for the crew, cost of equipment and supplies, travel, editing, processing, and postproduction costs, and salaries not agreed upon as above-the-line costs before production starts.

A BUDGETING CHECKLIST

Over the years I've developed a number of checklists to try to be sure I account in advance for everything I'm going to have to pay for on a production. I've consolidated these into the checklist that follows. I have tried to make this as comprehensive as possible, but don't blame me if I've left out something that you need, because every production is different. Treat this as a starting point and a memory jogger and then add to it the specifics of your production to create your own budgeting system.

I.   General (run-of-the-production expense)
    A. Production Company
       1. Producer
       2. Director

   3. Producer's assistant/secretary
   4. Bookkeeper
   5. Office rent
   6. Telephone
   7. Utilities
   8. Furniture and equipment
   9. Supplies
  10. Licenses
  11. Other
 B. Transportation
 C. Legal
   1. Contracts, releases, etc.
   2. Rights
   3. Copyright
 D. Insurance
   1. Office and equipment
   2. Errors and omissions
   3. Liability
   4. Production or negative insurance
 E. Payroll company
   1. Tax, benefits, workers' compensation, etc.,
      throughout the production
II. Preproduction
 A. Research
   1. Text researcher
   2. Cost of books, research materials, microfilm
      reproduction, photocopying, etc.
   3. Film researcher
   4. Cost of viewing and duplicating footage and stills for
      review
 B. Script
   1. Scriptwriter
   2. Interviews
   3. Storyboards if needed
 C. Production planning
   1. Director of photography

    2. Casting
       a) Casting director
       b) Videotape casting sessions
    3. Locations
       a) Location coordinator
       b) Location research
    4. Others
       a) Sound
       b) Art director
       c) Production manager
       d) Etc.
  D. Travel
  E. Payroll company
    1. Tax, benefits, workers' compensation, etc.
III. Production
  A. Crew and equipment (if contracted as a package)
  B. Crew (individuals as needed)
    1. Assistant director
    2. Director of photography
    3. Camera operator
    4. Camera assistant
    5. Sound recordist
    6. Sound assistant
    7. Electrician/gaffer
    8. Grip(s)
    9. Scriptwriter
    10. Production assistant(s)
    11. Editor
    12. Makeup artist
    13. Property person
    14. Wardrobe person
    15. Driver(s)
    16. TelePrompTer operator
    17. Other
  C. Talent
    1. Host/spokesperson

   2. Featured actors
   3. Extras
   4. Animals
D. Equipment
   1. Camera and support
      a) Camera(s)
      b) Film magazines
      c) Lenses
      d) Matte box, filters, etc.
      e) Batteries and charger(s)
      f) Tripod(s)
      g) Dolly, Steadicam, crane, jib-arm, etc.
      h) Special mounts (car, helicopter)
      i) Special rigs such as underwater housing
      j) Video recorder(s)
      k) Video playback
      l) Video assist
      m) Monitor(s)
      n) Slate, connectors, etc.
   2. Sound
      a) Recorder(s)
      b) Microphone(s)
      c) Wireless system
      d) Audio mixer
      e) Microphone boom or fish pole
      f) Cables and connectors
   3. Lighting and grip equipment
      a) Grip truck
      b) Lighting instruments
         (1) Spot/flood
         (2) Broad
         (3) Soft lights
         (4) Battery lights
         (5) Other
      c) Grip stands, sandbags
      d) Shiny boards

    e) Cables
    f) Clamps, gels, dichroic filters, etc.
    g) Background paper
    h) Large color-correcting gels for windows
    i) Generator
  4. Miscellaneous
    a) TelePrompTer
    b) Communication (walkie-talkies, cellular phones, headsets, etc.)
    c) Trailers, honey wagons, etc.
E. Transportation
  1. Cars
  2. Vans or trucks
F. Props and wardrobe
  1. Props as needed
  2. Wardrobe items
  3. Vehicles
G. Location and studio costs as required
  1. Location fees
  2. Licenses as needed
  3. Studio rental
  4. Set construction
  5. Set decoration
  6. Storage and transportation
H. Processing
  1. Laboratory processing of film
  2. Transfer and sync sound
  3. Work print or transfer to videotape
  4. VHS windowprint dubs for review
  5. Shipping
I. Travel
  1. Travel costs
  2. Rooms
  3. Per diem
  4. Shipping equipment and supplies
J. Supplies
  1. Film or videotape

      2. Audiotape
      3. Batteries for everything
      4. Gaffer's tape, camera tape, shipping tape, etc.
      5. Replacement lamps
  K. Meals and snacks
      1. Cast and crew meals as required
      2. Snacks and drinks available during production
  L. Contingencies
    A percentage of the production budget set aside to
    handle unexpected and unbudgeted expense
  M. Payroll company
      1. Tax, benefits, workers' compensation, etc.
IV. Postproduction
  A. Stock footage and stills
      1. Work tape
      2. Reproduction quality
      3. Rights
  B. Review of footage
    The director, along with the editor (if the director is
    not doing the editing) and possibly the producer, will
    want to review what has been shot to select the best
    takes, eliminate the unusable footage, and begin to
    organize the structure of the documentary. Allow time
    for this.
  C. Editing facilities
    The production company may have editing facilities
    available, or may rent a film-editing room or editing
    system or a video off-line editing room or system by the
    week or month until postproduction is complete.
  D. Off-line editing (video) or rough-cut editing (film)
      1. Editor
      2. Assistant editor
      3. Off-line (rough-cut) editing equipment
      4. Supplies
        a) Splicing tape for film, cores, split reels, marking
          pencils, etc.
        b) Mastering tape and work tapes for video

E. Graphics and special effects
　1. Animation
　2. Paintbox, computer graphics, etc.
　3. Special photographic or video effects
　4. Character generator
　5. Other
F. Music
　1. Composer
　2. Library music
　　a) Selection
　　b) Rights
　3. Music director
　4. Audiotape as required
G. Audio postproduction
　1. Record narration
　2. Voice talent
　3. Looping if required
　4. Record music
　5. Record sound effects
　6. Audio sweetening and effects (video)
　7. Sound mix (film)
　8. Audio layback
　9. Audiotape and/or videotape as required
H. On-line editing
　1. On-line facility by the hour
　2. Mastering tape
　3. Work tape
　4. Protection master
　5. Dubs to VHS for review
I. Completion on film
　1. Negative cutting
　2. Answer print
　3. Release print
　4. Internegative
　5. Shipping and insurance
J. Payroll company
　1. Tax, benefits, workers' compensation, etc.

V. Distribution
   A. Prints for release as required
     1. Theatrical standard
     2. Television network standard
     3. VHS video release copies, including labels and boxes
     4. Shipping

Use this checklist as a starting point. Specific items will change as the technology changes and as your approach to making documentaries evolves. The most important thing is to have a reference point for creating the budget for a documentary. There is so much to do, and there are so many different costs involved, that without some kind of checklist you can easily forget to include something that could cost a lot of money you didn't plan on spending.

And you'll have to live with that.

PRODUCTION

Every technology has its discipline, and you

have to learn it. A writer, for instance,

doesn't type with black ink on black paper.

. . . .

—*John Massi, The Annenberg School*

of Communications

16

RECORDING PICTURE
AND SOUND

You can't make a documentary without a certain minimum knowledge of the technology that is required. Unless someone on the documentary team has that knowledge, even the best of ideas won't get recorded. If someone doesn't know how to set the proper exposure, how to choose the appropriate videotape or film stock, what lens to use and how to get it in focus, and how to record legible sound, it really doesn't matter what you do with the camera. There won't be anything recorded worth showing to an audience.

ZERO-LEVEL KNOWLEDGE

I call this zero-level knowledge. You have to have it before you can produce anything. In doing documentary, you almost always have to trade off between technology and ideas. You can't shoot where there isn't any light. And you can't record where the noise level is so high that what you are interested in is drowned out by other sounds. But perhaps, if the reason to do so is compelling, you can accept a less-than-perfect image or get the sound you want in another location, or at a different time.

To that extent, technology must inform your documentary idea to make it workable.

Not a Hardware Primer

This chapter is not going to be a primer on production hardware, for several good reasons. The first is that production technology is evolving so rapidly that the half-life of change is roughly equivalent to the time it takes a book to go from manuscript to print. So if I included a lot of information about specific video or film cameras, recorders, and postproduction equipment, at least half of it would be out of date by the time you read this.

The second reason is that while I have performed just about every job on a production crew except makeup artist, for the past several years I've concentrated on writing and directing. I hire a camera crew when I direct, and when I direct postproduction, I use a technical editor. Today, I'm neither a shooter nor a film or video editor. And if you want to become expert with a technology, you should learn it from the people who work with it every day.

Fortunately, that's not difficult. You'll find several works on production technology in the bibliography to this book. Or you can take courses. Many college continuing education programs now offer an introduction to video or film production the way they once offered creative writing courses. Or you can do an apprenticeship.

Do You Want the Responsibility of Technical Knowledge?

You must decide if you want to be one of the technical people on your documentary crew. If you are the person with the camera, for instance, you have the responsibility for getting good pictures in every shooting situation. If you're the video editor, you not only have to know how to run the editing computer to edit scenes together, you must constantly be aware of color balance, video levels, and a hundred and one other things that have little or nothing to do with the content of your documentary, and everything to do with the technical excellence of the finished piece.

I know people who only want to operate a camera, and others whose joy in life is to record pristine sound. I know good technical editors who don't want to shoot or direct, but who love to make the production come to life on the screen. And I know of documentary teams where one person operates the camera and another the sound and they function so closely together that they are codirectors during production and coeditors later in post.

I also know writers who just want to write and do not care to direct. And I know directors who want to put together the best possible technical team on each production so that the documentary they've been imagining becomes the documentary on the screen. I know a director who used to be a pretty good camera operator who now says, "I'm not good enough to shoot a documentary for me." And I know another director who started out as a film editor who now says, "I've learned not to try to edit a documentary I've directed."

There are a lot of ways to realize a documentary vision. One is to be able to raise the money. Another is to direct a team of technical people to use their skill and professional knowledge to bring the documentary you've been dreaming of to the screen. And certainly another is as a technical participant.

Video and film are corporate media. It is not essential that each person working on a documentary be a master of all the contributing technologies. But, since eventually it all has to fit together, you do need to know how everything works. If you don't, you could end up with a lot of false assumptions that could cost you money, waste time, and lose you the respect and cooperation of the skilled people you're working with.

Technology and Art

Back when there was grant money around for any kind of wacky idea that could be expressed in standard English in a proposal with social value overtones, I was invited to a meeting of an organization composed of artists and engineers. I would be the filmmaker, presumably an artist. The idea for the organization, from whomever wrote the grant proposal and whatever funding agency put up the bucks, was that it would be good for the stuffy, nuts-and-bolts, calculator-toting engineers to be exposed to some artistic ideas.

And it would benefit the woolly-headed, esoteric, pie-in-the-sky artists to come up against some harsh, realistic, technological concepts. But that's not how it worked.

The engineers—who were all working pros in things like creating animated computer simulations for NASA—didn't waste a second talking about how wire A goes on pin C. They understood all that, and assumed everyone else did. What they wanted to talk about were the aesthetics of what they were doing.

The artists, on the other hand, had spent years mastering the aesthetics of their work, and only talked technology. They knew what they wanted to do artistically and were spending most of their time mastering the technical demands of their media. And that's all they talked about. They knew that to be good at a craft, it's not enough to have a clear idea of what you want to accomplish. You have to master the tools for doing it.

RECORDING FOR EDITING

When I started out, I thought a documentary was made with expensive equipment, fast film stock, and something called *content*—which was the result of brilliant directing. I was doing a lot of documentary filming on location—low-light or available-light stuff. The image would look okay in the rushes—not great, but okay; after all, I was doing documentary—but by the time the film went through an internegative to a release print, a number of the scenes in the movie would look strange.

The first thing I had to get over was the idea that a documentary is something you shoot. It isn't. It's what you show.

The main distinction between professional productions and home movies or home videos—quite apart from the cost of the equipment and the skill of the users—is that a professional production is *always* done to be edited and reproduced. That's what makes home movies so deadly. You have to sit through all the bad stuff to get to the few seconds that count, while the person who insists on showing it to you keeps saying, "This doesn't count, wait until you see what's coming, never mind that—I don't know why I did that—THERE IT WAS! DID YOU SEE IT?"

When you are recording for reproduction, the only thing th counts is what the final copy will look and sound like. Film becomes more and more contrasty as you add generations. The ideal film original actually looks somewhat soft and mushy. On the other hand, if you are shooting film original to transfer directly to digital video, you can tolerate a much harder look. Video loses resolution and definition as it goes through generations. So you want to start with the best possible video original. Sound *always* gets worse as it is rerecorded.

A documentary is what the audience sees on the screen. Everything you do in the production process is aimed at getting you and your documentary concept to the point where you have an edited production to show to an audience. So it is important to start with the best possible pictures and sound you can get, using the finest equipment you can get your hands on, recorded on the highest quality recording media.

A DOCUMENTARY IS MADE WITH LIGHT

It's one thing to understand that it takes a certain minimum amount of illumination to record a videotape or film, and quite another to accept the fact that a documentary is made with light. I would guess that between the two concepts lie about five years of experience at working with the tools and trying to get the image on the screen to look like the image in your head. If you have a good coach, you may move up in class faster. If you have to do it all on your own, it may take longer.

Lighting for the Print

The *amount* of light available establishes the existence of an image on video or film. If there's not enough light for an exposure—no image.

The *quality* of the light—balance, highlight and shadow areas, position of light sources, lighting contrast ratio, color temperature, and so on—determines the look of the image.

The better the lighting, the better the final copies of your documentary. Some video cameras will record a recognizable image in extremely low light. But since the original camera image will deteriorate slightly with each generation in video editing or film printing, if you start with a marginally lit picture—even though it may look acceptable on first video or in the film work print—it may not be good enough by the time you go through the generations to a distribution copy.

In analog video editing, each time you rerecord, you add a generation. So the release dub (fourth generation) is a copy from the dubbing master (third generation), which is a copy from the on-line master (second generation), which is a copy from the first-generation camera original.

Digital video editing has solved some of the problems of generational deterioration. In digital editing, each succeeding image is considered to be a clone of the original, because each generation is re-created using the digital code of the original.

Nevertheless, the better the original, the better the copies.

Location Lighting

On location, it's the quality of the light, far more than the amount of light, that counts.

As a documentarian, you don't normally face the problems of your feature film cousins in trying to match shots made on location exactly to shots made in the studio. In this case, the actuality of documentary works for you. But the fact that your production is a documentary is not an excuse for shoddy lighting.

In general, your goals in lighting a documentary are these:

To Achieve Sufficient Light for an Adequate Exposure. This will depend mainly on the recording medium and the camera. The goal is to have a decent depth of field in most situations without requiring an immense amount of light.

To Balance the Light for Proper-Looking Color. You may have more than one kind of light source at the location. For example, in a classroom or office building, you might find overhead fluorescents plus sunlight coming in from a bank of windows along one side of the room. And there might still be dark corners that will need additional lighting from your tungsten lights.

Yes, you may be able to white balance a video camera to accept three different light sources. But as you turn more toward the sunlight coming through the windows—or away from it—you'll go out of balance. To the extent that you are able, you want to reconcile the different light sources so that the camera is essentially working with the same kind of light no matter where in the room it is pointed.

When Shooting Film, to Minimize High-Contrast Effects. Contrast builds up at every stage of printing as film goes from camera original to printing negative to print, resulting in some loss of detail in highlight and shadow areas. Therefore, you usually want to eliminate hot spots and deep shadows, except where you have created them on purpose for dramatic effect.

To Keep Artificial Lighting to a Minimum. Lights are a distraction to your subjects. Lights are hot. Lights draw a lot of electricity, and adding lights can easily overload available electrical circuits. Keeping the overall level of illumination as close to the level of the ambient light as possible helps in maintaining a natural look while providing sufficient overall illumination for good camera and subject freedom.

To Give the Location a Natural, "Unlit" Look. Feature film cinematographers spend a lot of time on each set deciding how to *motivate* the lighting. Even though their lighting instruments may be mounted on an overhead grid or on lighting stands sticking up above the scenery, they have to decide:

- what the theoretical source of the lighting is—sunlight through a window, overhead fluorescents, a chandelier, room lamps on tables, or whatever

- how strong the light from that source should be
- what other sources there might be for fill lights
- how shadows will fall in the scene

As a documentarian lighting a location, you face more or less the same problem, except you are not starting with an empty set. And you may have to use just the natural light that's available.

The location itself can serve as a model for your lighting. Look it over carefully before you begin adding lights. Note the main sources of illumination, and use them to motivate your lighting. Your goal is to increase the illumination in the room to a comfortable level for shooting, without appreciably changing the way the room will look on camera.

To Give the Camera as Much Freedom as Possible to Follow Action. In certain kinds of documentary shooting, you really don't know what is going to happen next, or where it will happen. So you would like to have enough light everywhere in the area in which you are shooting, so that you can take decent pictures anywhere within that area.

To Give the People on Camera as Much Freedom of Movement as Possible. Again, in many documentaries, you don't want to intrude on your subjects to the point of asking them to "hit a mark" or to remember not to walk out of a certain area. So you want to maintain a useful minimum level of shooting illumination throughout the area.

To Provide a Dramatic Effect. It is the play of light and shadow that gives images on video or film their specific look. Not every scene needs to be lit to a flat level of constant illumination. Sometimes, such as in night scenes, you *want* dark areas. Sometimes you may want a subject partially in shadow. Sometimes you might like to have a subject walking from a pool of light into shadow and back into another pool of light. Sometimes you want side lighting, or back lighting, or even lighting from below.

Lighting for VHS Copies

If your documentary will be distributed on VHS video, lighting can be critical. Chrominance has some tendency to bleed in VHS dubs, especially in reds and blues. When this happens, a woman's lipstick may look like it is smeared all over her face instead of defining her lips. Or the color of a blouse or jacket may bleed beyond the edges of the clothing, so that your video image looks like Sunday comic pages that have been printed with the color out of register.

In lighting for VHS distribution, you need to be sure you have enough overall illumination, and that you have good lighting contrast to separate people and things from the background. If you have any control over clothing and items on the set, try to avoid red.

CAMERA WORK

The camera—whether video or film—accumulates the bits and pieces of visual evidence that will eventually make up the documentary you will show to an audience. Like a computer, a camera is a marvelous instrument for the storage and retrieval of information. And like a computer, it can only do what it is told to do—when and how it is told to do it.

Cameras Don't Make Documentaries—People Do

The point to all camera work is to let the audience see the scene in the way you would like to present it to them. When the image is too dark, or out of focus, or blurred from rapid camera or lens movement, the audience can't see the scene. And if the camera work hasn't been done with a sensitivity to the fact that the footage will eventually be edited for presentation to an audience, the editor, the director, and quite possibly the audience will be painfully aware of the fact.

If you are doing the camera work yourself, you have to keep all these things in mind as you shoot.

Using a Camera Operator

If you are using someone else behind the camera, you have to take time to be sure you both are in basic agreement as to how the footage is to be shot. It is not enough that the camera operator is a professional. For example, in my documentary shot in Wilkes-Barre, I employed two cameramen at one point. Both were professionals, not only in the sense that they were paid for camera work but also in the sense that operating a movie camera was what they did full time to earn a living. But on a scale of one to ten, the footage one of them delivered at the end of the day was a ten, while what the other handed in was a two, or at best a three.

One was a truly superb cameraman named Andy Dintenfass, now a director of photography in Hollywood. Andy could start a scene with a wide shot of people talking close to the camera and make an unrehearsed slow pan across the room, tilting up to the audience in the balcony and zooming in for a tight shot of a single person sitting there. And every frame was sharp and legible.

If that doesn't sound so hard, try it sometime.

The other, whose professional experience was gained mainly in shooting TV news, delivered six hundred feet of rushes so full of bumpy pans, fast zooms, and focusing adjustments that the footage was almost completely unusable.

In selecting a camera operator, ask to see some unedited footage shot in situations similar to those of your documentary.

And talk. Don't assume that what seems so clear to you is equally clear to your camera operator. If you're using a new camera operator, try to start with some fairly simple things, so that you can see in the footage if there are problems or misunderstandings. You want to get them corrected before you get into the critical stuff. Because, unless you're going to micromanage by headset from a monitor—which I don't recommend—in any hot shooting situation, your camera operator becomes a de facto codirector.

A *Shoot with a New Camera Operator*

I was making a sponsored documentary for a health plan, which was to be made up primarily of interviews with foreign-born adolescents and their parents, and my client requested that I use a specific camera operator. I knew the person and had seen samples of his work, but we had never worked together. Since I would be conducting the interviews, the camera operator would be, in effect, directing the shooting. Therefore it was important that he know, as clearly and completely as possible, exactly what I wanted in the footage.

Normally, when shooting interviews, I instruct the camera operator to change camera angle or focal length each time I ask a question, so that it is easy to edit out unwanted portions of the interview without a jump cut. In this case, I decided not to do that. Because I hoped to be probing some fairly sensitive areas, I thought it might be important not only to have the subjects' answers, but also their reactions to my questions. I decided we'd shoot formal cutaways after the interviews and have them available for editing.

Here are the instructions I sent the camera operator several days before we were to shoot:

SHOOTING NOTES—

1. During the interview, hold on the interview subject or subjects, mainly close-ups and medium shots. Obviously it is the camera operator's option to go wide or move very close, but *make no sudden moves*. Everything smooth, everything in focus.
2. We'll cover with a very formal cutaway protocol on a separate roll of cutaways:
   a. Two-shot of interviewer and subject.
   b. Subject listening, seen in long shot over interviewer's shoulder.
   c. Subject listening in close-up.
   d. Interviewer listening, seen over subject's shoulder.

  e. Interviewer listening (reacting) in close-up and medium shot.

  f. If possible, we'll try to get reaction shots of parents, friends, etc., who may also be present.

3. We'll need establishing shots of the area in which each interview is done.

4. We need to be on the lookout for backgrounds for head and tail titles.

5. If possible, let's get a visual slate at the head of each videotape for identification. Also audio identification.

6. Where several people are being interviewed at once, the camera should *not* "go hunting" for every person who speaks. If it appears the person is going to talk for a while, get him in the shot smoothly.

7. *If there are any unmotivated zooms, I'll break your arm.*

We always shot the cutaways after the interview had been completed. The reason is simple: In shooting cutaways I was, in a sense, asking the subject to *act*. When the camera was on him during cutaway shooting, he'd be asked to listen and not talk. When the camera was on me, he'd be asked to talk so that I could listen and react. By putting this kind of *acting* at the end, I was able to keep the subjects' reactions during the interview spontaneous and unbiased by any feeling that they were being directed.

Because it was a video shoot, we put the cutaways on a separate videotape from the interview for ease in editing.

Lenses

Documentaries are normally shot with a camera with a good, fast, sharp zoom lens, because that offers the most convenience and flexibility. I've learned that on location there's not likely to be much light or much space. So I prefer a fast zoom lens with the widest possible focal length at the wide angle end. I've done a lot of location work with the 9.5mm to 57mm f/1.9 and the 10mm to 100mm f/2 zooms. You can shoot in a small room at about 10mm without much noticeable wide angle distortion, and you're not likely to need a longer focal length than they provide.

I also like to carry along one or two prime lenses for special work. The Angenieux f/1.1 10mm lens is very fast with an almost infinite depth of field. A macro lens for close-ups of very small things can be useful.

If you're shooting video, you're likely to have less lens selection. But don't assume you have to use the lens that comes with the camera until you've discussed the possibilities with your camera operator or director of photography.

Camera Support

Andy Dintenfass could shoot rock steady with a twenty-pound camera handheld on his shoulder or under his arm—and did when the situation demanded it. But he would use a tripod for shooting whenever he had the opportunity. His goal, at all times, was to get the best possible images to be edited into the documentary.

Handheld shooting is fine and often necessary for covering action, for moving quickly from event to event, and even for providing complete coverage of people talking or doing things. An audience will accept a little camera wiggle and bump when the scene reeks of spontaneity. But they don't expect to see stationary objects such as buildings, signs, bookcases, furniture, and so on bouncing around on the screen when they don't bounce around in real life—and neither do I. So I have the camera operator use a tripod wherever practical.

In addition to a standard tripod, it can be nice to have a set of baby legs or a high hat along for low-angle shooting with tripod stability.

Videotape or Film Load

I make it a rule to start each new sequence, especially if it involves spontaneous behavior, with a fresh load of videotape or film—and a new reel of audiotape when we're doing double system sound. I don't want to have to stop and reload in the middle of the action if I can avoid it.

When I'm shooting film, I try to keep several spare magazines loaded and ready for a quick change if the first one runs out while the action is hot. The short ends of film or videotape remaining unused when you switch to a new reel to start a new sequence can be used later to shoot cutaways, close-ups, reaction shots, and relatively short set pieces that don't involve spontaneous behavior.

Show the Evidence

The first concern in composing a camera shot for documentary is to show the evidence. If the composition is too close or too far away, the audience won't know what they are looking at.

The second is to show the evidence as artfully as possible.

Always in that order.

In general, make all camera moves fairly slow and deliberate. A sudden zoom, pan, or tilt, followed by refocusing, is distracting to the audience and may make the shot unusable. Shaky-cam in documentary is always the result of poor camera work.

As I told my camera operator in the interview shoot, don't chase the speaker. When you are recording several people and you've been holding close on one person talking, don't think you have to quickly turn the camera to the next person, just because they've started talking. Many times you'll pan to them just as they've finished speaking and the person you just had framed up starts to reply. It's much better to slowly come wide until you have both speakers and then think about again going for a close-up of one or the other.

Other Camera Considerations

The Camera Is Always On. As far as the people in front of the camera are concerned, my answer to the question "Is the camera on?" is that the camera is always on and always loaded (whether it is or not).

Shoot Establishing Shots and Cutaways. After you've recorded the behavior you came for or covered the unique event, take time to finish the coverage. Shoot the exterior of the building you've been working in (from a tripod). Get the flavor of the location—furniture, bric-a-brac, signs, pets, whatever. Other cutaways might include close-ups of the subjects' hands as they toy with a pencil on the table, reaction shots of other people in the room, and so on.

The Camera Doesn't Talk. Whether you are the camera operator or have hired one, always remember that the camera never talks. Once you start, you'll find it hard to stop. And when you look at the footage, you'll find that the voice from the camera has ruined the scene.

Slating Takes. Slate takes where you can, but don't let the slating process interfere with the spontaneity of the scene. Slating is more important for double system film than for video, because the slate serves as a reference point for syncing picture and sound. But having someone step out in front of the people whose behavior you want to record, yell, "Scene seven, take one!" and slap a clapstick together is a good way to induce galloping performance anxiety. Remember, you can get a good sync point by shooting a close-up of the sound recordist tapping the microphone. If you have to go in hot, with no chance to slate, you can always slate at the tail.

DOCUMENTARY SOUND

Too many documentarians—especially those who have come to the position of producer or director via experience as a camera operator or editor—seem to approach location sound with only two imperatives in mind: (1) don't record any camera noise, and (2) keep the microphone out of the picture.

While these are good, they are not at all sufficient—or even absolutely necessary. Sound work, like camera work, has as its purpose the recording and accumulation of useful hunks of documentary evidence that can be used in the final edited version of the documentary.

Effect of Rerecording Sound

Recorded sound can go through many generations between the original recording on location and the mixed video sound track or the optical track on the final print of the documentary. And sound almost never improves with rerecording from generation to generation. It gets worse.

I say *almost*, only because in one case, the rerecording process did improve the sound in a film of mine. I had been filming in a public building, which had an air conditioner that couldn't be turned off. The air conditioner was putting out a high-pitched whine—not terribly loud, but very definitely there. That, in itself, wouldn't have been so bad. Once we got used to it, we barely noticed it, so we thought an audience wouldn't mind it either. But in editing I decided to intercut those scenes with scenes from other locations. Naturally, each time we saw a scene from that room, there was an immediate and noticeable high-pitched whine on the sound track. No help for it. That's what we had, and that's what we used. The tracks were mixed and the film was sent off for printing.

Then a wonderful thing happened. When I put the first answer print of the film on the projector and ran it, the whine was gone! All along it had been pitched above the 6,000 Hz cutoff of the optical sound track, and it simply fell away when the sound was transferred to optical film.

You get one or two technical miracles in a lifetime. The rest of the time you have to protect yourself.

Recording Audio

At a minimum you need to record legible audio in which the voices and other important sounds are sufficiently separated from the background and from each other that you can recognize and understand them. Which is simply the audio equivalent of saying that you want your pictures properly exposed and in focus so you can tell what you are looking at.

Your ultimate goal, of course, is the cleanest, most natural audio you can possibly get, so that you have the maximum control in editing and the least possible loss of quality in duplication.

Begin by getting rid of unwanted ambient sound, wherever possible, before you shoot. Turn off motors, radios, humming refrigerators, whistling light fixtures, air conditioners, fans, and the like. If the crew has to be able to move around on a bare floor, have them wear sneakers or go in their stocking feet.

Using automatic gain control (AGC), which is available on most audio and video recorders, will yield poor quality sound. AGC works by boosting the recording level until it reaches some predetermined point. When the sound you want is occurring right in front of the microphone, AGC works fairly well. But when the people stop talking, the AGC immediately raises the level of the background noise as high as it can. This can give you a sound track on which there's a loud whooshing sound in the spaces between people speaking. It sounds terrible, and it's difficult to edit.

Have your sound recordist adjust the recording level manually, keeping the level shown on the VU meter as high as possible without going into the distortion range.

The sound recordist should wear earphones to monitor the quality of what is actually being recorded. Sometimes, while shooting an interview or other sound take, a plane will go over or a truck will drive past, making noise that I can hear. When we stop shooting, I'll ask the sound recordist if the noise affected the track. Quite often the answer is that it didn't. The placement of the microphone and the level of sound close to the microphone will often block unwanted noise from recording on the track. But you'll only know this if the sound operator is wearing earphones. Similarly, your sound person may hear offending noises that are not apparent to you.

Do a Reality Check

When I lived in Hawaii, I was asked to produce some documentary-style testimonials for a political candidate on one of the outer islands. The video crew, supplied by the candidate's campaign, was one person from the local cable company, with a little bit of obsolete equipment. We shot a potluck dinner and rally for the candidate where there was a lot of background noise. I kept asking the operator how the sound was, as he was shooting, and he said "fine." But we had no playback, so it wasn't until I got back to Honolulu to start editing that I learned what he meant by "fine" sound. He had reproduced the noise in the room faithfully. Unfortunately, that meant we couldn't understand the candidate when he was speaking. The rally footage was good for background and nothing else.

So, if you haven't worked with the sound person before, do some reality checks. Ask for playback at the end of a scene. Listen in on a headset yourself. In planning the shoot, ask if the sound person can give you your own headset.

Microphones

The choice of microphones for location sound depends on the shooting situation and what you have available. I once thought that the only proper microphone for a documentary crew was a powerful shotgun mike that could reach into the scene and pull out legible audio. Today I mainly use individual lavaliere mikes feeding wireless transmitters.

When using a handheld microphone, the sound recordist has to keep out of the way of the camera in two ways. The first is to keep the mike out of the picture, if possible. The second is to stay out of the way of the camera operator. In one of the first documentaries I shot, I had a volunteer sound recordist who would invariably be standing right where I wanted to be to shoot. At the end of the first day's filming, I took him aside and told him what was happening. I said, "In each scene, figure out the best place for the camera to be, and don't be there."

Sound is an important part of the modern documentary. Plan your audio recording as carefully as you plan your camera work. Use the best sound equipment you can manage. And, above all, get the best sound recordist you can find. A poor one can make a day's shooting worthless through unusable sound. A good one can make your documentary come alive!

17

WORKING ON LOCATION

I've always thought that one of the most exciting and interesting titles for a book or movie—and it was both—was Irwin Shaw's *Two Weeks in Another Town*. It holds out the promise of something new and different, and the possibility of adventure.

That's working on location.

Most documentaries are made on location because that's where the action is. The location, of course, may be a house down the street or a wildlife preserve halfway around the world. And working on location is not at all like shooting in your own backyard or studio. Fortunately, the kinds of people who make documentaries are the kinds of people who tend to work on location anyway.

PREPARATION

When you go on location, you have to bring just about everything you'll need with you. Don't expect the people at the location to provide anything more than electricity for your lights. And if there's any doubt about that, you'll need to bring along a generator or arrange for an independent hookup from the electric company.

Carry spares of hard-to-get and easy-to-use-up items, such as fuses, batteries, clips, and clamps. You should have a comprehensive supply of audio and video connectors and adapters.

Unless you have a makeup artist on the crew, you should always bring along a basic makeup kit—a sewing kit and scissors, too—just in case.

Know where the crew is going to live, where you'll eat your first few meals, and where and how you'll handle lunch when shooting.

Have your local transportation arrangements made. I prefer a couple of cars or station wagons to one large van. That way the equipment vehicle can stay at the shooting location while your gofer or driver uses the other to run errands, pick up lunch, and so on. At an out-of-town location, give serious thought to hiring a driver/gofer/production assistant who knows the local area.

BE A GOOD VISITOR

Be careful about such things as where to park, observing no smoking rules, not trampling the flowers, and cleaning up the area after you have finished shooting.

If you've borrowed furniture or props from other rooms, put them back where they were. Leave the location the way you found it.

Be sure you have adequate liability insurance to cover any possible damage you may do in the location. You never know—lights fall down, furniture gets scarred, shrubbery gets mangled, and you have to be prepared. You also *must* be covered in case someone gets injured.

Almost certainly you will blow a circuit breaker or a fuse at some point. Plan for it. Locate the fuse box or circuit breaker panel ahead of time. And know how to contact an electrician if things go wrong.

Stay on schedule. And if you can't, for some reason, let everyone know that you are running behind and will probably be making changes to the schedule.

In the next several chapters we'll be looking at your relationship to the people at the location. Briefly, it should always be professional, thoughtful, and cordial.

TIME OFF WHILE ON LOCATION

Theoretically, you and the crew have off the time between the end of one day's shooting and the start of the next. In practice, the crew gets this time off while the documentary producer-director has a hundred and one things to do, from looking at the day's footage to setting up additional shooting, to putting together the shooting schedule.

Remember that almost everything about making a documentary takes longer than you hope it will. And it's stressful. You'll burn up a lot more energy through the intense concentration and long hours required during shooting than you may be used to. You need to be in good physical shape to go on location. And you need relaxed meals and a good night's sleep to keep in shape. So don't try to do too much.

Have a clear understanding with the crew ahead of time about how long the working day will be and what is and isn't included. You should expect them to get breakfast before you start the day's work and dinner after you wrap. But if you've got a split day, running into a night shoot, then work out an agreement as to when you'll be working and when the crew will get meals and rest. And stick to it.

CLIENTS, FRIENDS, AND FAMILY

Shooting on location is hard enough without adding a lot of other problems. If you're going out of town and the location is in or near a city where you have other clients or other business, there may be a temptation to try to schedule business meetings while you are there. If you can do so after the obligation to your documentary is complete, fine. But don't get yourself into the position of trying to rush shooting so you won't keep an important client waiting.

By the same token, if the location is attractive as a place to visit, you may be tempted to bring along family or friends to enjoy it with you. If you do, make it clear that they will be on their own and that they may not see you from the time you arrive until it's time to go.

You never want to find yourself in the editing room wishing you'd gone ahead and shot one more take or filmed the piece of business you'd had in mind but gave up because it was getting late and you had someone waiting for you. Remember that the real excitement of going on location is in the work—and the work is very demanding.

18

BUILDING AN
INVISIBLE WALL

In his excellent book on the documentary movement of the 1960s, *The New Documentary in Action*, Alan Rosenthal profiles the intimate portrait of a marriage in Alan King's documentary *A Married Couple*. The film was shot over ten weeks, mainly in the couple's home. Richard Leiterman, photographer and associate director, tells how they handled filming in such an intimate situation for such a long time:

> We went in with a kind of ground rule that we would have no communication with them nor would they communicate anything to us. We put up an invisible barrier between us. . . . If we came at any time, they were not to act surprised or to change what they were doing to something else, and they would not make any exception to what they were doing just because of our presence. (p. 46)

And King, who directed the documentary, comments on making a film about friends:

> We established also that, while we were all friends and knew each other, it wouldn't work if we had dinner with

them, or if Antoinette was obliged to make coffee or provide the kind of hospitality one normally extends to people in one's house. We decided to dispense with all this and to avoid conversation with Bill and Antoinette as much as possible, so that interactions of that kind wouldn't interfere with our ability to observe and record. (pp. 26–27)

Not every documentary of behavior is a protracted study of whatever happens in the lives of two people, as in A Married Couple, or in the life of a family as it goes through various crises, as in that magnificent, controversial, often flawed tour de force documentary series An American Family, or even in the lives of the various members of an entire community, as in Herbert Smith's Mayan documentary.

DOCUMENTARY SITUATIONS

Most of us, most of the time, will be working on less ambitious, if no less worthy projects than those mentioned above. So it is probably worthwhile to examine some different documentary situations, and how they will affect when, where, and how you place the invisible wall.

Just an Interview

In some cases, all you actually want from the shooting situation is an interview with someone. That means someone representing you and the audience is going to conduct the interview. Nevertheless, you want the answers to the interview questions, the way the questions are answered, and the reaction of the person being interviewed to be as spontaneous as possible. I try to do interviews in a location where the subject will be comfortable—which usually means on his or her home ground—and that will be visually interesting for the documentary.

This means we may intervene in the subject's life to the extent of setting a place for the interview, deciding who is to sit or stand, and where, checking lighting, and even wiring the subject with a lavaliere microphone. But once these preparations are completed, the invisible wall goes up. From then on, no one gives the subject stage directions and no one talks to the subject except the designated interviewer.

Filming Specific Behavior

Sometimes you are looking for certain kinds of behavior. In making A Young Child Is . . . , we wanted to show certain kinds of development and learning in very young children of different ages. Ideally, we might have spent four or five years tracking the progress of several kids from birth to school age. And I'm still willing to do that if anyone wants to put up the money. But in this case, time and budget forced us to select several children of different ages and try to record them in situations in which we thought their behavior would be significant.

Most of the time this meant discussing the kinds of things we would be looking for with the children's parents, and planning the shooting schedule around events that would naturally occur in the lives of the children. We decided what we were going to film, and where. Sometimes we discussed with the parents what would probably be happening, so we'd know where to set lights and the best probable camera location to start with. But this was always done on the basis of, "You tell us where you want to be, and we'll figure out how to shoot it."

We rejected all suggestions from the parents that they could have the child do whatever it was in some other location that would be more convenient for us, or that they alter the process in some way that they thought might make things easier or better for us. This was always the first step in putting up the invisible wall. The parent would make the suggestion. I would ask, "Where (or how) would this normally be done?" They'd tell me. And I'd say, "Then we won't change it. We'll shoot it normally." Once that was made clear, it was relatively easy to put the invisible wall firmly in place for shooting.

Documenting an Event or a Process

Sometimes you are documenting an event or a process, and the *specific* behavior of the people involved in the process is less important than just being certain that *whatever* behavior occurs is valid and spontaneous. This can often be the easiest kind of situation for the behavioral documentarian, because you can claim, with absolute honesty, that you are just interested in shooting whatever happens. And the invisible wall goes up with no problem.

There are exceptions, of course, and you have to deal with them as they come up. There are always the people who will stop in front of the camera and ask when this will be on TV, or what channel you are from. They are usually no real problem, and someone from the crew can take them aside, answer their questions, briefly, and move them out of the way.

There are muggers and show-offs, and you handle them as best you can. Often it's enough just to point the camera in their direction for a few seconds, even if you're not shooting at the time. But this can backfire, especially with teenagers, if they go tell their friends they were "on TV," and all the friends show up mugging and yelling, "Hey, mistah, take my pitchah!"

You have to be sensitive to what's going on. Sometimes you may get a sense that the whole thing is being staged for the benefit of the camera. When that happens, if it seems relevant and might fit into your documentary, you may want to capture some show-off behavior.

Or you may just decide to go home.

My Favorite Muggers

The most delightful muggers I ever filmed were some very young Puerto Rican kids who found me with a camera on my shoulder and wouldn't let me go.

I was shooting at a day-care center for the children of migrant farmworkers. All the kids were outside, and I was shooting them at play. A five-year-old boy appeared in the frame and immediately sat down. Within seconds he was joined by a half dozen other kids, all sitting, all smiling. No sooner would I point the camera in another direction than the little boy appeared again, soon to be joined by the others, all sitting still on the ground and smiling at the camera. I can only assume that these kids had no experience with motion media, but had learned that if they wanted their pictures taken, they were to sit still and smile.

This went on for about ten minutes, until it seemed to me that the little boy had somehow figured out where I would decide to point the camera next, and was getting there ahead of me. I finally had to quit shooting for a while, until the kids got interested in playing in the sandbox, and then I walked all the way across the playground to an older group of children before I began filming again.

There was no way I could work that two hundred feet of film into the final version of *Season for Learning*, but I still have it, and I treasure it as an example of some delightful, spontaneous behavior for which I have never found a use.

You Have to Do It

It sounds easy, but it takes a lot of self-control to keep putting up the invisible wall and to maintain it. But you have to keep doing it, because its existence is really the only answer you have to the critics who question whether anything done in front of a documentary crew can be *real* and to the people who believe that only footage shot with a hidden camera is valid evidence of behavior.

TEMPTATIONS

Nevertheless, there are many ways in which a documentary crew trying to make an honest record of the behavior which occurs before their camera may be tempted to break through the invisible wall between them and the people whose behavior they are recording.

Interesting People Are Interesting

The people you are shooting are probably interesting in some way, or they wouldn't have been chosen to be in your documentary. The temptation is always present to try to get to know them better, off camera, than you do on camera. And there's nothing wrong with that, once the documentary is finished.

When I started making documentaries, I thought it was a nice idea to take the people we were recording out to dinner after the day's shooting was finished. I don't do that anymore—at least not until the end of the last day of shooting. Take the school principal I mentioned in chapter four whom I tried to interview for *Schools for Children*. It was at dinner the night before we were to film him that he spoke so eloquently about open education. Possibly, if we had not discussed it in detail in advance, I'd have gotten a better interview the next day.

Filming Friends

The people you are recording may actually be friends already. And it's hard to remain aloof just because you're filming them. Getting it settled in advance, as King and Leiterman did in shooting *A Married Couple*, can help. Each shooting situation is different, and your behavior and that of your crew must be guided by the goals of the documentary and your purpose in shooting the scene.

You have to construct the invisible wall as high and as wide as the situation requires. And it's up to you to maintain it. Your subjects will take the cue for their own behavior from the way *you* behave. If you stay on your side of the invisible wall, they'll stay on theirs.

Showing Off and Apologizing

For relatively inexperienced documentarians there are the twin temptations of showing off while you're working and of apologizing when things don't go according to plan.

The people you are filming assume that you know what you're doing and how to do it. In fact, when you walk through the door with a crew and a lot of expensive equipment, they assume that you know everything there is to know about every aspect of video and film production. This can be a problem if you let them draw you into answering a lot of questions about the last movie they saw, how special effects are done, and the private lives of the people in Hollywood. That just becomes a kind of showing off.

But the presumption that you know what you are doing can work for you when you have technical problems or something or other starts to go wrong. Generally there is no need to explain what has happened, let alone apologize for it, to the people you're shooting. Actually, it's when you allow yourself to show off by playing an expert that you then feel some compulsion to explain or apologize when things don't go perfectly. Instead, just stay on your side of the wall.

The best way to show off is just to do the job you came to do in a thoroughly professional manner. If you've prepared carefully for the shoot, briefed your crew thoroughly, and allowed plenty of time to get the job done—including time to solve the problems that inevitably crop up—then you won't have to apologize for anything.

Accepting Hospitality

What about accepting the hospitality of your subjects? It's hard to refuse a cup of coffee when it's already made, or a piece of pie when it's sitting out and being sliced, but if you accept that, where then do you draw the line?

There's a scene in one of the episodes of *An American Family* in which it is clear that Pat Loud and her mother are the only people in the house—except, of course, for the film crew. But one of the women makes cocktails and pours them into *three* glasses. Who is the third drink for? Pat has one. Her mother has one. So it must be for some member of the production crew. That's a mighty big crack in the invisible wall. Unless it is explained on film—which it wasn't—it alters for all time the way in which we understand the behavior of the people in the scene in relation to the documentarians showing us that behavior.

Adapting to Fit the Filming Process

The temptation to try to bend behavior to fit the filming process—and the catastrophic results which that can produce—has been amply described in the story of the Wilkes-Barre police captain in chapter four. It can be a perfectly natural error, especially for a crew accustomed to working with professional actors. Still, there can be only one solution for the documentarian: *never do it.* The moment you ask the people you are recording to be concerned about your production problems, you have torn down the barrier completely, and made your subjects part of your crew.

Getting Things Moving

There is often a powerful temptation to try to get things moving when nothing seems to be happening. Don't do it. The moment you start suggesting something to do, you remove the only element that makes the behavioral documentary worth all the time and effort—the spontaneity of the people you're recording.

Even worse than that, however, is the temptation to move into a power vacuum when one occurs in a project or event you are documenting and try to take charge of the whole thing. Avoiding this may take the most self-control of all. A documentarian is experienced at organizing people and equipment for a specific purpose and is a person who has learned how to make decisions. And sometimes the process or event that you are documenting is being run by people with neither of those skills. If you are documenting the behavior of the people involved in the everyday operation of a project, you may actually spend more time with them and get to know more about what they are doing and how they feel about it than the people who are supposed to be in charge.

Nevertheless, the value of documenting a project in process with the end in doubt is just that—that the outcome is uncertain, and the process itself will determine how it all comes out. If you can't make a commitment to documenting the process honestly and accepting the outcome, no matter what it is, then you shouldn't try to shoot it as a behavioral documentary.

Don't Let the Crew Take Over

Finally, don't let your crew take over. This can be a temptation if you are fairly inexperienced as a director and are working with a professional crew. It can be caused by neglect, if you have failed to brief the crew properly. Or it can be the result of a series of bad decisions, perhaps out of a desire not to rock the boat, as happened to me in Wilkes-Barre.

If you're the director, the final decision is always up to you. Some crews will give you everything they've got, all day long and into the evening, and some will spend an enormous amount of effort trying to convince you that the easy way is the best way.

Take charge. And remember the advice of an old director to a young man who was going to direct his first shoot. "If it takes digging a trench to get the shot," he said, "then dig a trench."

WHAT ABOUT A HIDDEN CAMERA?

The question of using a hidden camera often comes up in the initial stages of planning a behavioral documentary. And the more interested you are in the behavior of people, the more likely it is to arise, and the tougher it will be to dispose of. Someone will always want to know if you don't think it's a good idea to shoot the documentary with a hidden camera.

Hidden cameras can be a lot of fun, as the programs "Candid Camera," "Totally Hidden Videos," and others have proven since the early days of television. But the use of a hidden camera in shooting a documentary is rarely practical, often impossible, usually unnecessary, and probably unethical.

Problems with Hiding the Camera

The obvious problem with the use of a hidden camera is that you have to hide it. However you do that—by placing it behind a one-way mirror, by camouflaging it to look like something that would naturally be in the setting, by shooting through a peephole in an adjacent wall, or by concealing the camera in a vehicle—you have given up the one great advantage of modern equipment: its portability. Essentially you have gone back to the shooting situation used in Hollywood during the early days of sound films—locking the camera away in a separate room, so that the action in the scene has to come to the camera, instead of the camera following the action.

A normal lens covers an arc of about twenty-four degrees. That means a locked-off, hidden camera with a normal lens can record only one-fifteenth of the activity available to a portable camera placed in the center of the action and able to point anywhere. Going to a wide angle lens might double the viewing arc, but the increased viewing angle is gained at the loss of detail. So much for facial expression and subtle nuances of behavior.

Even if the camera is placed behind a one-way mirror or the equivalent, so that a camera operator can point it more or less anywhere within a 180-degree radius, you're still shooting from a fixed position. You can change focal length, you can follow focus, you can pan and zoom, but you can't change camera angle. If someone is standing with his back to the camera, you're going to spend your shooting time getting pictures of the back of his head and the texture of his shirt. If someone moves in close to the camera position, so that his body covers your field of view, you're out of business until he moves away.

Lighting Problems

The second problem with a hidden camera concerns lighting. If you're shooting outside in daylight, you're probably okay. But few films of human behavior can limit themselves to exterior shooting.

Which means you're going to have to shoot under artificial lighting at some point.

The ambient lighting in most public buildings and offices with even illumination from overhead fluorescent lights generally falls within a range of about sixteen to forty footcandles. In homes and other informal settings it may be much less. This may be enough to get a *legible* image on videotape or with very fast film stock, but the quality of the light may not be very good. It may be a mixture of daylight and tungsten light. And it may be way out of balance for good pictures.

In low light you'll have to use a fairly wide open aperture, resulting in a narrow range in which the picture is in focus. This is because the depth of field of any lens decreases as the size of the aperture increases. Depth of field also decreases as the focal length of the lens increases. So as you move from a wide angle to a longer focal length to frame a two-shot or a close-up, you again have a very narrow range in which the image will be in focus.

Therefore, if you want your pictures in focus—and that's the point to the exercise, isn't it?—you have to have enough light to shoot by. If you bring in enough lights to raise the ambient light in the room to a hundred footcandles or more, there's hardly any point in hiding the camera.

Yes, you can go to faster film, and yes, some video cameras can shoot in extreme low-light situations. But you don't get something for nothing. In general, you'll have to accept some loss of image quality to work with low-light video or ultrafast film.

The point, of course, is not whether it can be done—"Candid Camera" proved it can years ago, when a lot more light was needed than today—but whether it is worth the extra effort and the sacrifice of mobility and image quality just to fool the subjects of your film into believing there is no camera present.

Ethical Problems

Another problem with the use of a hidden camera falls within the not very well defined area of image ethics. Clearly, our society still frowns on invasion of privacy. Deliberate eavesdropping is a social no-no. And filming someone without his or her knowledge or consent—or even simply observing someone, whether you are recording or not—is deliberate eavesdropping. At some point you have to come out of your hiding place and admit you've been filming. And at some point you have to ask the person to sign a release so that you can show the footage you shot.

When do you do that? At the end of the day's shooting? But suppose you want to come back to shoot in that location again. Suppose the footage you got is so good you want more. Suppose you want to shoot some of the people again but not all of them. Do you ask the ones you won't need anymore to keep the secret from the others? Suppose they refuse. What do you do then?

If anyone in the scene you've shot from hiding refuses to sign a release, you can't use the footage. That's it. Do you keep shooting, piling up expensive days and a lot of videotape or film, in the hope that everyone will agree, later on, that the project is worthwhile? Could you find a sponsor to fund a documentary project under such conditions?

And do we have the right to observe and record what someone does when he thinks he is alone? That's a tough question to try to answer. The one thing I'm certain of is that the ethical resolution turns on what the person believes the situation to be, not on what he was doing while we were observing.

"Candid Camera" and its successors get away with filming from hiding just because they are, primarily, big practical jokes. And a joke is one of the few acceptable ways to violate social rules. Even so, I'm sure that some people they filmed failed to see the humor, and at the very least refused to sign a release. But these programs are prepared to shoot many, many setups to get a few scenes that can be used on television.

No Real Need

Actually, I've never felt the need to use a hidden camera. The powerful images of *Chronicle of a Summer* or *Brother's Keeper* or

The War Room, all shot with cameras in the open, have convinced me that there is no advantage to hiding away. I've viewed videotapes of psychotherapy and family therapy sessions shot both with a concealed camera and with a small camera mounted in sight but out of the way, and I saw no difference in the behavior of the subjects.

And I've seen films such as Ed Mason's *Referred for Underachievement*, in which the camera operator sat in a chair right in front of the members of a family during an initial intake interview for family therapy. Again, there was no difference in the kinds of behavior recorded by the hidden and the obvious camera. But there was a big difference in the kind of documentary that resulted. The footage shot by an active, participating, decision-making documentarian working in the open was better because of the freedom to capture the best images possible.

One Final Reason

The final reason I'm against using a hidden camera is that I've always been more than a little suspicious of the motives of the people who have suggested it. A very thin line separates the behavioral scientist from the Peeping Tom. I grew up in the tradition of the social documentary, in which there are often good guys and bad guys. I've always wanted to be on the side of the good guys.

And good guys don't shoot from hiding.

. . . .

19

DIRECTING PEOPLE
WHO ARE NOT ACTORS

As the previous chapter showed, when you are recording behavior, your function as the director is mainly to convince the people in front of the camera that you will *not* direct them—that whatever they do is absolutely okay with you.

But not all documentaries are concerned with human behavior. There are productions in which the primary concern is to document and explain events, processes, and ideas. There are training films and tapes. There are reports on everything from scientific investigations to the release of new industrial or consumer products. And any of these can call for people who are not actors to appear on camera.

The decision to use people who are not actors may occasionally be a matter of budget—by the time you've accounted for the cost of crew, equipment, stock, and incidental expenses, there just doesn't seem to be any money left over to pay actors. The problem with that kind of budgeting decision is that it can turn out to be false economy. The cost in crew and equipment time while you try to get a decent reading out of an unpaid amateur can often turn out to be several times as much as you would have spent to hire an actor in the first place.

But usually you find yourself working with people who are not actors for the very basic reason that they can do whatever it is they do better than an actor can. In a training film about trucks, for instance, an actor who can speak lines but can't drive an eighteen-wheeler just won't do. Or sometimes it is this person—who is not an actor—that the documentary is about.

Directing people who are not actors requires a production plan that recognizes the value of these people as well as their limitations. A good shooting plan will emphasize their strengths—the things that they know how to do, the things that they are able to talk about—but won't call for them to act. You are the professional, and the situation requires you, as the director, to do a lot more than just check lighting and set camera angles.

HOLD AUDITIONS

Unless you're stuck with the company president, or *must* include the director of research in your documentary, try people out.

I once had to borrow a school and shoot a film about a seventh-grade class in the middle of July. I had hired a professional actress to play the teacher—she had a lot of lines to say—but I also needed a class for her to teach. We got kids for the film by putting an ad in the local paper, asking anyone interested in being in the film to show up at the school Friday morning. Mostly we needed spear-carriers—kids to sit in the seats and look like a class. But there were a few speaking parts where the kids had to appear to be involved in classroom activities.

So I had each youngster practice the single toughest line in the script, and then deliver it in front of the rest of the "class." I figured that anyone who got nervous in front of a bunch of other kids would never make it in front of a camera. In a short time I had gone through twenty-five boys and girls and found out who was going to giggle, who was going to freeze up, and who wouldn't talk above a whisper. I also had a handful of kids who could say the line as if they meant it. And they were just fine, in short scenes, over two days of work.

I hadn't left everything to chance, however. In case I needed someone to say a specific line, I had brought along my own kids who had been drafted into appearing in my films, and those of my students, even before they could walk. Sure enough, there was one bit that caused trouble. It involved a boy taking a survey, who was asking questions of a girl.

BOY: How old do you think you should be to get married?
GIRL: Forty-two.
BOY: Are you kidding?
GIRL: Are you proposing?

None of the local boys seemed to be able to play that scene without breaking up—perhaps because they knew the girls and it was just too close to home. So I used one of my sons, and the scene went off perfectly. Interestingly, none of the girls had any trouble at all in auditioning for this scene, even when they auditioned with the local boys.

Audition for Interviews

When all you want is an interview, the principle remains the same: Find the people who will do well and eliminate the ones who won't. Videotape the auditions, if you can. At the very least, audiotape them. A person who freezes up in front of a tape recorder will probably become catatonic when the lights come on and the camera starts to roll. If you can't videotape, make some still pictures to see if the camera will reveal hidden beards or bulges.

YOU HAVE TO BE THE PROFESSIONAL

Your contract with people who are not actors is that you will not abuse their amateur standing. Right from the start, it is up to you to keep them confident and secure.

Keep Technical Manipulations to a Minimum

Sure, you've got to set the lights and check the sound. Just don't make a big deal about it. Tell the people you're using that it's going to take a few minutes to get set up. Let them go for coffee, or go into another office to get some work done while you get ready. Or let them stay on the set and watch. But don't keep them waiting in place while you fiddle around.

Prepare for Sound Checks

Have something ready for the person to say when you go to set the audio level on the recorder. "Mary Had a Little Lamb" is good—everybody knows it. Or give the person something written out that he or she can read. If it's an interview, let the interviewer get in place and ask a few innocuous questions about football, family, or fashions—just something to keep the person talking—but *never* the real interview questions.

And recognize that rigging a lavaliere microphone can be a potential moment of embarrassment for people who are not used to having it done to them. Most sound recordists have developed a deft touch that lets them tape a tiny lavaliere to a woman's skin under her blouse in a totally asexual way. But while they're doing it is no time for the crew to watch and make jokes.

Grooming

Even if you don't have a makeup artist on the crew, give your subjects a chance to check their grooming before you shoot. Provide a mirror of decent size if you are on location away from restrooms and dressing rooms.

Keep the Lighting Soft, Simple, and Easy on the Eyes

Try to avoid hot lights. Actors have to learn how to live with the lights. People who are not actors don't. I use soft lights or umbrellas whenever possible to keep the set cooler and avoid harsh light in the subjects' eyes.

Don't keep people under the lights too long. Call a break when you have to change lighting or tinker with the technology. Light the entire area the subjects will be working in, so that if they have to move—or want to move—they can.

Be Reassuring

Above all, use a good crew that can work around the people you are filming without threatening them or distracting them.

Use Audiotape Lavishly

In a film situation where the subject is explaining, describing, or demonstrating something, I may do extensive audio recording, off camera, getting the subject to tell his or her story completely. Audiotape is cheap. I'm not worrying about the cost of the interview—as I might be if expensive film were running through the camera while the subject circled around the point of the interview without ever getting to it—so I'm relaxed, and the subject eventually relaxes and starts to talk.

I may do the same thing if I'm shooting video, without telling the subject that the camera is actually running.

In effect, the subject is rehearsing what to say before we shoot the interview. And I've gotten plenty of good sound to use as off-camera explanation if the interview on-camera goes badly.

When I do this, especially with a nervous subject, I'll often have the camera in position, lights on, and everything ready to go. When I've gotten all the audio I want, I'll surreptitiously signal the camera operator to start shooting. At the same time, I'll say to the subject, "Now I'd like to go over what you said about such and such. How does that work again?" The interview simply continues, and quite often the person doesn't realize he or she has been talking for the camera until I call for a tail slate.

Use Tail Slates

Whether or not you do an audio preinterview, consider using tail slates on your sound takes when you're shooting film. This is particularly useful when the subject is doing a demonstration or is otherwise involved in some activity that may require several takes. Otherwise, just as you start shooting, if the subject hears, "Scene fifty-four, take thirteen," he'll be convinced he's done it wrong the previous twelve times. And you stand a good chance of having him freeze up.

ACTING NATURAL

Remember that acting natural on command is the hardest thing in the world to do. It is almost impossible to get a person who is not an actor to walk, sit, or gesture naturally when asked to. So don't ask. If you must have someone enter a room and sit in a chair, don't tell them that's what they're doing. Just say, "Go over to your desk and get to work." They know what that means.

When working with people who are not actors, remember that whatever the person does in the scene is always right. If it isn't what you want, *you* have to work out the problem. It is *never* the subject's responsibility.

Here's the difference between professionals and people who are not actors. I was recording a narration track, using an experienced professional narrator. The way he was reading one line bothered me. I knew it wasn't right, but I couldn't quite explain what was wrong—or what I wanted. Finally, I asked him to give me some variations on the line. He read it a half dozen different ways, putting the emphasis in different places, making his voice go up one time, down the next, and so on. Eventually I heard exactly what I wanted and told him, "That's it." As a pro, he was able to replicate that reading exactly through several more takes.

But you can't expect that from someone who is not an actor. You have to come up with specific, nonacting directions. For example, if you need more time in the shot of the person crossing the room and sitting in the chair, you might have to say, "Go over and get the daily schedule from Mike's desk, then go to your desk and get to work."

Don't Forget the Background

You can get to concentrating so hard on the one or two people you're working with right in front of the camera that you forget there are other people and other things that are—or should be—visible elsewhere in the scene. If there are people back there who are busy doing something, fine. But be sure they know to stay busy. It can be pretty disheartening for a director finally to get a perfect take of the action in the foreground, only to realize that all the people in the background stopped what they were doing to watch.

The purpose of the documentary you are shooting will determine how far you go in manipulating the situation. For a behavioral documentary, you set up the invisible wall early and keep it in place. Whatever happens in the background happens, and is part of the scene. For a training film, you may need a combination of documenting behavior and shooting preplanned shots.

For some kinds of shots you may want to dress the set with some extras. For example, for a health education video I needed a shot of a person having blood drawn for a blood test. I wanted to shoot it right in the laboratory for verisimilitude. But the chair where the person sat was against an uninteresting black wall.

By moving the chair to camera left a foot or so, however, we could now look beyond the person having blood drawn into another part of the lab where there was a receiving counter and some telephones. One end of the counter was partially blocked by a wall. As I was setting up the shot, a woman who was standing and talking on the phone but who had been hidden by the wall took a step backward so that she came into view. It was a nice piece of business, and I incorporated it into the scene. I told her to stand so that she was hidden by the wall and when she heard me say, "Action," she was to count two seconds and take a step backwards. That was all. But it added immensely to the verisimilitude of the scene. Even in this case, I wasn't really asking the woman to *act*. Beyond counting, "One one thousand, two one thousand," she was simply doing something she did all the time.

Record Your Rehearsals

People who are not actors tend to peak early and then lose their enthusiasm. It can often happen that you'll get the best take the first time they try the scene. When I'm working with videotape, I record everything. Tape is cheap. With film, some compromise may be necessary. But since I tend to work in short takes with people who are not actors, it usually isn't a strain on the budget to shoot the rehearsal as take one. I tell the subjects that this is a rehearsal for the camera. That way, they go through the business of the scene without feeling camera shy. Then, when they find out I've shot the rehearsal, they're often relieved. The pressure of doing it right for the camera the first time has been eliminated, and we can go on and do several more takes with no problem. Even so, it often turns out that the first take is the one that is used in the final production.

SEVEN DEADLY SINS

I originally listed these as seven deadly sins in working with people who are not actors. But, with the exception of the first one, they're really ways you can get in trouble regardless of whether you're working with volunteer amateurs or professional actors.

One: Treating Amateurs as Actors

The essence of amateur volunteers is that they are not actors. So don't ask them to memorize long speeches, to emote, or, in short, to act. Set up a situation in which they can behave naturally. If they must speak lines, keep the lines short and shoot them in short takes.

Two: Failure to Explain What You're Doing and How Long It Will Take

All producers have a tendency to underestimate the amount of time it will take to shoot a scene, and then to shave it a little more when asking for volunteers to be in the production. Even when you are working with paid actors, common courtesy demands a realistic explanation of the task and the time it will take.

Three: Failure to Discuss Wardrobe and Makeup

We're gradually getting past the day of the TV-blue shirt, but checks and patterned fabrics still cause moiré patterns on video and some colors will bleed in VHS dubs. Makeup is a matter of individual taste, but it should be discussed. Dark beards and transparent skin still cause problems on film that could be helped with a shave and some makeup.

Four: Putting Pressure on the Person

A friend of mine, a physician, was asked to make a statement in a film about patient treatment. Just before the scene was shot, the director said, "We're almost out of film, so we have to do this right." Of course the doctor fluffed a line, and the director blew up. But being low on film was the director's problem, and he had no right to put the pressure, or the blame, on my friend.

Similarly, failure to explain that retakes have to be made for technical reasons may make people wonder if they've done something wrong.

Five: Stopping the Process to Get Them to Do It "Right"

Anything that calls attention to people who are not actors is another way of putting pressure on them for a performance. If they fluff a line, assure them that it's all right, you'll pick it up in the close-up. If they stumble when they enter the room, tell them not to worry, you want to shoot it again from a different angle.

Most professionals will stop when they go up on a line and immediately get ready to shoot another take. In fact, sometimes when they don't like a reading, they'll deliberately fluff a line so you won't use that take. But even with professionals, it's best to keep the pressure off and maintain an attitude of "We're getting closer, and you can do it."

Calling attention to errors just tends to magnify them, until it is the error that the person remembers, not the way to do it right.

Six: Letting the Crew Take Over

When the crew starts to give directions to the people you are recording, you're in trouble. By all means discuss the scene thoroughly with your crew and ask them to bring up any potential technical problems. Make sure the crew understands that when something goes wrong, they are to talk to you, and you'll decide what to say to the talent—regardless of whether you are using a professional or an amateur. It may be that you've been working with your on-camera person, very carefully, building toward something you know you've almost got. That's not the time to burden him or her with a technical something-or-other from your camera operator or sound recordist.

There can be only one director on any shoot. Keep it that way.

Seven: Concentrating on Your Needs Instead of Concentrating on How to Get What You Want from the Person You're Directing

Even a professional actor won't give you what you want just because you want it. That's what directing is all about. With a person who is not an actor it's even more important to make no demands and to find a way to get the person to do what you want—naturally and unselfconsciously.

LEARN FROM WORKING WITH CHILDREN

Kids can be totally natural, completely spontaneous, and absolutely gorgeous on film or videotape. I really enjoy working with children. Some directors don't, probably because they see working with kids as a problem rather than as a creative challenge. Here are some of the things I've learned in shooting nonfiction films and tapes with children:

- Be sure they have something to do. A child working on something he or she is interested in will forget the camera. One with nothing to do will mug.
- Keep them absorbed in what they're doing, even if what they're doing is acting in a film. Tell them stories about the part they're playing, explain your technical problems, but keep them interested. Do all you can to treat them as collaborators, not furniture.
- Show them your equipment and explain what you're going to do when you start shooting. They're interested in the production as much as they care about their parts in it. But if you haven't explained what is going to happen, they'll sneak looks at the camera while you're recording.
- Audition for speaking parts. Find out who can talk—and is willing to.
- Never talk down to kids. Assume that they are intelligent people with a sizable amount of experience with the world. Talk with them exactly as you would with adults and explain anything they don't understand.
- Never lose your temper, or you'll lose your actors. Most kids will want to be in the production and will want to cooperate with you. If they don't, get rid of them.
- Be alert for signs of restlessness. When otherwise cooperative kids start to fool around, talk among themselves, or become annoying, they're probably either bored or tired.
- Never keep kids working too long. Keep lots of snacks on hand.

Call frequent breaks. Let the kids relax while you change
setups.
- Let them do it their way as well as your way. In my first
experience filming children, I used my then-five-year-old son
to play the part of a child playing in an abandoned amuse-
ment park. I had an idea of what a kid might do with the
abandoned equipment. But so did he. So I had to film him
doing it his way before he would do it my way. When we cut
the film, we used all the takes that were his way. They were
better.
- Keep their speeches short, unless you're doing an interview or
having the child explain something in his or her own words. A
few words are easy to remember and don't call for much
acting.
- Cover the scene with several takes—master scene plus close-
ups of each speaker. Shoot the entire scene each time. You can
then edit around fluffs and other mistakes. And by shooting
close-ups of each speaker, you'll have natural reaction shots
without *acting*.

Finally, if this makes sense when you're working with kids, then
it's a pretty good set of instructions for working with adults, and
especially adults who are not actors. We're all a bit like children
when we get into a new situation. And for most of the people you'll
be working with, being in a documentary is definitely a new situation. If you treat them with the courtesy, kindness, consideration,
and patience you would extend to children, you'll find that working
with people who are not actors can be a lot of fun and can result in
excellent footage that could be gotten in no other way.

20

WHEN YOU MUST WORK
WITH ACTORS

The small-crew behavioral documentarian never sees an actor, except for the occasional brief appearance of an on-camera host or spokesperson. But when you are making a historical documentary or reenactment, you'll need to use actors.

CASTING

Where do the actors come from?

In general, when you begin trying to cast actors, you have your choice of three different approaches:

- using a casting director
- using the services of one or more talent agencies
- doing it all yourself

Casting on your own is too difficult and too time-consuming. It's better to turn to an expert.

Using a Casting Director

My preference is to use a casting director. This is a person who keeps up-to-date files on the actors and models available in your locale. You pay the casting director to work for you—either on a daily or hourly rate, or on a flat fee for the production.

The casting director has no special loyalty to any specific actors or talent agencies and can call on anyone, from anywhere, to audition for a part.

The casting director should know something about the work experience of any talent you are interested in and tell you the bad along with the good.

The casting director should know what is a fair rate to pay for the talent you want and should help in negotiating with the talent or his or her agent. In this way, the casting director works for you just as a talent agent works for the actor. The casting director may be able to leverage a better rate for your production than you could yourself, simply because you may represent only an occasional opportunity for the talent to work, but the casting director represents a continuous flow of jobs.

Using a Talent Agency

In most metropolitan areas, you'll find a list of talent agencies in the phone book. In my town they're in the Yellow Pages under "Modeling Agencies," "Professional Talent Management," and "Theatrical Agencies." There are also some schools for models and actors—which may be run by a talent agency—listed under "Dramatic Instruction" or "Modeling Schools." These are always a potential source of talent for your productions.

Like a casting director, the agency will make all those phone calls to line up talent for an audition. But unlike a casting director, an agency usually will not make any direct charge to you for its services. It gets paid a commission by the talent you hire. However, if the agency supplies special services, such as videotaping auditions, there may be a charge for these. Ask.

In my opinion, using a talent agency is far better than trying to set up your own casting department. But there are drawbacks.

One is that every agency likes to give its newcomers experience. Not just experience in front of the camera, but experience in an

audition. So you may find that in order to see the few really quali-
fied candidates for a part, you have to sit through some poor auditions by inexperienced neophytes.

The agency may not have people for all the parts you want to
cast. So you face a choice between accepting someone who is not
quite what you had in mind or starting all over with another
agency.

An agency casting session won't tell you much about an actor's
overall experience or how he or she will do on the set as you go
through take after take. Unlike a casting director, the agency will
want to play up each actor's assets and minimize any liabilities.

AUDITIONS

You may rely on the talent agent or casting director to select a pool
of actors for you to consider for the parts you need to cast. But the
decision as to whom to cast in what part remains yours. Unless you
are thoroughly familiar with each actor's capabilities, you'll want to
hold a casting session or audition. The casting director or talent
agency may provide facilities for the audition and may offer to
videotape the auditions for you. In any event, for a casting session
you'll need:

- a room big enough for the candidates to move about in with
  chairs or other furniture to simulate the set
- a waiting room, outside the audition room, for the other candidates
- sufficient copies of the script for all those being auditioned to
  have their own copy for study ahead of time—obviously, you
  don't need to give them a full script, just a page or two with
  the scene to be auditioned
- props as required by the scene, including costume props, such
  as a cape or large hat

You'll need some kind of an evaluation system. This could be
just a tablet on which you write each actor's name and your notes

about the performance. Or it could be a more formal set of evaluation criteria.

Videotaping Auditions

I'm a firm believer in videotaping auditions. You get a chance to see how the talent behaves in front of a camera—who is mike shy, who is bothered by the lights, who tenses up under the pressure of being recorded, and, on the other hand, who shines through with a better performance when the camera is on.

And you get to see what each actor actually looks like on camera. You may like the way the person reads the lines, but they may not look right. The camera may add weight, making a normal person seem pudgy. Or the person may not move well in the confined space of a video picture. Or they may tend to overact, which might not be apparent in person but comes across strongly in a camera close-up.

The close-up can also reveal blemishes or other cosmetic problems that may not always be apparent in person. For example, I was seriously considering a young woman for a part, until I played back the audition tape. When she smiled in close-up, her teeth, which I didn't remember as having any problem, appeared as sharp, pointy fangs. The camera revealed a flaw that might have been overlooked if we had not videotaped the audition. And if we had selected her, all her scenes might have had to be reshot.

What to Look For

Obviously, you are looking for specific people to play specific parts. But when you start the session, you don't really have any idea which of the people auditioning will be right for which part. You may have a strong preconception of what you want, but you will almost always have to modify this in terms of the talent available.

These are the things you are looking for:

How Does the Actor Move and Speak? Can this person move and speak at the same time? Block out a scene involving both. Have each person do this same scene, so that you have a standard for comparison.

Can the Actor Remember Lines? For some people, the script is a real problem. They just can't remember it. Some have an even worse habit. They get the wrong reading seated in their minds, and it is almost impossible to dislodge it. So be sure to have each candidate do at least one bit without the script.

Can the Actor Follow Directions? I'm willing to give actors a reasonable amount of latitude in interpreting a role. That's their profession. But when a difference exists between the actor's interpretation and the reading I want, the one we're going to go with is mine. So it is critical to find out if the actor can shift gears. And it is important to find out if the actor can understand your directions and follow them. During the audition, change your directions and see if the talent can give you what you ask for. There are actors who can only give you one interpretation of a scene. You ask for something different—they give you the same reading as before. A real pro recognizes that there are a lot of different ways a line can be said. Does the person seem real or seem to be acting? Does he or she seem natural? Believable?

Can the Actor Replicate? Once you have gotten the actor to give you the reading you want, can he or she deliver it consistently, take after take?

How Does the Actor Handle Props? If business with props is important to the part, get the actor to handle props at the audition. Use the real props if possible. But don't be shy about handing the actor something and saying, "Pretend this is an accordion"—or whatever.

When you have made preliminary casting decisions, have the people read together. See how they work together. See how one reacts to another's lines. Switch them around to see which is the best combination. Above all, don't be afraid to change your mind. The program you are casting may be around for a long time.

Notifying the Actors

Everyone who auditioned should be notified of the outcome of the casting session immediately after the final casting decisions have been made. Let the casting director notify the actors or their agents.

Auditioning Voice Talent

Even if you're just casting a voice-over narrator, it's a good idea to do an audition, however short. You just can't rely completely on sample tapes. I had a bad experience this way. I was doing a video for IBM and had selected a narrator I didn't know, based on a sample tape he had sent in. It was a great, strong voice, with a lot of credibility and a good range. The problem was that when I got the talent into the studio, he couldn't deliver.

He had trouble reading basic words about computers. He had a very limited range of expression. And he lacked the professional's ability to bring enthusiasm and emotion to the task. We had to bring in another narrator and do the job over.

WHAT DOES A DOCUMENTARIAN KNOW ABOUT ACTORS?

As you begin working with the actors, you'll discover that you do have something to contribute.

For instance, anyone who has shot and edited a documentary of human behavior probably knows a heckuva lot about how people actually behave. Certainly you know as much or more than most actors do, and probably more than most directors do who only work with actors.

I'm thinking of a high school play in which one of my sons appeared. There was a boy in the play who portrayed a middle-aged New York cab driver. He had the makeup and the props to go with the part. In spite of his youth, he was an experienced actor who had done a number of plays and had made several television appearances. He had most of the traits of his character down cold, but there was something wrong with his performance. It didn't quite permit the willing suspension of disbelief that would have allowed the teenage actor to become the middle-aged cab driver.

As I watched him, I realized what it was. He didn't *walk* like a middle-aged man. He bounced. He moved too quickly. The character he was playing might have an impatient mind that raced ahead at the speed of sound, but his aging body would always hold him back.

A good documentary director would know this.

A good stage or film director who works with actors would know it as well. My point is that a documentary director doesn't have to come in the back door. Your knowledge of the way the world works, and the way the people in it behave, is something the director of actors spends a lot of time trying to learn.

COSTUME AND MAKEUP

There are no fixed rules about who provides makeup and wardrobe for the actors. In today's documentaries, the general rule is that the actors provide their own wardrobes if it's just street clothes for normal wear.

However, if the production calls for special clothing—uniforms, special work clothes, hard hats, boots, heavy gloves, and so forth— then the wardrobe should be provided by the producer. Similarly, if damage to the clothing is a likelihood, the costume should be provided by the producer—or you should arrange in advance to reimburse the actor for cleaning or replacement.

Finding costumes for a period piece is always a problem. If you are putting together a Civil War film, you may have to rent all the costumes; or you may be able to borrow in some cases, rent in others, and even, occasionally, have the actors provide their own. Be sure you are insured against damage to borrowed costumes.

Makeup is another problem. Most experienced actors have

learned to do their own. But that doesn't mean they are good at it. Stage actors tend to go for strong makeup that will hold up under stage lighting. This may look fine to the audience of a play, viewing from a distance, but it will look coarse and false on camera.

I generally budget for a makeup artist for any production involving actors, unless it is obvious makeup won't be necessary.

DIRECTING ACTORS

The whole purpose in directing actors is to get the actors to create a scene the way you want it.

Therefore, you have to know what you want.

You have to communicate it to the actors.

And you have to keep at it—in rehearsals, retakes, or whatever—until you get what you want.

A common mistake is to look at the script and assume that everyone sees the scene the way you do. They don't.

It can come as a great surprise that an actor you have selected, who gave such a great reading at the casting session, could interpret a scene so differently from the way you see it. But it happens all the time.

So, the more specifically you have blocked out exactly what you want—in your mind and on paper—the easier it will be to communicate it to the others involved and to get it in performance.

But be flexible. An actor may come up with an interpretation that is exactly what you want. Or he or she may be way off base and in need of direction, or may come up with an interpretation that is not at all what you had in mind, but is just as good as, or even better than, your idea.

In short, know what you want, but be open to improvements.

Try to Budget Extra Time for Rehearsal

I suspect that in most film and video work, not enough time is given to rehearsing the actors. One reason is that you usually record a few lines at a time, and they can get up in those lines fairly quickly. Another is that there is so much technical stuff to be handled, that working with the actors is only one of the director's responsibilities. Another is the idea that film is a director's medium, which would seem to de-emphasize the importance of the actors.

Work out the fine points of performance before you get on the set, if you possibly can, so that the time spent setting lights and planning camera moves is not taken at the actors' expense.

On the set you'll need some full rehearsals of camera, cast, and crew. When shooting on videotape, which is relatively cheap, I tend to record these rehearsals. You never know when you'll get exactly what you want the first time. If I'm shooting film, I may choose not to record the rehearsal, since film materials have gotten terribly expensive.

Communicating with Actors

When the actor you are directing gives you exactly what you want and can replicate all day long through retake after retake, you are in director's heaven. But most of the time it's not so simple.

The things an actor will do during a scene are:

- move
- look
- do something
- speak
- react

Gross Movement—the Blocking of the Scene. I generally attend to movement first. Where does each actor start? Where does each actor end up? How does the camera move—if at all—to cover the action? How will you edit within the scene? And how will you edit this scene with the scene that goes before, and the scene that follows?

Generally, you want the motion within the scene to be fluid, well-motivated, and continuous from prior action to following event.

I try to get everyone who has to move in motion before the scene begins. Usually, I'll do a countdown to the start of the scene: "Five . . . four . . . three . . . two . . . ," with the count of *one* understood and the action of the scene itself beginning at *zero*.

As you block the scene, each person, and possibly the camera, will have a number in the countdown on which to start moving. This way all the necessary motion has already been started at the point at which you'll cut into the scene. During rehearsal, I make adjustments to starting positions and starting count until I get the movement within the scene exactly the way I want it.

Where to Look—the Eyes Have It. Where does your actor make eye contact? Is it with the camera, as if he or she were speaking directly to the audience? Is it with another actor, either in the scene or off camera? Or is the actor looking at something else?

Decide in advance, because it has to be right in the master scene or you'll find yourself in a lot of trouble when you go for close-ups.

Doing Something. In real life, people can walk, speak, and do things with their hands all at the same time. What does your actor have to do? When is the appropriate time in the scene to do it?

Doing something specific requires planned, fluid movement just like gross movement. It should neither start too soon nor occur too late. When a person walks to a car and opens the door, his hand comes up just before he reaches the car in anticipation of grasping the door handle. When a person spots something on a desk and reaches for it, the sequence must be to see and react to the object before reaching out to get it.

Speaking—Placing Words in Context. I may surprise you by putting speaking lines way down in fourth place on a list of five items. What is said and how it is said are certainly important. But ever since our first kindergarten play, so much emphasis has been placed on remembering and saying the words that we have almost been trained to ignore the other elements that breathe life into a scene.

If, however, we can get the actor moving properly, doing things naturally, and looking in the right places, we'll already be building up a natural rhythm to the scene that will make it easier to get the words out properly.

The mark of an amateur is a letter perfect recitation of the speech—in a vacuum.

Most dialogue is written not the way people actually speak, but the way they wish they did. Just as doing something often involves making awkward movements in a way that looks natural, so it is with speaking. Your actors must take words written by someone else and use them as if they were their own. They must enunciate clearly—without seeming to. They must pause as if to think, even though what they will say next is so well memorized they can say it in their sleep. And they must say the same speech through a hundred retakes if necessary—and make it seem fresh and original each time.

James Garner calls this saying your lines "as if it were the first time you have ever said those words."

Listening and Reacting. Much of the impact of words comes from the effect they have on someone else. In directing actors to react on camera, you may simply have them react to the actual speech. But you may also want to have them give you a variety of specific reactions from which you can choose in editing the documentary. To show an amused reaction, you might ask for a long, slow smile, as well as laughter. The important thing to remember is to direct your actors in both the actions and speeches they must perform and in their reactions to the behavior and words of others.

ONE-ON-ONE

How do you direct actors? What do you do? What do you say?

Probably at one time or another you'll do just about everything.

For some actors you can say as little as, "Let's try it again." For others you may need to give a full on explanation each time.

In communicating with actors, I try not to act out the scene. I want the actors to use their skill to interpret my directions. I certainly don't want a good actor trying to imitate my bad acting.

Ego Massage

You usually can't hurt actors by massaging their egos. I've never gotten mad at an actor, or abused one. I've read about directors doing this to get the performance they wanted, but I've never felt I could predict accurately enough what would happen. I go on the theory that if I treat the actors like adult human beings, they'll probably return the favor.

Don't Settle for Less Than You Need

On the other hand, I don't carry ego massage to the point of accepting takes that aren't good enough. I've done that in the past. And every time, I relearn, to my sorrow, that when you get into the editing room, you have to live with what you've shot.

There can be a lot of pressure on you to accept a less-than-perfect take. Expense is one. You may have an executive producer or sponsor or boss who doesn't understand what is going on, who wants you to "get on with it." You just have to grit your teeth, broaden your smile, and keep shooting until you've got what you need. The same people who are hurrying you to finish shooting won't for a minute accept any responsibility if you have to go back for retakes.

I don't consider it an insult to the actors to ask for another take—or for several more. I do try to let them know why we're doing retakes. If the reason is technical—sound or picture problems—I tell them that. If it's a fluff in the lines, I tell them that.

I try to get an acceptable take as early as possible. (That's one more reason for recording rehearsals.) When I have that, I can tell the cast and crew, "Okay, we've got an acceptable take, now let's go for perfection."

One important thing to remember is that if you don't like what you're getting, let everyone know. Figure out what's wrong, and what's needed, and then work on getting that.

And realize that your behavior will affect the actors. If you act bored, for instance, they may assume what they're doing is not important. I recall being on the set of a shoot in which the director was not getting the performance he wanted from the actors. It was a comic bit, and what he said he wanted was more excitement, more energy, and a faster pace. He was watching each take on a monitor in a room off the set as it was shot. After the take, he would come out and talk with the actors and crew and then go back for another take. And each time, as he would disappear back toward his video monitor, he would chant in a sing-song voice, "Everybody up, now. Lots of energy, lots of excitement."

What he got each time was a sing-song performance.

Positive Feedback Can Get You There

Put yourself in an actor's place. Imagine you're standing on your mark while the professionals work the technology to record whatever you do and say. And imagine that two-thirds of the way through your bit, you make a mistake. What would you like to have happen? Actually, the last thing you need is to have a lot of attention drawn to:

· the fact that you made a mistake, or
· the line or action you did wrong

Whenever I can, I'll let the actor complete the scene, and then ask for a retake.

Of course, if there have been problems with one line or one piece of business, you may want to try picking up a repeat as soon as it goes bad, and keep trying until you get it right. What I'll try to do in this situation is to say, in a calm voice, "Keep rolling. We'll pick it up from the start of your speech. And . . . action." Then if it goes bad again, I'll say, "Again . . . Position One, quickly . . . And . . . action." And we'll keep it going until it either comes out right or it becomes clear that some other change has to be made.

What I don't do is yell, "Cut!" so I can be heard in the next county. I expect electronic equipment to fail and actors to make mistakes. So there's no reason to act disgusted when either happens.

Ask for What You Want

It can happen that the actor is reading the lines correctly and going through the movement properly, and you're still not happy with what you're getting. Then you have to make a change. And you have to tell the actor what you want changed. Say, "The way we rehearsed it just isn't working. Let's try this."

I've had it happen that I get so focused on what I'm looking for that I forget to tell the actor what I need. Or sometimes a subtle change will creep into the performance. I may notice it and think, "Well, he won't do that next time." But if I don't say anything about it, that little change may become a part of the scene. And I may keep asking for retakes without realizing that I haven't told the actor that I want him or her to quit doing that.

Break Up the Action

One of the things you can do with film and video, of course, is to work in small units of script. This is especially helpful when your actors are not very experienced. You can have the actor say just one line, and say it exactly the way you want it, whether he or she understands it or not. Then you go on to the next line.

Generally, this is the way I plan the shoot, unless I'm thoroughly familiar with the capabilities of the actors. As we gain experience with each other, I'll add length to what we try to accomplish in one take. It sometimes turns out, delightfully, that what I had blocked out as three or four different shots can be done in one long take. I don't count on it; I just accept it with gratitude when it happens.

FILM AND VIDEO ACTING VS. STAGE ACTING

There are definite differences between acting in films and acting on the stage. And this can cause problems if the actors available to you primarily have stage experience.

The Stage Is One Big Wide Shot

There's no such thing as a close-up in the theater. You see the whole stage and everyone on it all the time. In general, you are seated somewhat above and looking down. There is very little visual relief. The plot advances mainly through the words said by the actors. That's one reason why the stage is a writer's medium, just as film is considered a director's medium.

The Stage Requires Overstatement

In the theater, everything is aimed at the people in the back seats. Voices project. Gestures are broad. Makeup is strong. What is appropriate for the stage can come across as overdone on film.

Acting on the Stage Is Done in Sequence

A theatrical performance runs from the beginning of the play to the end and is a collaboration between the actors on the stage and the people in the audience. It's live. It's now. The actors build their performance in real time. And once the curtain goes up, the director is out of it. Stage actors may have trouble shooting scenes out of sequence and with the director always there and in control.

Film and Video Bridge Time and Space

What appears on the movie screen or the tube of a TV set can come from anywhere and be made up of anything. You see an actor in close-up, followed by a shot of the Grand Canyon or the mountains of the moon. Film and video are *not* locked into one time, one place, or one dimension.

Acting on Film or Video Takes Understatement

Acting on camera requires a subtle approach, underplaying and reacting rather than projecting. Normal stage projection will come across as overacting, while the powerful language of the stage is often too much for the screen. It seems forced and artificial—which, of course, it is. Different media require different conventions.

A Film or Video Is Shot Out of Sequence

The actors in a film may never all be in the same place at the same time. In fact, it's possible—though rarely desirable—to have a dialogue between two actors who actually never are on the same set, in front of the same camera, at the same time.

A Film or Video Is Always Shown After the Fact

The audience, while kept in mind from script to screen, comes to view the finished work long after the fact. Because of this, the director is the unifying force in film and video. To provide the integrity and direction that will sustain a work through all the phases of production, you must be clear about what you want, and work with crew and cast until you achieve it.

21

THE DOCUMENTARY
INTERVIEW

The lights are set. The Knowledgeable Person has taken his place comfortably behind his desk. You've checked the sound levels, checked your notes, and you're ready to do an on-camera interview.

CUT!

Let's freeze the scene and ask a Stanislavskian question usually thought more appropriate to actors in dramatic fiction than to documentarians doing an interview:

What's the motivation for this scene?

What part does the scene play in your documentary? Why are you doing an interview at all? Why are you talking with this particular person? Why is he sitting behind a desk? What is he going to say? Couldn't it be said quicker, easier, and cheaper by a voice-over narrator?

Presumably you have answers to all of these questions. If so: Roll sound! Roll camera! And . . . Action!

But if not, you may be on the verge of wasting an afternoon and a roll of film or videotape.

WHAT IS AN INTERVIEW?

An interview is a relatively spontaneous, more or less unrehearsed dialogue. On one side is the interviewer, who is in control of the form of the dialogue and who suggests topics, asks questions, and prompts responses. On the other side are one or more interviewees or speakers, who generally have control of the content and information value of the interview.

Why Not to Do an Interview

What disturbs me is the trend toward constructing a documentary out of interviews. PBS, which for twenty-five years has had too much money and too few ideas, has encouraged the documentary of talk—so that the documentarian has people telling the story rather than showing it to us. Every now and then the documentarian throws in a few visuals for relief. This kind of documentary treats visual evidence as a cutaway.

National Endowment grants provide welfare for academics by requiring the involvement of humanities professors and art historians in documentary projects. And I guess the documentarians feel that as long as they are paying the academics a fee, they might as well put them on camera—whether they have anything to contribute to the film or not.

Can this be the reason we find the biographer of a president talking about baseball?

. . . And Why You Might Do One

Interviews are done for a wide variety of reasons:

- You may just want to show the person on camera. Company presidents, politicians, and celebrities often fall into this category. Their physical presence in the documentary may be more important than anything they say.
- Sometimes the speaker is an expert on some topic or holds a

strong opinion about it, and you want to hear what she has to say, in her own words.

- Sometimes an interview is used as a substitute for action footage you don't have and can't get. When a ship sinks at sea, you interview the survivors. It's the best evidence you have.
- You may want an on-camera interview to be able to prove that the speaker said whatever he said, especially if the statement is controversial or can be shown to be untrue. You may want to cross-question the speaker to probe his statement for flaws or inaccuracies or for the strength of his convictions.
- You hope that the person being interviewed will reveal her thoughts, hopes, dreams, and feelings as part of the texture of your documentary.
- Finally, you may want to use pieces from an interview to supplement or replace narration, in order to give your film a feel of spontaneity and a look of reality.

Whatever your reason for shooting an interview, remember that its *use* in the final version of the documentary has to be justified on the same basis as any other scene. That is, it presents evidence, provides information, or enhances the feel, mood, or flavor of the production, *and* it helps to move the documentary along toward its resolution and ending.

Otherwise it belongs on the cutting-room floor with the other shots that didn't work.

PREPARATION

To do a successful interview, you have to prepare.

Every expert on interviewing says the same thing: Do your homework. So *do* it. Find out what you can about your subject ahead of time. Most important, find out what you don't know. That's the basis for your questions. Gather documents. No matter what the topic of the interview is, something has probably been written about it. Talk to your interviewee's associates. They may give you personal glimpses or a different slant that the speaker won't provide.

Quite often you can have the interviewee prepare a list of suggested questions for your use. This is a common device of talk show hosts, and you may find it valuable. Just make it clear that you won't be limiting the interview to the questions that are provided.

You may want to do a preinterview to find out what the person has to say and how she or he says it. But be careful this doesn't lead to the situation, on camera, where the speaker begins each statement with, "As I told you before, . . ." The preinterview is a good time to get the correct spelling of the speaker's name and the exact title. You'll need this for subtitles on the screen.

Take time to explain to the interviewee your purpose, the purpose of the documentary, your slant, if any, who the documentary is being produced for if there is a sponsor, and the intended audience. If it's a hostile situation, tell your subject what others have said, or are expected to say, and give him or her a chance to refute them.

Explain that it's customary to overshoot an interview. Be sure the person understands that you may shoot a half-hour interview, but you will probably use less than a minute of it in the documentary.

ON LOCATION

Do the interview in a place where the speaker is comfortable. Get everything—lights, camera, sound equipment, sound checks, extra tape, lens cleaning, and so on—taken care of ahead of time. Let the interviewee know in advance that you'll need a half hour or so to set up.

Have your crew well briefed and well trained. This means starting the interview with a fresh magazine of film or a new roll of videotape and checking that everything is running properly. Don't let the camera operator direct the scene or the sound recordist indulge his or her curiosity. You control the interview, and you ask the questions.

No one else.

Find a comfortable place to sit or stand to ask your questions. Settle ahead of time whether the interviewee will be talking to you or to the camera.

Avoid Dumb Situations, Dumb Questions, and Dumb Interviewees

The man-in-the-street interview is the classic dumb situation. You grab somebody off the street and ask him what he thinks about something. What you get is noninformation.

The dumbest question I can think of is the one I hear almost every night on TV news. The interviewer asks the survivor of a fire or a car accident, "How do you feel about it?" No information. So define your purpose. You can't really ask dumb questions if you know what you're there for.

Every now and then you'll interview a person who is just no good on camera. There's nothing you can do except wind it up quickly and move on. Preinterviews should eliminate the people who will freeze up. But some people go through a personality change when the camera begins to roll. There exists such a thing as the talk show syndrome. People watch "Oprah" and all the others and they think that's the way it's done. So they try to sound like someone on TV, and you're in trouble.

Or they start to talk on the record. I've already written about the school administrator I liked very much who talked quite intelligently about problems in education until he got on camera. Then he turned into an educationist, speaking unintelligible jargon.

And, of course, there was the Wilkes-Barre police captain who retreated to talking on the record out of insecurity.

If you're in a grab situation—a unique event, a disaster, or whatever—stay away from college graduates and professional people unless you're very certain about how you want to use them. They usually want to give you the cosmic framework within which the event happened, when all you're after are the facts. Find a working person—a waitress, a truck driver—or else a kid or a housewife. They'll tell you what they saw and what they did. It may come out a little disjointed, but it will make good footage on the screen.

Be sure to have each person say and spell his or her name on camera, including rank or title where appropriate. And it's always a good idea to have the interviewee give you permission on camera to use the interview.

SHOOTING OPTIONS

Shoot the interview before you shoot other kinds of action with this person. This keeps the behavior of the interviewee fairly spontaneous and free of any bias toward acting you might introduce later on.

Try to do the interview in an interesting location that helps to build the visual evidence of your documentary. In general, the least interesting place you can shoot someone in is his or her office, with the subject sitting behind a desk. Can you get someone riding a golf cart around the plant? Shopping in a supermarket? At a little league game? Gardening?

While on location, go for documentary footage that provides visual evidence to go with the interview. You know what the speaker talked about, so you should have no problem planning what to shoot. For example, if the subject was discussing the operation of a new pollution-control device that has been installed, get your shots of it while you're there at the location.

Shooting to Edit

If you plan to edit out the questions that are asked, have the camera operator change camera angle or focal length only while you are asking questions. This will give you more flexibility in editing the interview down to a short, on-camera sequence without any apparent jump cuts. It may also do away with the use of unmotivated cutaways. An unmotivated cutaway is purely an editing device. It is not used to show the audience something important, but merely to cover a sync-sound edit point and eliminate a jump cut.

If, however, you think you may want to keep the questions as part of the scene, then the reaction of the subject to the questions as they are asked may be as important as his or her answers. You'll want to keep the camera changes to a minimum so that the audience can see the reactions as they happen. Therefore, you may have to cover edit points with cutaways.

If you, or someone, keeps track of the questions that have been asked, you can move the camera around to the subject's point of view after the interview is over and reshoot the interviewer asking the questions on camera.

Shoot cutaways after you have completed the interview. This is the point at which you may be asking the interviewee to *act*, so it should come after you've gotten his or her spontaneous answers and reactions.

Editing Options

Enough has already been said about talking heads. You'll know when the face of the speaker is the most exciting thing you can use, and you'll know when it's dull. Most of the time it is enough to establish the speaker on camera for twenty or thirty seconds and then cut away to something that shows what he or she is talking about. The less you show the person talking, the easier it is to edit the sound track. That's why it's important to shoot that other stuff and not just the moving mouth.

Interview Audio

Sound is the heart of an interview. Get the microphone close to the speaker and keep it there. If you're in a grab situation and working with a handheld mike, get it in close to provide good separation between the speaker's voice and the background noise.

But don't hand the mike to the speaker. The person who has it controls the interview, and you may not be able to get it back without yelling, "Cut!" and stopping the entire process.

ASK THE RIGHT QUESTIONS

Your questions should be specific enough to point a direction for the speaker and vague enough that he or she has to fill in the details. Try to stay away from leading questions, to which the interviewee can answer "yes" or "no." Instead, ask questions such as:

> "Tell me what happened."
> "How would you explain this situation to people?"
> "What would you like people to know about this?"
> "What do you see in the future?"
> "How did this come about?"

Don't show off your knowledge of the topic. You're asking questions in the name of your audience, and you want answers from the speaker that will inform them. Don't be embarrassed to say, "I don't know about that," or "I don't understand," even if you do. It's a good way to get more information.

Sometimes you have to play the devil's advocate and take a position that seems to oppose the speaker's views—or your own—in order to get good explanations and clarification.

Listen, Listen, Listen

After you've asked a question, *listen to the answer.* Let the speaker know you're interested. Follow up any interesting points your subject brings up. The only reason you have written questions is to have something to go back to if the interview slows down.

Don't rush to ask another question as soon as the speaker pauses. Wait a bit. A silence may prompt the interviewee to elaborate on what he or she is saying in important ways that would otherwise be missed. And that can often be better than the first answer given.

The Two Most Important Questions

When you come to the end of everything you've planned for the interview, you still have two questions to ask.

The first is: "Is there anything I should have asked you that I just didn't know enough to ask?" This gives your subject one last chance to show that he or she knows more than you do about the subject.

The second is: "Is there anything that you'd like to say that you haven't had a chance to?" Sometimes your subject has been thinking about the interview and rehearsing little speeches, but feels he or she should only answer the questions you ask.

Occasionally one of these questions may open the floodgates, and you'll get more than you ever dreamed of. But be sure to brief your crew that you're going to ask this. One crew shut down the camera and recorder as soon as they heard me ask the first of the questions, because they thought I was gathering information off the record. Keep the camera running. You only get one shot at the answer to these questions.

PRACTICE

Finally, if you want to be a good interviewer, practice. The hardest thing to learn to do is to listen. Try to think about what the speaker is saying and where it's leading, not about what you're going to ask next. Learn what kinds of questions prompt good answers and what kinds tend to shut off the response. See if you can't find ways to nudge the speaker into revealing more without asking a direct question. Interview your friends, your relatives, and people you meet at parties. Don't just talk to them, interview them.

And when the time comes to do it on camera, you'll be ready.

· ·

22

SOME OTHER PRODUCTION CONSIDERATIONS

This short chapter deals with some other things to think about as you plan and execute a documentary production.

IT'S HARD, PHYSICAL WORK

Making a documentary can be real work, and you need to be in good physical condition to do it. With a small crew, *everyone* ends up carrying equipment from the car or van to the location setup and back. The technical crew may be used to that. And even if you are not carrying equipment, just spending an eight- or ten- or twelve-hour day on your feet can be draining if your normal activity includes lots of sit-down time. You may be a very active person, but if you spend most of your working day in an office, in meetings, or in an editing room, the physical demands of production can be a radical change for your body.

It's hard to be creative—or even effective—when you're fatigued. You make bad decisions. And you tend to skip things that you'll wish later on that you had done. So work out. Do some aerobics. Run. And get in shape for the work ahead.

Dress for the Job

Wear comfortable clothes that you can work in. All other things being equal, crew people tend to wear jeans, sneakers, and T-shirts and carry along sweatshirts and jackets to layer on if it gets cold. If you are the producer or director, you may not want to be that casual—and under some circumstances you may not want your crew to be that casual either—but you shouldn't need to spend a long, busy day in a three-piece suit or heels and hose.

Wear comfortable shoes that you can stand in for a long time. Most aerobic shoe manufacturers now have a dress version of their walking shoes that's comfortable and gives a lot of support.

And don't be stupid. If you'll be outside in the sun, wear sunscreen and a hat. If it's cold, wear a hat, coat, and gloves. During my fourteen years in Hawaii, I saw a lot of people come from the mainland to do a shoot, and someone on the crew *always* thought it was a great opportunity to get a tan. Of course Hawaii's tropical sun will burn most people crimson in an hour and put them in a hospital in two. Your job is to do your job, and that's hard when you're badly sunburned.

Or frostbitten.

Get Enough Rest

Because shooting a documentary is physically demanding, you need to get a good night's sleep. And you need to take short breaks during the day.

When the adrenaline is pumping from excitement and the location clock seems to be dinging away the hours like a runaway gas pump, the tendency is to try to squeeze in just one more location, one more setup, or one more shot. And sometimes you have to.

But my experience is that you lose time when you're fatigued. And you work more quickly and more effectively when you're rested.

Meals, Snacks, and Drinks

Eat well when you're shooting. Coffee and an English muffin may take you easily to lunchtime at your desk, but when you're doing physical work you need fuel.

Eat breakfast. Keep snacks on hand—fresh fruit and health bars as well as donuts and chips. And keep a cooler filled with drinks. Stock it with bottled water and fruit juice as well as sodas. Make sure there's plenty, and make sure that everyone in the cast and crew knows it's available.

Once you've gotten set up on location, you usually don't want to stop down and lose momentum by going off to a restaurant for lunch. Consider having a caterer bring meals to the set. Or send your driver or gofer for takeout food. But definitely take a break to eat and have some personal time at mealtimes.

YOUR HOTEL OR MOTEL

The ideal place to spend the night is a ground-floor motel room facing a parking lot where you can back the equipment vehicle right up to the door. There's always a lot of stuff to carry from the vehicle to the room at night and from the room to the vehicle at the start of the next day. You don't want to have to haul it to a second-floor room or even through the lobby to an elevator and from the elevator to your room. And you don't want to be dependent on bellhops to move your fragile and expensive gear in and out every day.

BE TRUTHFUL AND BE PUNCTUAL

Be honest with people about when you will arrive at their location, how long you'll stay, and how much disturbance you and your crew will create.

And then be punctual.

If you find that your crew tends to arrive at seven-fifteen for a seven o'clock call, adjust the schedule to get them there on time.

If you find that the production always seems to be running late and that everyone seems to be waiting for you, make some adjustments. Stop trying to squeeze in one extra phone call—or whatever—and start trying to be the first person ready to go.

WRITE THANK-YOU LETTERS

When you've finished with a location, send a thank-you letter to everyone who helped. Don't just blow in, shoot, and vanish.

Do the same with your crew members when shooting is over. Send them a written acknowledgment saying how much you appreciate their contribution to the success of the production.

I promise you that it will pay off big time—you just never know when.

PART IV

Postproduction

Postproduction. The time after production,
when editing, looping, scoring . . .
mixing, etc., are done. In other words,
everything you need to finish the film.

· · · · · · · · · ·

—*Ralph S. Singleton,*
Filmmaker's Dictionary

. . . .

23

PREPARATION FOR POST

At last your documentary is shot, except for a couple of scenes you may have to go back and pick up or may decide you don't need. You have the footage. You like what you've done. And you can't wait to begin shaping your documentary.

But you still have a few things to do to get ready for post.

· PROTECT YOUR ORIGINAL FOOTAGE

If you've shot on film, the film has gone to a processing laboratory where it has been developed. Then either you've had a work print made from the original or you've had the footage transferred to videotape. Most likely you've had your lab make you a Betacam copy of the original.

Now protect the original. The best way is to leave it in the vault at the processing laboratory until you need it, while you edit with the work print or the video copy.

If you've shot on video—or if you've had a video transfer made from film—the next step will be to have a VHS windowprint dub made from your footage. This is a copy of the picture and sound from the original videotape with a window inserted into it electronically in which you can read the running time code of the original camera tape in hours, minutes, seconds, and frames. The windowprint is like a film work print, a copy of the original that you can work with, run back and forth, and even occasionally destroy, without risking damage to your precious original. Because it's on VHS, the windowprint can be viewed on an inexpensive recorder and TV set without tying up expensive production equipment.

When you make windowprint dubs, use one VHS tape for each original videotape. If you've shot on thirty-minute Betacam tapes, make your window prints on VHS T-30s. Yes, it's possible to dub three or four Betacam tapes to one VHS T-120, but it's false economy. You'll save a few dollars in VHS tape stock and waste hours of your time or your editor's time just shuttling back and forth to find the scenes you want.

GET ORGANIZED

Your footage is only as good as your ability to find what you need. So get it organized. Have a specific place to keep all of the materials related to this documentary. Label all your film or tape, both the original and the dubs. Be sure to label both the film cans or tape boxes and the film leader or videotape cassette. Put the background information you've collected in file folders and label them.

LOGGING FOOTAGE

Next you need to find out what you've *really* shot. And that means someone has to look at, and log, all of your footage. That someone is probably you, especially if you are the director or editor or both. You need to know everything you have. At the very least you should be able to say to your editor (or director), "Don't we have a shot of _____ that might go in here?"

Logging is simply making a record of what is on each roll of film or reel of tape. This will include:

· the time code address of the start of each shot
· scene and take number, if any

Figure 23.1

Timecode	Description/Comment
12:08:25	Tilt down off ironwood trees to a collapsing shack.
12:08:54	Several Laysan albatrosses. Pan left across ironwood trees to the shack.
12:09:23	Laysan albatross among a lot of corrugated metal that's starting to rust. Tilt up to an abandoned house.
12:10:04	Looking at a nesting area with a lot of red plastic caps in it, along with feathers and things.
12:10:34	CU of red plastic cap with plastic bottle. Pull out.
12:11:00	Goony bird in front of yellow flowers. VERY NICE. Pull left and we see a cinder block wall.
12:11:32	Stencil on the wall is: Brackish Water Pump House. CU.
12:11:40	Some goony birds, yellow flowers, and an abandoned building in the background.
12:11:58	More abandoned stuff.
12:12:17	Looking at a crack in concrete. So close, you can't tell what it is.
12:12:25	Tilt up and we see that it's the remains of a runway. Probably on Sand Island.
12:12:55	More of the remains of the runway. Different angle. Pan right. There are trees, bushes, and yellow flowers growing out of that runway.
12:13:36	We see albatrosses, trees, and bushes, and the remains of the runway.
12:14:04	CU of the face of a Laysan albatross. Pull out and we see a lot of wood kindling, that sort of thing behind him. A tree stump. Albatross walking. GOOD WALKING.

Figure 23.2

Timecode	Scene	Take	Description/Comment
09:00:50	10	5	Super Suite; model down stairs; no good
09:01:16	10	6	Super Suite; model down stairs; good
09:01:51	10	7	Super Suite; model down stairs; good
09:02:22	10	8	Super Suite; model down stairs; really good
09:02:52	10	9	Super Suite; model down stairs; the best
09:03:18	38	1	Convention Information booth
09:04:00	38	2	Conven. Info. booth; ped.down
09:04:53	38	3	Conven. Info. booth; ped.down
09:05:12	38	4	Conven. Info. booth; static
09:05:30	38	5	Conven. Info. booth; ped.down
09:06:11	38	6	Conven. Info. booth; talent walking into picture
09:06:44	38	7	Conven. Info. booth; talent walking into picture from right
09:07:12	38	8	Conven. Info. booth; talent walking into picture from right; good
09:08:15	37	1	Allstate car rental; good
09:08:50	43	1	Smiling desk clerk; girl
09:09:27	01	1	Glimpse of Genie
09:09:46	01	2	Glimpse of Genie
09:10:01	01	3	Glimpse of Genie
09:10:44	42	1	Genie talks animately with several people
09:11:17	02	1	Handsome male genie

- a brief description of what happens in the shot
- any comments you have about the shot.

Figure 23.1 shows a page from the log for one videotape from *Defenders of Midway*. Figure 23.2 shows a page from the footage log of a scripted documentary shot in a Las Vegas casino. Note that comments haven't been made on every scene. In the *Midway* log comments have been typed in capital letters, wherever they occur. In the casino documentary, the scene has already been fully described in the script and is identified by scene number, so the description is just a brief reminder. Of course if something had changed from what was called for in the script, that would be shown in the description. In this log, comments have been made after the description of the scene.

It doesn't matter how you do the log, just as long as you are consistent and complete and it works for you.

Computer Logging

I dictate the log into a tape recorder as I view the footage. Then the log can be typed into the computer later. Quite often I will have the footage log typed into a database program. This gives me the ability to sort the shots by scene and take number, by location, or by topic. Then, in addition to a sequential log of shots as they occur on the film or tape, I can create custom logs:

- showing the scenes in the order in which they will be edited, and identifying the best takes
- showing all the footage shot at a specific location, regardless of what tape it is on
- showing all the shots dealing with a specific topic or person

The better and more versatile your logs are, the easier it is to find a specific shot when you need it or to find a replacement shot when what you thought was a good idea doesn't work.

There are now computer programs that will let you connect the

VHS playback to your computer so that as you view the footage, you can capture the time code and a still of the scene in a logging database.

Seeing What Is There

When you log your footage, you have to forget what you intended to shoot and look critically at what you've actually recorded. In chapter five I told the story of Miss Darling and the scene that wasn't there, even though I kept hoping that it was. Finally, I had to admit that what had been shot was okay for what it was, but it wasn't the lovely moment I'd been carrying in my head all those months.

If you consider your footage to be visual evidence and build your documentary as a visual argument, then you will rarely make the mistake of putting in a shot that doesn't belong simply because it's a *visual* that seems to *illustrate* something being said on the sound track.

Most people see what they are looking for, not what they are looking at. I'm always fascinated by the way people look at snapshots. As far as they are concerned, all that is important in the picture is what they *want* to see. They'll show you a crowd, underlit and partially out of focus, and say, "Here's Jennifer and the baby." Or a close-up of a bush, which they say is a snapshot of Uncle Jasper. And if you look closely, sure enough, you'll see a tiny Uncle Jasper way in the background.

But an audience probably won't know to look for Jennifer and the baby or Uncle Jasper. They'll see a crowd shot and a bush. And that's what you have to see as you log the footage. If a scene is no good, mark it as such.

NARRATION, GRAPHICS, ANIMATION

If your documentary is fully scripted, you may decide to record narration before you begin editing so that you'll have it for timing as you edit the picture. This is common practice in editing commercials and information videos.

In making a documentary, however, I almost always prefer to record the final narration after the program has been edited. There are two reasons:

- When the pictures are strong, you may be able to get away with less narration than was written.
- As you edit, you may find you need a few words of narration to cover a change from the script or to explain something not covered by the script.

So my choice is to do a scratch track for timing and do final narration before the on-line.

The same is true of creating graphics or animation. If you are certain of exactly what you will need, there's no reason not to have it made before you start editing so that you'll have it to use as you put the off-line together. Except . . .

. . . you rarely know *exactly* what you will need. So, again, my preference is to see how the footage goes together and then have graphics and animation made to fit.

DOING A PAPER EDIT

Once you have logged and studied your footage, you may want to organize it in a kind of off-off-line or paper edit. Sometimes I'll have the computer print out each good take in the log as a small paragraph as if it were on a Post-it or a 3 × 5 card. Then I'll move these around on a planning board until they form an organization of the material that seems to make sense.

This gives me something to start with when I go into the editing room.

HOW LONG TO ALLOW FOR EDIT PREP

You need a couple of days just to get organized and get things labeled and put away.

Logging will take three to four times the running time of the footage, plus time to type it into a computer.

A paper edit can take as long as you want it to. But the longer you take, the better. John Holt, who wrote several excellent books on learning in young children, said that one thing he found from watching kids was that the good problem solvers spent a lot of time just playing aimlessly with whatever it was they were doing. A *lot of time*. Longer than most teachers thought they should. And even longer than he thought they would. But at the end of this long process, they had gotten to know whatever they were working with very well. They knew its shape, how it felt in their hands, what it looked like, which things seemed to be like other things and which seemed to be different.

And when they had gotten to that point, they were usually able to solve the problem quickly and creatively.

The kids who didn't go through this play phase of becoming familiar with the materials, but went right to trying to solve the problem, usually took longer and sometimes never found a solution.

Editing a documentary is often a lot like building a jigsaw puzzle. If you take your time and carefully get all of those odd-shaped pieces to fit together the best way, you'll end up with a beautiful picture.

24

EDITING THE
DOCUMENTARY

There is no escaping the responsibility for the edited film or video. It is the absolute result of the documentarian's judgment as to what to show and how to show it. Since, in editing, the documentarian essentially starts with an empty reel and fills it with images and sound in sequence, there is nothing in the final print that is not put there deliberately.

As a director and photographer you work with potential, a lot of ifs—if the light is right, if it doesn't rain, if you can get the shot, if the product manager can remember his lines, if, if, if.

As an editor you work with concrete reality—the footage and recorded sound that exist after shooting is complete. No matter what you intended when you were filming, you have to edit what you actually got.

And that can be a lot of stuff. Shooting ratios for documentaries have increased radically as the direct cinema documentary ended reliance on shooting from a script and the use of videotape allowed overshooting to become an inexpensive addiction. You know going into the editing room that you have far more footage than you can actually use. So a major task in the creative editing of a documentary is to cut away the parts you can't use or simply won't have the time to use.

The story goes that Michelangelo was asked how he could begin with a huge block of solid stone and end with a masterpiece of sculpture such as his *David.*

"It's simple," he answered. "I just chip away everything that isn't David."

In that sense, creative editing is a lot like sculpture. Robert Flaherty, I was told, edited *Nanook of the North* by projecting his rushes over and over again, gradually taking out the scenes he decided not to use.

Film Editing

Today, editing a documentary—no matter if it was shot on film or video—is much more likely to be done in a video editing room than on a film editing console. And in some ways that's too bad.

Actually editing film was hand work. You cut the image away from its home on the camera reel and attached it to another image on an editing reel. You had to physically match the audio track to the roll of picture it went with and then play it to check on the sync. You physically cut the scenes you were not going to use off the reel and stored them on an OUTS reel. And you usually took all the scenes that went together, regardless of what camera reel they had come from, and spliced them together, creating a new roll of film, which you labeled DRUGSTORE or JENNIFER or whatever.

I think old-fashioned film editing had several benefits.

One was that you simply had to handle the material a lot to get it synced, logged, and sorted. And you got familiar with it as you went along. Because you moved the outs to a separate reel and never looked at them again, you spent most of your good time working with and learning about a smaller set of footage from which the documentary would be made.

Another was simply that it was called *film* editing, and you tended to think in terms of the *pictures* you would use. Few if any film editors would dream of lining up a long sound track from an interview in the synchronizer and then promiscuously adding in *visuals* to fill out the picture side.

And because it was a hand skill, and was actually referred to as cutting the film, you really understood the idea that in editing, you cut what you needed out of all the stuff that was recorded, to create something new that didn't exist before.

And film editing was risky. You actually cut the stuff you were working with. Each time you made a splice, you sacrificed a frame of picture. So just possibly you looked at the footage an extra time or two before committing to a cut.

It's too bad we don't do it anymore.

Video Editing

Video editing is an intellectual exercise that is more like running a spreadsheet on a computer than sculpting a work of art. If in film editing you cut away what you can't use, in video editing you select what you want from the database of everything that was recorded.

I do not mean to imply that a video editor is not an artist. I've known many who are. And I've known film editors who weren't. But I am suggesting that the process of creating video art is different from the process of doing it on film. And I think the best documentaries are sculpted rather than assembled.

At the same time, video offers unlimited possibilities for play. Because you rerecord rather than physically cut the original, you have the freedom to try *anything*. You can put two scenes together just to see what happens. You can add in a few frames of this or that and possibly create some magic.

Nonlinear Editing

The availability of AVID and other nonlinear editing systems brings new possibilities for playfulness to video editing. Already it is possible to load all your footage into your personal computer and do an off-line at home.

Certainly nonlinear editing has speeded up the off-line editing process without substantially increasing the cost. So you may be able to budget more time for playing with the footage without actually increasing the cost of the production. This means that you'll need good footage logs so that you can find what you need, quickly.

Today you can bring your laptop with your footage log in it to the AVID suite and find the shots you need by computer search.

Tomorrow you'll be able to interface the laptop with the non-linear system, search out what you're looking for in the log, and bring it up on the monitor with a keystroke or two.

Why the Emphasis on Play?

Good cuts don't just happen. They are the result of knowing what you've got to work with and experimenting with the ways it might go together. In film grammar, the cut is often seen as a collision of ideas in a kind of visual dialectic that produces a new synthesis. And when it is well done, the audience gets it.

In video, however, a cut is often thought of as a jarring transition. Video editors will ask, "Don't you want a dissolve here?" and are sometimes surprised when I say, "No." There's a huge philosophical difference between a jarring transition which might upset the audience and visual evidence in the form of thesis, antithesis, synthesis.

Whether you care about these philosophical distinctions or not, play with the footage and hold off on making final decisions until you are really familiar with what you've got. It will make you a better editor. And you will make a better documentary.

TRANSCRIPT EDITING

I have no problem with shooting a lot of interviews as part of the process of recording your documentary. I have no problem with having the interviews transcribed so that the log of the interview footage shows what has actually been said. But just because you've shot the interviews, you don't have to use them, or at least you certainly don't have to use big pieces of them. Balance in documentary editing is not politically correct. You don't have a quota that says this interview is 5 percent of the footage you shot so it has to make up 5 percent of your documentary.

Interviews are research conducted on camera. You shoot them because you hope that in all the talk, you'll find something really good that you can use in the documentary. Mostly, you won't. Mostly, you'll just get people talking, the dullest thing next to a test pattern that you can put on a screen.

Don't feel you have to use it. If you can pull twenty great seconds out of a thirty-minute interview, it was worth shooting the interview.

And if you think in that kind of ratio, maybe you won't be tempted to paste pieces of transcript together to create the structure of your documentary.

A good documentary is carefully constructed from visual evidence.

A transcript is not visual evidence.

USING AN EDITOR

As with every other phase of the documentary process, you have to face the question of who is going to edit your program. Will you do it yourself? Will you hire an experienced creative editor to organize the film? Or will you direct the edit, working with a technical editor who will push the buttons and make the editing system work?

My friend, Paul Galan, made his early reputation in documentary as a highly skilled film editor. Then he went on to direct a large number of outstanding network documentaries. He told me, "I have learned never to try to edit a documentary that I directed. It's just not as good."

A creative editor brings a fresh set of eyes to the problems you've been wrestling with for months—or even years. Your editor lives in a world of concrete images. All he or she has to work with is what has been recorded on the film or videotape. Good intentions no longer count. Footage is everything. And a good creative editor can help you understand exactly what you have, and what you don't have, and how to use it.

Not all of us can afford the luxury of bringing in an objective editor to cut our documentaries. The trick is to remain objective and still be creative. When you cut your own, you have to step away from the documentary you've been planning all this time, forget everything that happened while it was being shot, and look at it with a different set of eyes—the eyes of the audience.

EDITING FROM THE SCRIPT

There are two situations in which you come to postproduction with a finished script. The first is the historical documentary or reenactment that has been fully scripted in advance. The second is the behavioral documentary or documentary of a unique event—such as *Defenders of Midway* or the little restaurant opening video I wrote about in chapter nine—in which a scriptwriter has been called in after production to write a script from the footage.

Most other documentary projects arrive in the editing room as a mass of footage loosely connected by an idea. This may be a vision residing solely in the director's head, or it may be expressed in a proposal or treatment.

Editing a Reenactment

The problems and challenges of editing a fully scripted documentary are exactly the same as editing any other fully scripted production, from a thirty-second commercial to a feature film. The script lays down the organization and structure for the program. The footage has been shot to numbered scenes, and each scene has been covered as well or as poorly as the director and crew could manage.

In this situation I would be tempted to hire a creative editor experienced at cutting from a script. The structure is already set and the creativity is in the margins. But even in this situation, the script is a guide to editing the documentary, not an Eleventh Commandment, carved in stone, to be followed at all costs. Obviously, the more detailed the script, the more likely it is that every word and image has been laboriously approved, and the less freedom you may have to depart from it. But you should be prepared for the fact that a sequence that reads well on paper simply may not play well on the screen. And that can be true even if *you* wrote the script.

So be flexible.

Editing the Direct Cinema Documentary

If you are editing a behavioral documentary or a freewheeling documentary of a unique event, you'll rarely see a finished script before postproduction is finished. Instead you'll have a statement of purpose, an indication of style, a suggestion of the flavor of the documentary, and not much else. It will be up to you—or you and your editor— to organize the material and make it work as a visual argument.

What is most important is to have a clear sense of the documentary's purpose—how it is meant to affect an audience. And then to find the visual evidence which supports that purpose.

WORK ON THE WHOLE DOCUMENTARY

The editing process can be thought of as a series of approximations, each of which should get you closer to the documentary you are trying to make, the documentary that will communicate to your audience what you want it to.

At first, the approximation is very rough—the scenes are too long, they're in the wrong order, the rhythm is off. But in selecting the shots to edit, you have, at the same time, eliminated a lot of footage and are now, presumably, working with the best of what you shot. Moreover, the very fact of having edited the documentary into a rough order lets you see better what is wrong and how to fix it.

In the rough cut—the first edited version—everything is tentative. You're experimenting with the way bits and pieces can be built up into master scenes, and how the master scenes can go together to make the whole documentary. But you don't have to start at the opening and slog on through in sequence to the closing titles. You don't even have to edit everything onto the same reel.

Start with a sequence that will be easy and fun to put together and go on from there. Build up a sequence in the way you think it should go. Then set it aside and start another. The important thing is to be thinking about the whole documentary, from beginning to end, even while you're working on a small part of it.

Structure

In the back of my mind I carry around, while shooting and editing, a notion of the structure of a documentary. It's not much more than a string of blank spaces with labels to be filled in during editing:

Opening. This is the point before which nothing needs to be said. That's a simple statement of a profound idea, because it gives you a kind of subjective yardstick for any proposed opening. You can ask yourself, "If I leave this out, will the audience really miss it?"

The opening should catch the viewers' attention, excite their interest, and suggest what the documentary is about.

The opening titles may come before the opening or after it, but should not stop the progress of the documentary. In shooting, you want to be on the lookout for an interesting sequence that might be used as background for the opening titles.

Explanation, Exposition. This is where you weave in a brief presentation of the purpose of the documentary and the problem or problems it deals with—the basic information your audience needs to understand where you're going.

Have faith in the audience and explain as little as possible. Let them have the delicious experience of reaching their own conclusions based on the evidence you have presented. If you can, include this explanation-exposition function either in the opening or in the following section.

Evidence Related to the Theme. You've gotten the audience interested. You've given them a notion of what the documentary is about. Now you need to present some hard information to keep them interested. This may be evidence that supports the theme—or some part of it—or it could be evidence that appears to contradict the theme you've established.

This is the middle. It is a logical and emotional argument constructed out of the visual evidence that you've shot. It builds the story you have to tell, while exploring conflicting elements of the situation.

Resolution. This is really the point to the documentary, toward which all of the evidence has been leading. In a documentary of a unique event with the outcome in doubt, it is the point at which the audience learns the outcome. In *Unzipped* it's the successful presentation of the Mizrahi collection. In *Defenders of Midway* it's the outcome of the battle, the point where the documentary totals the devastating enemy losses and compares them to the very light American casualties. In *Roger & Me* it's the point at which Michael Moore finally confronts Roger Smith, the chairman of General Motors. In *The War Room* it's the emotional high of election night, with Clinton winning.

Ending. This is the point beyond which nothing needs to be said. It is a final sequence within or after the resolution that ties up the loose ends, drives home the theme, and completes the documentary for the audience. In *Defenders of Midway* it's the point where the veterans reflect on the meaning of the battle and are seen dedicating Midway as a national historic landmark.

In *Hoop Dreams* it's the end of the process, as the two boys go off to college and talk about their dreams of playing in the NBA. William says, "If I had to stop playing basketball, right now, I think I'd still be happy. I think I would. That's why when somebody say, you know, 'When you get to the NBA don't forget about me,' and all that stuff, I should say to them, 'If I don't make it don't you forget about me.'" The resolution ends with a denouement in which roll-up titles inform the audience of what has happened to the two boys at college.

In *The War Room* it's Clinton's acceptance speech, in which he praises "the members of my brilliant, aggressive, unconventional, but always winning campaign staff. They have earned this," as the staff goes crazy with shouts and applause.

The closing titles may come during the ending, or after it.

Selecting Footage

As I view and log the footage, I'm constantly looking for pieces that will fit into various parts of the structure. What will make a good opening? What will make a good ending? What will make an interesting background for opening and closing titles? What should be the first evidence to be presented? What would happen if I ran a piece of this interview right after the mayor's speech? And so on.

At the same time, I try to eliminate the scenes that are no good for one reason or another—scenes that are out of focus, have bad sound, accidentally include people who do not want to be in the documentary, and so forth—and scenes in which nothing happens of interest, or which are otherwise inappropriate.

I would include under "inappropriate" the interview with the police captain in Wilkes-Barre, for instance, which I considered an untrue and unfair portrayal. I'd probably also include almost any scene in which someone was mugging at the camera—unless, of course, I wanted to show that doing that was their natural style—or any scene with an unfortunate background, say, a high school cheerleader walking down the street under a theater marquee advertising "Sex, Drugs, Rock & Roll."

THE IMPORTANCE OF A GOOD OPENING

I'm convinced that what happens in the first few minutes after the lights go out has an immense bearing on the audience's reaction to the documentary. You've got everything going for you before the projector starts. The audience expects the experience they're about to have to be worthwhile, or they wouldn't be there. Even captive audiences assume there must be some value, or they wouldn't have been *captured* to look at the production. They assume that the documentary they are about to see is professionally and competently made, and that the documentarian is in control of the material.

Respect the Audience

I have never subscribed to the belief that it is a documentarian's responsibility to do all the work for your audience. You have no business confusing them, of course, but you shouldn't have to do all their thinking for them.

You do, however, have the responsibility to set them on the right track at the start of the documentary. As Sol Worth used to say, "You should teach the audience in the first few minutes how to look at your film."

Audiences have come to expect a unity of style and form, an internal logic to the documentary, which is foreshadowed by the way the documentary opens. And they'll pay close attention to those first couple of minutes as a guide to whether or not there is anything here that is of interest to them. If they see any evidence of lack of control, poor planning, technical problems, inaccurate information, or a dull approach, they're likely to decide that their time will be better spent trying to calculate all the prime numbers between one and five hundred.

Where to Start

Don't get locked into thinking that because you shot the documentary in a certain order, or because the events to be shown occurred with a certain chronology, you must present the information in that same order. Starting in media res (in the midst of things) was a good technique when Spenser wrote *The Faerie Queene*, and it's still a good technique today.

Your job is to make your audience want to see what will happen next. The best way is to start with a problem and work out from it in as many directions as it takes. If you can unsettle the world of your audience, just a little, in the first two minutes, you're going to find them still with you a half hour or two hours later when the documentary is ending. So ask a question, present opposing points of view, show a problem, or make a statement that goes against common sense—but one that you can back up with documentation later on, of course. Which you choose will depend on the rest of the documentary, because the opening, in addition to provoking interest, must be consistent with the style and content of what is to follow.

Edit the Opening Last

I believe that documentarians should make it a rule to edit the opening only after the rest of the documentary has been cut. There are at least two good reasons for this. The first is that the genesis of many documentaries comes from an imagined opening scene that the documentarian loves and has planned in meticulous detail. Without the concept of that opening scene, the rest of the documentary might never have been made. But that opening may no longer have anything to do with the documentary as it has evolved, and therefore should be scrapped. Unfortunately, it has squatter's rights. And there it squats—right at the start of the documentary.

The second reason is more formal and has to do with the style, pace, and feel of the documentary. These change as the documentary goes through the editing process. And an opening scene edited before the style is set reflects a documentary that never was, rather than the documentary that is to follow.

Problem Openings

If you want to lose your audience right at the start, here are some ways to do it:

Technically Atrocious. The image is out of focus, the camera shakes, the color is weird, or the sound is impossible to understand.

And if this is the best the documentarian could find for the all-important opening scene, the rest of the documentary is likely to be a disaster area.

The Man at the Desk. This used to be a standard opening for nonfiction films. They'd start with some sort of certifiable expert telling you about the documentary that was to follow. You're there to watch a movie, but, instead, he's going to tell you about it.

Panning the Gargoyles. There's music. And there are these images that seem to go on forever—scenery, architecture, close-ups of statue parts—and it is all really rather attractively done. But there's no information. The documentary is supposed to deal with some kind of interesting problem or event. But if it can't get started, how is it ever going to come to grips with anything of substance? Maybe some documentarians feel that if they start with the actual topic, they're being too obvious.

My friend Andy Edwards shot his first documentary in Saudi Arabia—a beautiful video called *Falcons of Arabia.* But for some reason he chose not to show us an actual falcon until four and a half minutes into the program. And the beautiful shot of a falcon flying, which I think should have been the opening, doesn't occur until forty-one minutes into the show. When I asked him about it, he said, "I know. I wouldn't do that now."

Dumping Exposition. This opening is like the public speaker who stated, "Before I begin my speech, I'd like to say something." There's a whole lot of stuff the documentarian, or someone, thinks you have to know before you can watch the documentary. So they dump it all at the front and pretend the documentary hasn't really started yet. Almost always this sort of thing is not needed. Raise an issue and explore it with good visual evidence and the audience will stay with you right to the end.

False Starts. It's a human failing. Very likely we all do it. We start the documentary, and then after awhile we start again, and sometimes we start a third time. There's nothing wrong with doing that while the documentary is taking shape in editing. The fatal flaw comes in failing to make a decision about which start you like best, so you can leave the others on the cutting-room floor.

Titles with Irrelevant Music. Personally, I lean in the direction of not using background music anywhere in a serious documentary, but when it is used—with head and tail titles, montage sequences, and so on—it should be appropriate. Better to use musical wallpaper from the stock library, which nobody will notice, than a highly distinctive but totally wrong theme. It's a matter of taste, I'll admit. But when the documentarian and I differ on taste at the opening titles, we're going to have a hard time getting together later on.

Columbus Discovered America! Or Breathlessly Stating the Obvious. Every manual on effective communication suggests you start with what the audience already knows and build on it. But if you try to play it safe, to be sure you've included something familiar for every member of the audience, you're likely to lose more souls to boredom that you'll save with misplaced relevance. A documentary on hurricanes, for instance, began by telling the audience that when Columbus discovered America, the natives in the Caribbean worshiped the wind god Hudda-kahn. Using the short definition of an opening as the point before which nothing needs to be said, you can ask, "Do I have to tell this to the audience? If I leave it out, will it be missed?" While it was nice to know where the term hurricane came from, this was not the sort of thing that would propel an audience eagerly into the topic.

MIDDLES

The middle shows all the good stuff dealing with the documentary topic that you have room to include. Ideally it will consist of a combination of factual information, dramatic events, and human emotions.

You won't necessarily know the proper order of presentation of this material until you've put the scenes together and looked at them. Quite often either moving a scene to a different place—or sometimes eliminating it—will solve problems of awkwardness and understanding.

Recurring Themes

In *Roger & Me*, Michael Moore will show someone from business or government making an optimistic prediction about the future of Flint, and then cut to a sheriff's deputy evicting people from their homes. This is dramatic conflict. And between these milestones, he'll go off to explore some new facet of his story.

In *A Young Child Is . . .* , each new sequence deals with a child a little older than the previous one and builds upon what the audience has seen in the previous sequence about learning in young children.

In *Basic Training: The Making of a Warrior*, we see the recruits learning various aspects of infantry training and then applying them in practical situations.

Balance in Editing

Sometimes you have to strike a balance between what actually happened when you were shooting and the way it appears in the edited version of your documentary. I ran into this problem in my first documentary, *The Trouble with Adults Is . . .* , about a group of white high school and college students involved in a summer project on white racism. They were loosely affiliated with a Protestant church group, and in their zeal and immaturity they had alienated the members of a suburban church.

The climax of the documentary was a confrontation between the kids and the church members at a meeting of the congregation. This erupted into a free-for-all when one of the young people, a seminary student, began reading aloud to the congregation a passage from a book of black literature that included the then-taboo word *fuck*. The church had not permitted us to film the meeting.

We did have an audiotape of what happened at the church and a ten-minute sequence we had filmed back at the project headquarters immediately after the meeting broke up.

We turned on the camera as the kids stormed into the house very much like combat pilots entering a debriefing room after a mission. They were laughing and talking, and their speech was sprinkled with meaningless profanity and an occasional obscenity. After a couple of minutes, they calmed down and described how they had been threatened, yelled at, and in some cases physically thrown out of the meeting room at the church.

In the rough cut, I left most of this sequence just as it had been filmed. But when I began to show it for comments, I noticed a strange thing. The people who saw it not only missed the point of the scene—my intended point, anyway—but they described it in terms that had very little to do with what happened on the screen. They talked about "a bunch of wiseass kids with no manners, just trying to get a rise out of people." And about "somebody jumping up and yelling an obscenity in church."

It took me almost a month to discover that the edited version was way out of balance with the event it was intended to show. The occasional rough language of the kids as they entered the house was so upsetting to some viewers that they missed the explanation in words—and in pictures taken in the parking lot of the church before the meeting—of how and why this all came about. Quite literally, the viewers went deaf and blind for about two minutes. And just about the time they got their senses back, they heard the young seminarian reading *that word,* and they went off again. Essentially, they weren't *seeing* my documentary.

I wanted the sense of turmoil that the opening of that sequence provided, so I couldn't just eliminate it and start with the calm, rational explanation that followed. The solution I found was to balance the scene according to the expectations and conventions of the intended audience, so that the use of the word *fuck,* when it appeared, would become data, and not just a shocking experience.

I shortened the introductory scene and trimmed the rough language to two *hells* and a *damn.* Suddenly, the people I showed it to started talking about what was there, not about some other documentary that existed only in their heads.

Not all of them liked it. But they now understood that sequence as the crucial event of the documentary, against which everything else that happened should be evaluated. If they disliked the kids it was because they found them unlikable throughout the documentary, not because of shock at their language in one sequence. And many viewers now found a sympathy for the students' idealism, even though they may have questioned their judgment.

And that's the most I could hope for—a fair presentation of a controversial subject.

Crossing the Line and Other Technical Rules of Editing

Like every other aspect of film and video production, editing has become saddled with a list of rules that has grown longer and longer over the hundred years since the invention of motion pictures. One is the rule against crossing the line, which comes from the idea that in order for the audience to understand what they are looking at, the camera should never cross an imaginary line running through the people or event being shown. There are lots of others.

I've never learned them, and I suggest you don't either. There are a number of principles of good communication that should be followed in editing a documentary. But as to technical rules of editing, there are just two questions you need to answer:

- Can you see what's happening?
- Does it make sense?

Writing Narration as You Edit

Documentary narration, if used at all, should be written as late in the production process as possible. Give the visual evidence a chance to state the case before you feel you have to have a narrator explain anything. And then use narration only to explain whatever the audience needs to know that they can't get from viewing the images.

I try not to write any narration until the fine cut. That's the point at which you can see what information is actually missing or what needs to be explained. Until then make notes as to what narration might be required, but without actually writing the words to be said. Hold off on narration as long as you can. And then write as little as possible.

THE ENDING

In one of Hollywood's many fairy tales about itself, there's a producer who says, "All I want is a picture that ends with a kiss—and black ink on the books."

Take it as a metaphor. You want to end your documentary in a way that satisfies the expectations of your audience. It doesn't have to be a happy ending. But it does have to bring a sense of completion to the viewer.

SEVEN SINS OF EDITING

These are some things that can turn your documentary from a fascinating exploration of an important topic into something else entirely.

One: The Documentary Is Too Long

Most documentaries are too long. When you're convinced that your documentary is absolutely and finally completed, go back over it and try to cut it by 10 percent. You'll be amazed at what happens.

Two: Relying on Sound to Carry Meaning

Good sound is always a blessing, but a documentary should be a *visual* experience. Edit the documentary to *show* an audience what you mean, and you'll find there's a lot less you have to tell. This is important, because a reliance on words slows down the documentary and makes it longer. Which is why you don't write the narration until you start editing the fine cut.

Three: Using Inappropriate Images

The use of inappropriate images is often the result of relying on telling instead of showing. I've mentioned the protest film in which the narrator said that twenty thousand people showed up, while the picture on the screen showed a bored policeman and an empty street. The initial impression was that no one came to the protest march, even though later scenes proved there was quite a crowd.

Four: Repeating the Same Shot for No Reason

Maybe you like the look of it, or maybe you just have to have something to cover a sound edit, but be careful. Repetition of a shot tells the audience that what they are seeing is important. When it isn't, they get confused.

Five: False Structure or the Cute Cut

False structure is putting shots together because they are similar visually but have no good communication reason to be next to each other. You'll know you've done this if you catch yourself saying, "Yeah, that's kind of cute."

Six: Mickey Mousing the Music

You've got a piece of music with a good beat to it, and you think, "I've got a great idea. I'll cut each shot on the downbeat."
   Don't.

Seven: Talking Heads

It's so easy to get lots of pictures of the faces of people talking. The problem is when to use them. Occasionally, the most interesting thing you could show your audience is the face of the person speaking. Usually it isn't. Most of the time, talking heads slow down the documentary—they're dull—and make it longer, because when you show the person talking, it's hard to cut the babble away from the good stuff.

FINE CUT

After the rough cut comes the fine cut, where the documentary is edited to the desired length, awkward cuts are polished, and sequences are speeded up—or, occasionally, extended. In film, this is a continuation of the editing process leading up to freezing the work print. On videotape it will be the last off-line edit before finishing the program in on-line.

It's possible that there will be one or two bothersome scenes in the documentary that you don't know what to do with. If time permits, it's often a good idea to put the documentary away for a few days. This gives you time to get back your objectivity. It may be that the bothersome scene is bothersome because it actually doesn't belong in the documentary, even though it has been there since the first rough cut. Eliminating the scene entirely or substituting something different may solve the problem for you.

Or it may be that when you show the current edited version, your viewers are missing the point to an important scene because something in a previous scene is leading them off in the wrong direction.

For instance, I cut an opening sequence for *These People*, a documentary about mental health problems, which used a long, slow pan across the empty beds of a crowded ward in a mental institution, ending with one lone mental patient slumped in the shadow. The narrator explained that research showed most patients preferred to be treated in their community rather than in an institution.

This was the point to the documentary, and it was the best opening I've ever done. The scene was so dramatic that everyone who saw it was moved by it. But everything that followed—I mean the rest of the documentary—seemed an anticlimax.

The problem was that, structurally, that scene was an ending. It completed the visual argument for the audience. So I pulled it out of the opening sequence and used it as the last scene of the documentary, where it worked beautifully.

GETTING FEEDBACK

Show the edited documentary to people with as little comment as possible and try to gauge their reaction to it in terms of the way your intended audience will respond. Seeing the edited version with an audience—even an audience of one other person—will also help you to see it with fresh eyes.

But remember that anyone asked to look at a cut of a documentary unconsciously casts himself in the role of an expert and feels he has not discharged his obligation to you unless he *helps* you. The less he knows about making a documentary, the more generous he is likely to be with his help. You can't take these comments literally as instructions on how to change and improve your documentary. You have to read between the lines if you are to extract something useful.

I use a four-step method of analyzing audience reaction from the comments people make:

1. Viewer says, "I don't like it," or "I don't understand it." *Message:* She doesn't like it or doesn't understand it. There's a lot of work left to do.
2. Viewer talks about technical problems, fuzzy sound, abrupt cuts, color, composition, and so on. *Message:* The documentary doesn't hold interest. He had time to look for flaws.
3. Viewer talks about how well made the documentary is and

says, "You've done a really good job." *Message:* The documentary is okay but not finished. It doesn't move the audience.

4. Viewer doesn't talk about the documentary, but talks about matters related to the problem explored in the documentary. She says, "I know a person like that man in the documentary. He's really hard to get along with." *Message:* The documentary is getting the desired reaction. It is essentially finished.

It may be a little hard on your ego, but the highest praise is no praise at all. When the viewer ignores all your hard work and starts a discussion where the documentary leaves off, you're communicating.

Don't Expect to Be Loved

One final word of warning. If the documentary deals honestly with a controversial subject, don't expect everyone to like it. In fact, you can expect negative comments from people on all sides of the question—some complaining that the documentary goes too far, others complaining that it doesn't go far enough.

When that happens, you can take it as evidence that you've done an honest job of organizing the material to communicate with an audience.

25

. . . .

FINISHING
THE PRODUCTION

When the reaction to the edited version of your documentary indicates that you've accomplished your goals, it's time to finish up and send your program out into the world.

At this point, your documentary exists either in a film fine cut or a video off-line, edited to final length and content. In either case, there still may be some elements missing:

- titles, both head and tail
- graphics or animation sequences
- photographic special effects
- final versions of stock footage or stock photos
- final narration
- sound effects where needed
- final music
- mixed or sweetened sound.

APPROVAL SHOWING

If you have a sponsor, underwriter, or distributor with the right to approve the documentary, this is the point at which you need to hold a formal approval showing to get the money people to sign off on the documentary for content and editing. Even if there are no

money people, it's a very good idea to hold a formal approval showing for yourself and your colleagues. You are about to go into the
expensive stage of postproduction, and any changes that have to be
made beyond this point will be costly.

Check for Accuracy

You need to be certain that what you have said and what you have
shown is accurate:

- Do you have the correct spelling of people's names?
- Do you have their correct titles?
- In editing, have you cut out any explanations or qualifying
  statements, thereby changing meaning?
- Have you added anything that might change meaning or give
  the wrong impression?
- Is the narration correctly written and properly recorded?

I've learned the hard way that it's good to have someone who
has not been involved in the day-to-day production look at the cut.
By this time, you know what you meant to do and assume you have
done it. A new viewer may raise questions you thought were already
answered.

FINAL ELEMENTS

Now you need to complete all the elements that go into your documentary, so that you will have them to finish the production.

Final Sound

Up to now you may have been getting by on a scratch track narration read by someone on the crew. Now is the time to bring in the
good narrator and record a final narration track.

The same with music. Once you have frozen the fine cut or final off-line, your music director or composer will have exact picture and timing to work from.

Sound Sweetening

And once you have frozen the off-line, you can remix the sound in a sweetening session. This lets you bring in final narration and music, of course, but it also lets you clean up location sound to get rid of unwanted noises. And it lets you add wild sound or sound effects as needed. The final mixed track can go directly to the on-line as a layback track so that you don't have to spend time rerecording and mixing the sound again in on-line.

Stock Footage and Stills

For editing, you have probably been getting by with a low-quality dub of whatever stock footage you are using. Now you'll order it in production quality.

The stock library probably gave you photocopies of the stills you thought you might use for editing. Now that you know exactly what you are going to use, you can order production copies.

Graphics and Animation

Do you have any special graphics planned or computer animation, such as a map with a moving line showing the route that was taken? If so, you have probably already completed these in the last stages of off-line editing. In any event, you need the final version for the on-line.

THE VIDEO ON-LINE

If you are finishing on video, you'll go to on-line. This is the point at which you rerecord everything onto a new, edited master tape in its final distribution form.

Be Prepared

Go into the on-line with everything you need, properly identified and in a form in which it can be used:

- all your field tapes
- any work tapes that have been created
- whatever stock footage you've ordered
- any stills that you are using, transferred to videotape using a good camera (I recently learned, to my chagrin, that the graphics camera attached to an on-line suite may not be adequate for fine work)
- the final script
- all the finished sound

Working from an Edit Decision List

From your final off-line, you should have an edit decision list (EDL) that describes the way the documentary goes together. It tells the source for each image and each bit of sound used in the off-line. It will not, of course, include images or sounds to be added during the on-line or during an audio-sweetening session. The EDL is computer-generated and can be moved electronically or by disk from the off-line computer to the on-line computer.

A digital editing system will assemble the on-line picture and sound from your source material using the edit decision list. Because the EDL shows not only where everything has come from but also the exact location where it is to go on the master, it can rerecord all the shots from reel one, then all the shots from reel two, and so on.

You'll have to add in anything that was not included in the off-line, such as superimposed titles from a character generator. And you may have to remake transitions such as dissolves and wipes.

At the End of the On-line, Your Documentary Is Done

You'll walk out of the on-line session with a finished master tape, which is your documentary in all its glory. Done. Finished. Ready for distribution.

FINISHING ON FILM

Most documentaries these days will be finished on videotape, regardless of how they were shot.

If you have shot on film and intend to finish on film, you are probably thoroughly familiar with the process. I've reviewed the process for finishing on film in chapter eight.

GOING TO DISTRIBUTION

Again, if you have a sponsor, underwriter, or distributor involved with your documentary, have a formal approval showing and get them to sign off on the finished work before it goes into distribution.

Protect Your Master

Once you have a perfect master—either edited film original or digital video—make a protection master from which to make copies. From this point on, you want to handle the original as little as possible. So print an internegative of your film or clone dubbing masters of your tape. Let them take the heavy wear of making prints.

ENJOY IT—AND MOVE ON

You have been living with this project for months or years, and now, incredibly, it's finished. Enjoy everything that goes with it. The screenings for friends, colleagues, and backers. Entry in film festivals. All the hoopla of theatrical release if that's the direction you are going.

Stand for the applause.

Give the interviews.

And then get back to work.

Because the work is the only thing that counts.

. . . .

INTERNATIONAL
DOCUMENTARY ASSOCIATION

Documentaries are not made in a vacuum. Even the simplest documentary—made with a one or two person crew—will probably require the efforts of a variety of people and organizations before it is completed. Major productions can take many years and a whole lot of help to plan, fund, shoot, edit, and distribute.

If you are serious about making documentaries you need to belong to the International Documentary Association. It is your prime resource for everything from contacts in other states where you may be planning to shoot, to news about the state of the art in documentary production, to help with funding. Membership dues are relatively inexpensive, and the rewards can be great. Low cost student memberships are available.

PURPOSE AND BENEFITS

This is what the IDA says about itself, taken from its *Membership Directory and Survival Guide:* "The International Documentary Association is a nonprofit organization founded in 1982 to support the efforts of nonfiction film and video makers around the world and to increase public appreciation and demand for documentary films and television programs. Our international membership includes producers, directors, writers, editors, camera operators, musicians, researchers, technicians, journalists, broadcast and cable programmers, academics, distributors, and members of the general public.

"IDA and its cultural/educational arm, the International Documentary Foundation (IDF), work to raise public consciousness of the documentary's importance to a free society, and to encourage international understanding and cooperation through the medium of documentary film."

Membership Features:

- One year subscription to *International Documentary*
- Availability of IDA-sponsored health insurance
- Listing and biography in *IDA Membership Directory*
- Discounts to IDA awards, events, and screenings
- Discounts on *IDA Membership Directory*
- Discounts on advertising in IDA publications
- Complimentary addition to IDA résumé file
- Access to IDF as nonprofit fiscal sponsor.

International Documentary

The IDA magazine includes news about documentary projects and the people making them, information on festivals and competitions, classified ads for members, and information on funding sources, distribution, and employment opportunities.

Seminars and Workshops

IDA schedules a number of educational events each year, which are convenient for people in Southern California. Major events, such as International Documentary Congresses, feature well-known documentarians and draw people from all over the world. Even if you can't attend, there's always a report in *International Documentary*, and the proceedings of the major conferences are published and available for a fee.

Networking

Many of the people who commission, make, and distribute documentaries are involved with IDA. As a member, no matter where you are located, you're no longer alone.

Screenings and Awards

IDA holds screenings throughout the year, maintains a library of documentaries in conjunction with the Academy of Motion Picture Arts and Sciences, and confers the prestigious Distinguished Documentary Achievement Awards on several documentaries each year.

Membership Directory and Survival Guide

This document alone is worth the cost of membership—although you can order it at the nonmember price. The front part is a listing of IDA members throughout the world by specialty and location. If you need a camera operator in the Netherlands, a film researcher in Washington, D.C., an editor in Michigan, or a writer in Vermont, this is where you'll find them listed.

The second half is the Survival Guide, where you'll find information—including addresses and/or telephone numbers where appropriate—covering such areas as:

- Listing of U.S. and international broadcasters who buy or make documentaries
- Grant writing, including funding sources
- Publications and other sources of information
- Film/video/photo archives and stock footage libraries in the U.S. and other countries
- Companies which distribute documentaries
- Documentary film festivals, award competitions, and film markets
- Trade and professional organizations
- Film commissions: state, city, and international

- Helpful information on international production, production insurance, U.S. embassies, and U.S. government offices.

In addition, you'll find ads for stock footage libraries and production services.

Becoming a Member

For a membership application, contact IDA Membership, 1551 S. Robertson Blvd., Los Angeles, CA 90035. Telephone: (310) 284-8422. Fax: (310) 785-9334. E-mail: idf@netcom.com.

FILMOGRAPHY

This is a list of the documentaries mentioned in the text. Many of the more recent and better known of the films and videos may be available from sources such as Blockbuster Video. Older and classic documentaries may be available from a variety of sources, such as the documentary library at the Academy of Motion Picture Arts and Sciences in Los Angeles, the film library of the Museum of Modern Art in New York, and elsewhere. I've included some sources, with their addresses, following the list of films.

89 mm from Europe (1995). Written and directed by Marcel Lozinski, this beautiful short film received a 1995 IDA Distinguished Documentary Achievement Award. Distributed by Studio Filmowe Kalejdoskop (Poland) and Direct Cinema Limited.

Ages and Stages (1950s). This series of films on behavior in early childhood was produced and distributed by McGraw-Hill. It is responsible for perpetuating a libel against two-year-olds, by titling the film on that age *The Terrible Twos*. An example of visuals illustrating the sound track.

An American Family (1973). Shot and directed by Susan and Alan Raymond, this series for PBS was a landmark event in the evolution of direct cinema. The Museum of Television and Radio has some episodes.

Baseball: A Film by Ken Burns (1994). Directed by Ken Burns, this is a very long, very eclectic look at the game which used to be known as the national pastime. Various distributors, including Dave's Video, The Laser Place; PBS Video; and Video Library.

Basic Training: The Making of a Warrior (1994). Produced by Kevin Stead and directed by Ari Golan, this documentary about infantry basic training is awaiting distribution. Call Atomic Imaging: (702) 387-0800.

The Battle of San Pietro (1945). John Huston directed this classic documentary about a single battle in the Italian campaign during World War II. Various distributors, including Museum of Modern Art and Video Yesteryear.

Battleship Potemkin (1925). Classic reenactment documentary directed by Sergei Eisenstein. Various distributors, including Dave's Video, The Laser Place; Festival Films; Home Film Festival; Museum of Modern Art; and Video Yesteryear. (Silent film, see note on page 325.)

The Berkeley Rebels (c. 1964). Directed by Arthur Barron, this early-'60s documentary appeared on CBS. I have found no distributor.

Berlin, Symphony of a Great City (1927). A classic silent film, directed by Walter Ruttman, which has become a model for all city films. Various distributors, including Home Film Festival and Museum of Modern Art. (Silent film, see note on page 325.)

The Birth of Aphrodite (date unknown). I don't know where you're likely to find this film. I got it out of the Philadelphia Public Library twenty years ago.

The Blue Minority (1968). Paul Galan directed this documentary about police officers for Westinghouse Group W. I have found no distributor.

The Bridge (1928). A beautifully realized, classic documentary directed by Joris Ivens, who gives a clinic on how to observe an object with a camera. Available from the Museum of Modern Art. (Silent film, see note on page 325.)

Brother's Keeper (1992). A film by Joe Berlinger and Bruce Sinofsky about the murder trial of Delbert Ward, one of four hermit brothers in rural New York State. Available through Blockbuster Video.

Chronicle of a Summer, 1960 (1961). This is an early and exciting example of cinema verité in France from Rouch and Morin. I saw the film in French with English subtitles, but as of this writing have not been able to find a distributor.

The City (1939). Willard Van Dyke directed this classic American city film, which follows the format established by Ruttman with *Berlin*. Various distributors, including Discount Video Tapes and the Museum of Modern Art.

The Civil War (1990). The PBS series that made director Ken Burns a household name. Various distributors, including Dave's Video, The Laser Place; Festival Films; Home Film Festival; PBS Video; and Video Library.

Crumb (1995). Terry Zwigoff conceived and directed this offbeat theatrical documentary about underground artist Robert Crumb and his family. Various distributors, including Movies Unlimited, Inc.

Defenders of Midway (1994). Directed by Tim Bradley and written by Barry Hampe, this hour documentary on the greatest naval battle in American history was funded by the Department of Defense Legacy Resources Management Program.

Dialogues with Madwomen (1994). Director Allie Light's documentary of emotion is available through Women Make Movies, 225 Lafayette Street, #207, New York, NY 10012. (212) 925-0606.

Falcons of Arabia (1994). This is an interesting first documentary shot, directed, and edited by Andrew Edwards. Available from Falcon Productions and Expeditions, Inc., 850 South Rancho, #2-164, Las Vegas, NV 89106. (702) 870-5661.

FDR (1995). This four-and-a-half hour documentary, made for the PBS series *The American Experience*, was produced and directed by David Grubin. Available from PBS Video.

Frank and Ollie (1995). This theatrical documentary directed by Theodore Thomas looks at the lives of two of Disney's legendary animators. From Disney.

Harvest of Shame (1960). An early award-winning television documentary for *CBS Reports* from the team of Edward R. Murrow and Fred Friendly at CBS News. From the Museum of Television and Radio.

Hoop Dreams (1994). The most talked-about documentary never to get an Academy Award nomination started out to be a TV half hour, and became instead a longish theatrical documentary and PBS special. Produced by Kartemquin Films, 1901 W. Wellington, Chicago, IL 60657. (312) 472-4366. Various distributors, including Dave's Video, The Laser Place; Movies Unlimited; and PBS Home Video.

In the Street (1952). An early experiment in concealed photography by Helen Levitt, Janice Loeb, and James Agee. Available from the Museum of Modern Art.

Light in Art (1988). A documentary directed by Holly Richards and written by Barry Hampe for Hawaii Public Television, 2350 Dole Street, Honolulu, HI 96822. (808) 955-7878.

Lonely Boy (1961). Wolf Koenig at the National Film Board of Canada set the mold for films about entertainers and musicians with this direct cinema study of Paul Anka. Various distributors, including the Museum of Modern Art and the National Film Board of Canada.

A *Married Couple* (1961). An early direct cinema behavioral documentary directed by Alan King. I have found no distributor.

Mother Washing a Baby (c. 1896). This short observation of behavior was made at the Edison Studios at the turn of the century and can be found in a compilation called *Early Edison Shorts*. (Silent film, see note on page 325.)

Nanook of the North (1922). Robert Flaherty's classic film is arguably the first behavioral documentary. Various distributors, including Festival Films, the Museum of Modern Art, and Video Library. (Silent film, see note on page 325.)

Natasha and the Wolf (1995). A strange documentary for the PBS *Frontline* series by Kevin Sim and Olga Budashevska, set in Russia and full of interviews with simultaneous translation. Distributed by PBS Video.

Night Mail (1936). John Grierson carried the show-and-tell documentary about as far it could go with this classic film about a train. Various distributors, including Festival Films, the Museum of Modern Art, and Video Yesteryear.

October: Ten Days that Shook the World (1927). Sergei Eisenstein's recreation of the Bolshevik revolution. Various distributors, including Festival Films, the Museum of Modern Art, and Video Yesteryear. (Silent film, see note on page 325.)

The Plow That Broke the Plains (1934). Pare Lorentz made this film about the drought in the Great Plains and its causes at the height of the Great Depression. Various distributors, including Festival Films, the Museum of Modern Art, Video Library, and Video Yesteryear.

Primary (1960). Robert Drew thought there had to be a better way to document unique events than the standard show-and-tell documentary, and this film was the visual evidence. From the Museum of Television and Radio.

Referred for Underachievement (c. 1966). Dr. Ed Mason, a psychiatrist, made this documentary record of an intake interview with a patient and her family. I have found no distributor.

The River (1937). Another Depression-era documentary directed by Pare Lorentz, showing a flood on the Mississippi and its causes. Various distributors, including Festival Films, the Museum of Modern Art, Video Library, and Video Yesteryear.

Roger & Me (1989). Director Michael Moore uses his quest to bring GM chairman Roger Smith to Flint, Michigan, as a metaphor to show hard times in his home town. Various distributors, including Blockbuster Video; Dave's Video, The Laser Place; Home Film Festival; and Video Library.

Salesman (1968). Albert and David Maysles filmed this behavioral documentary about door-to-door Bible salesmen and shared the directing credit with editor Charlotte Zwerin. Various distributors, including Home Film Festival and Video Library.

Schools for Children (1973). Second of two films on learning in children, directed by Barry Hampe for the Educational Information and Resource Center, 606 Delsea Drive, Sewell, NJ 08080. (609) 582-7000.

Season for Learning (1972). A documentary about a summer educational program for children of migrant workers, directed by Barry Hampe for the Educational Information and Resource Center, 606 Delsea Drive, Sewell, NJ 08080. (609) 582-7000.

See It Now. A documentary series on CBS in the 1950s from the team of Edward R. Murrow and Fred Friendly. Episodes are available at the Museum of Television and Radio.

Sexual Intercourse (c. 1970). An observation on film of a couple making love, made for a medical school in the early 1970s. I have no information on distribution.

Sleep (1963). Andy Warhol directed this five-and-a-half hour observation of a person sleeping. It is part of the collection of the Museum of Modern Art. There may be some restrictions on rental—call for details.

The Sorrow and the Pity (1970). Marcel Ophuls directed this landmark documentary which explored anti-Semitism in France during World War II. Various distributors, including Home Film Festival and Video Library.

These People (1976). A documentary about the controversy over community care versus institutionalization of mental patients, directed by Barry Hampe for Horizon House, Philadelphia.

The Trouble with Adults Is . . . (1968). A well-edited, technically atrocious documentary about a group of students in the summer of 1968, directed by Barry Hampe for the United Church of Christ.

Unzipped (1995). Douglas Keeve directed this theatrical documentary about fashion designer Isaac Mizrahi. Distributed by Miramax.

VolcanoScapes (c. 1990). One of a series of documentaries about Kilauea Volcano, produced by Artemis and Mick Kalber; Tropical Visions Video, Inc. 62 Halaulani Place, Hilo HI 96720.

The War Game (1966). Peter Watkins directed this speculative documentary about the effects of a future nuclear war. Various distributors, including Festival Films, Video Library, and Video Yesteryear.

The War Room (1993). A film by Chris Hegedus and D. A. Pennebaker, which follows the Clinton campaign from the New Hampshire primary to the election. Various distributors, including Home Film Festival and Video Library.

Woodstock (1970). The first of the great concert films, directed by Michael Wadleigh. Various distributors, including Dave's Video, The Laser Place and Home Film Festival.

A *Young Child Is . . .* (1973). A behavioral documentary about early learning in young children, the first of two films on learning in children directed by Barry Hampe for the Educational Information and Resource Center, 606 Delsea Drive, Sewell, NJ 08080. (609) 582-7000.

Note: Silent films were shot to be projected at the silent speed of 16 frames per second rather than sound speed of 24 fps. If you view any of these silent films on video, be sure they were transferred at silent speed.

SOURCES

A sampler of video and laser disk sources and 16mm resources for documentaries.

Dave's Video, The Laser Place, 12144 Ventura Blvd., Studio City, CA 91604. (818) 760-3472. (800) 736-1659.

Discount Video Tapes, P.O. Box 7122, Burbank, CA 91510. (818) 843-3366.

Festival Films, 6115 Chestnut Terrace, Shorewood, MN 55331. (612) 470-2172.

Home Film Festival, P.O. Box 2032, Scranton, PA 18501. (800) 258-3456.

Movies Unlimited, 6736 Castor Avenue, Philadelphia, PA 19149-2184. (800) 466-8437.

Museum of Modern Art Film Library, 11 W. 53rd Street, New York, NY 10019. (212) 708-9480. The museum has 16mm films only.

Museum of Television and Radio, 25 West 52nd Street, New York, NY 10019. (212) 621-6600. The museum has a library of documentaries for study on the premises but does not lend out or distribute programs.

PBS Home Video, to order certain PBS programs. (800) 645-4727.

PBS Video, 1320 Braddock Place, Alexandria, VA 22314. (800) 344-3337.

Video Library, 7157 Germantown Ave., Philadelphia, PA 19119. (800) 669-7157.

Video Yesteryear, Box C, Sandy Hook, CT 06482. (800) 243-0987.

BIBLIOGRAPHY

Barnouw, Erik. *Documentary: A History of the Non-fiction Film*. Second revised edition. New York: Oxford University Press, 1992.

Barsam, Richard M. *Nonfiction Film: A Critical History*. Revised and expanded edition. Bloomington: Indiana University Press, 1992.

Crichton, Michael. *Rising Sun*. New York: Alfred A. Knopf and Ballantine Books, 1992.

Ellis, Jack. *The Documentary Idea*. Englewood Cliffs, NJ: Prentice Hall, 1989.

Grant, Barry K. *Voyages of Discovery: The Cinema of Frederick Wiseman*. Champaign: University of Illinois Press, 1992.

Guyann, William. *A Cinema of Nonfiction*. Cranbury, NJ: Fairleigh Dickinson University Press, 1990.

Haag, Judith H., and Hillis R. Cole. *The Complete Guide to Standard Script Formats, Part I: The Screenplay*. Los Angeles: CMC Publishing, 1980.

———. *The Complete Guide to Standard Script Formats, Part II: Taped Formats for TV*. Los Angeles: CMC Publishing, 1980.

Hampe, Barry. *Video Scriptwriting: How to Write for the $4 Billion Commercial Video Market*. New York: A Plume Book, Penguin Books, 1993.

International Documentary Association Membership Directory and Survival Guide. Los Angeles: International Documentary Association. Published biennially.

Jackson, Bruce, and Diane Christian. *Get the Money and Shoot: The DRI Guide to Funding Documentary Films*. Buffalo: Documentary Research, Inc., 1986.

Kline, Mary. *A Guide to Documentary Editing*. Baltimore: Johns Hopkins University Press, 1987.

Konigsberg, Ira. *The Complete Film Dictionary*. New York: A Meridian Book, Penguin Books, 1987, 1989.

Lipton, Lenny. *Independent Filmmaking*. Revised edition. New York: Simon & Schuster, 1983.

Nichols, Bill. *Representing Reality: Issues and Concepts in Documentary*. Bloomington: Indiana University Press, 1992.

O'Connell, P. J. *Robert Drew and the Development of Cinema Verité in America*. Carbondale: Southern Illinois University Press, 1992.

Pryluck, Calvin. "Ultimately We Are All Outsiders: The Ethics of Documentary Filming." *Journal of the University Film Association* 28, no. 1 (Winter 1976), reprinted in Alan Rosenthal (ed.). *New Challenges to Documentary*.

Reichman, Rick. *Formatting Your Screenplay*. New York: Paragon House, 1992.

Robiger, Michael, ed. *Directing the Documentary*. Second edition. Stoneham, MA: Focal Press, 1992.

Rosenthal, Alan. *The New Documentary in Action: A Casebook in Film Making*. Berkeley: University of California Press, 1972.

———. *New Challenges to Documentary*. Berkeley: University of California Press, 1987.

———. *Writing, Directing, and Producing Documentary Films*. Carbondale and Edwardsville: Southern Illinois University Press, 1990.

Singleton, Ralph S. *Filmmaker's Dictionary*. Beverly Hills: Lone Eagle Publishing Company, 1986.

Swann, Paul. *The British Film Documentary Movement: 1926–1946*. New York: Cambridge University Press, 1989.

Worth, Sol, and John Adair. *Through Navajo Eyes; An Exploration in Film Communication and Anthropology*. Bloomington: Indiana University Press, 1972.

Worth, Sol. *Studying Visual Communication*. Edited and with an introduction by Larry Gross. Philadelphia: University of Pennsylvania Press, 1981.

Zettl, Herbert. *Video Basics*. Belmont, CA: Wadsworth Publishing Company, 1995.

———. *Television Production Handbook*. Belmont, CA: Wadsworth Publishing Company, 1997.

INDEX